A Dog Barking
at the Moon

달 보고 짖는 개

Cho Moo-Jung
조무정

Book Lab Press
Seoul, Korea

A Dog Barking at the Moon(달 보고 짖는 개)

발행일	2023년 6월 7일

지은이	Cho Moo-Jung 조무정		
펴낸이	손형국		
펴낸곳	(주)북랩		
편집인	선일영	편집	정두철, 배진용, 윤용민, 김부경, 김다빈
디자인	이현수, 김민하, 김영주, 안유경	제작	박기성, 황동현, 구성우, 배상진
마케팅	김회란, 박진관		
출판등록	2004. 12. 1(제2012-000051호)		
주소	서울특별시 금천구 가산디지털 1로 168, 우림라이온스밸리 B동 B113~114호, C동 B101호		
홈페이지	www.book.co.kr		
전화번호	(02)2026-5777	팩스	(02)3159-9637

ISBN	979-11-6836-936-8 04740 (종이책)	979-11-6836-937-5 05740 (전자책)
	979-11-6539-728-9 04740 (세트)	

(주)북랩 성공출판의 파트너

북랩 홈페이지와 패밀리 사이트에서 다양한 출판 솔루션을 만나 보세요!

홈페이지 book.co.kr • **블로그** blog.naver.com/essaybook • **출판문의** book@book.co.kr

작가 연락처 문의 ▸ ask.book.co.kr

작가 연락처는 개인정보이므로 북랩에서 알려드릴 수 없습니다.

To

June (주영),

Korean ancestors, who have continuously refined their proverbs over centuries,

And

All my friends, who have welcomed my recent return to Korea for good.

CONTENTS

FOREWORD

The human 'mask' we all wear not only protects us from unwanted transparency and external threats but at the same time makes identification of the truth quite difficult in Western culture...we hide and avoid the obvious risks but leave ourselves less open to observing and learning.

We are assaulted by voluminous, indiscriminate, and unvalidated information through the Internet.   For many, more of a curse than a blessing.   But almost always confusing rather than very enlightening.

When we "fish" (for ideas, input, support) it's often with a hook that has been straightened by our own prejudices and defenses...so we don't get what we want and maybe nothing at all. See Entry #456.

Maybe for you too, it's time for a refreshing change. Dr. Cho is widely recognized in his professional circles for having very unique and valuable perspective on any number of topics—he's *different* in a very positive sense. Cho's contributions, including this latest volume, offer the wisdom of older and very different Asian cultures thru traditional stories and proverbs that expand and enrich our understandings...often shaping as well as reinforcing insights. He supplements these with his own thoughts and observations including from his experience in pharmaceutical research and the necessity it teaches of patience and persistence.

For a sheltered Westerner then, these volumes offer a quiet respite to consider different ways of looking at our shared world and deeper, more meaningful interactions with our fellow travelers who co-habit it.   ENJOY!

Douglas Mendenhall, PhD
a friend,
colleague, and
admirer of Dr. Cho
April 15, 2023

ACKNOWLEDGMENT

A Dog Barking at the Moon is a sequel to the earlier four books, *The Tongue Can Break Bones* (2018, written under a pen name, C. Bonaventure), *Easier to See Love Leaving than Arriving* (2020), *A Hole Gets Bigger Whenever You Work on It* (2021), and *Dragon is Easier to Draw than a Snake* (2022). These were published both in Korea and the United States. As before, this book also introduces 100 proverbs, starting with #401 and ending with #500. Unlike other fiction novels, each entry in these books is independent of the others and has no formal beginning and end. When one opens these books, every two-page essay starts on the left side so that one can open the book at any page for quick reading in a rush.

The previous four volumes were all published early in the spring. This time, I am one season behind the regular schedule. This was because June and I moved back to Korea during the wintertime beginning in December of 2022. We plan "to bury our bones" here.

Thus far I have written 500 essays on 500 proverbs. This is a good place to take a break at. The contract with publishers for each book will be over in two years, in the summer of 2025. During this period of a two-year pause, I plan to refine, and update if warranted, each entry. Newer versions will come out simultaneously this time, most likely with new publishers.

As I believe that the incidental interpretation of a proverb is the best way to offer its underlying nuance, I have heavily quoted the Korean (hi)story as well as happenings in the United States. Although I had planned to use more time-tested old events, there has been much distraction from contemporary news, particularly those political turmoil. They were certainly low-hanging fruits for this lazy writer to pick. Likewise, I have cited numerous novels and films that many readers may have read or seen. Even with my long life, I realize there is only so much I can cite from my own experience.

Donghae Silvertown
Gangwon Province
Korea
April 29, 2023

INTRODUCTION

The beauty of proverbs lies in their simplicity. Spoken and written in plain language, any child can memorize them as soon as they learn to speak. However, the deep-rooted meaning of these old sayings evolves as we age. Most likely, children hear a given proverb for the first time from an older and thus wiser person who relates it to one occasion, and then, they hear the same proverb spoken later by others in a slightly different situation. Soon, these proverbs become children's own.

At least, that was how I acquired the essence of Korean proverbs. There was no class at school, neither at the elementary school nor at the university, where teachers could have taught us what Korean proverbs are all about. The situation is quite different nowadays as we can learn almost anything online including someone's interpretation of a given proverb. But I do not want to read what others have to say lest they should affect my own understanding. One can thus say what is written here in these books is my own voice that I have found in a given proverb.

If there is one unique feature in Korean old sayings, it would be gentleness, often with humor derived from the everyday lives of average citizens. They are as if the sharp edges have been worn down through continuous use over many years. They are rolling hills under the blue sky peppered with lazy white clouds, never the Alps or the Himalayas under a windy snowstorm. They are small, gentle streams with the peaceful sound of a lullaby, never the deafening thunder of Niagara Falls.

Many Korean proverbs end with a question mark. Instead of stating outright, "The first spoonful of food will never give you satiety," my ancestors would ask, "Would the first spoonful of food bring about satiety?" See Entry #46. You will come up with the same conclusion in the end, but it asks you with some level of subtlety. The gentleness and subtleness that I identify Korean proverbs with must be from the people's life as well as the terrestrial surroundings of the Korean Peninsula. Describing these two factors alone in analyzing Korean proverbs would require a tremendous amount of research. Then, there is the historic backdrop for a given proverb, both societal and cultural, to study. I have neither ability nor time for such an academic endeavor. I will instead let these proverbs speak for themselves.

And the wisdom therein! The oral history of Korea goes back 5,000 years. The traceable history for the two millennia preceding the 15th century had been recorded in Chinese characters and our own alphabets, hangul, since then. Although many idioms were thus written in Chinese, especially those four-letter phrases in Chinese characters, I suspect that they could not have been very popular among our ancestors, since most of them were simply illiterate in Chinese.

The class division itself, between learned men, or 양반 (*yang-ban*), and the ordinary citizens, or서민 (*seo-min*), has been a popular subject among the latter, sprinkled with their ridicule and wit. These ordinary people, who shared barely won happiness as well as various adversities in their lives, invented and enjoyed their proverbs. They are the collective consciousness of Korean people, which defines who we are now.

Some 40 years ago, my sister who lived in Phoenix, Arizona, sent me *One-Thousand Korean Proverbs* in several loose pages. I do not know where they were originally from, but I knew that one day I would try to interpret them for English speakers. I have kept them in a drawer till 2017. As I tried to translate a few of them into English just to gauge the scope of the job, I immediately encountered the difficulty of keeping alive those rhymes that are perfect in the Korean language, which has survived for many generations. They are poetries. I do not know how to translate them into English. All I can say is that I did my best. In some fortunate cases, however, there are some English versions that are almost mirror images of Korean proverbs. I hurriedly copied them into this book. If there is an English version that is similar in its implication to a Korean proverb, I also introduce it in the text.

As to the implied meaning of a proverb, I take my prerogative: others may interpret it in different ways. The proverb may talk about an earthworm or spider, but I am more interested in learning about what their behaviors teach us about human interaction and those interactions among institutions, communities, or even nations. I will be the first to admit that my thought in the interpretation process tends to drift widely and wildly. Japanese kamikaze pilots may appear in a story involving tiger cubs. The story about smoke from a chimney introduces those cheaters in the contemporary sports world. Quite often, I find great pleasure in submitting my own opinion on various topics as I have not yet had the opportunity to do so. Be it cynical or sounding ridiculous, the writing is, to the truest sense, my voice: good as well as bad that has been accumulated during my life.

Language is a culture, which leads to the next problem of how to take care of the stark differences between the two cultures. I naively thought that I should be in a good position to address this issue since I had, after all, lived more than two-thirds of my life in the United States. It was once again my guesswork to determine to what extent I ought to cover cultural background in these essays. I apologize in advance if I have too many superfluous words or too little on Korean culture.

Then, there are many words with different nuances and meanings: krill and shrimp are completely different from each other, but we Koreans call them both새우, or *saewoo*. Tangerine and orange are both 귤, or *gule*.

Since the topic of proverbs varies widely and since there is no framework for sorting them in some rational manner, I list them at random. As far as I can tell, the *One-Thousand Korean Proverbs* that I received many years ago do not appear to have any discernable order either. I simply present them in chronological order with the date of the write-up at the end of each entry.

I have tried to avoid discussing ongoing events as much as I could. I wanted to cite time-tested, well-established historical accounts. However, I could not let the episodes involving the current political turmoil just pass by unnoticed. Many stories from Washington DC, often ridiculous and beyond my comprehension, provided an immeasurable amount of priceless examples of how one should not govern the nation and its citizens. I am thus thankful for the contribution of those politicians.

The most impressionable and formative period of my life in Korea was just after the Korean War (1950-1953). There was a large contingent of American soldiers in the country. Whether we liked it or not, their presence offered us a great deal of exposure to the American culture. We read Hemingway and Steinbeck, followed the fights of Cassius Clay (Mohammad Ali since then), admired Mickey Mantle's career at the Yankees, sang along with the Beatles, watched American films like *From Here to Eternity*, and even monitored closely what was happening in the political arena of the States.

At night, my ears were glued to the AFKN (American Forces Korea Network) radio station, which carried songs requested by the loved ones back at home for the American soldiers in Korea, largely what I later realized was country music. My poor English did not allow me to fully understand what the lady announcer was saying, but I figured it was all about boosting troop morale. I still vividly remember the alluring voice she spoke in. As I look back now, I understood America far better than they did Korea.

An imbalance in cultural understanding between nations has certainly added fuel to ongoing animosity, often igniting a full-blown war. Even at that tender age, I found myself wondering how many Americans knew anything about Korea, the exception being the Korean War and our cold winter. Years later, I discovered that the Peace Corps campaign by the John F. Kennedy administration was to help Americans understand the culture of developing countries. In token of a similar spirit, I hope that this book could contribute to the understanding of Korean culture among English speakers. It is one tiny grain of sand on the vast oceanic beach but is better than nothing.

Having been a scientist, it has become a habit to always reveal the source of a given piece of information in my writing. Here, I am greatly indebted to Google, Wikipedia, NAVER, and NamuWiki. Even with these online encyclopedias, whenever warranted, I went back to the primary literature to confirm that what I was writing is indeed correct. My Korean is no longer what it used to be when I was a college kid in Korea. Inevitably, I had to consult Korean-to-English as well as English-to-Korean dictionaries, both by Dong-A Publishing and Printing Company. To my delight, they sometimes introduce an English version of a Korean proverb. These occasions were like finding a 10-dollar bill between the cushions of a sofa.

I used a pseudonym, C. Bonaventure, as the author of the first volume, *The Tongue Can Break Bones*. It was published in the U.S. in 2018. As writing essays has never been my profession, my real name would not mean anything. Bonaventure was the Christian name given to me when I was baptized as a Catholic. There is neither more nor less significance associated with the pseudonym. Just accept it as is. Now that all of the first four books have come out in Korea, there is no reason not to use the name given to me when I was born. Some of my old Korean friends may still recognize the name.

I immensely enjoyed writing these essays. I hope that readers find this collection somehow meritorious and enjoy reading as much as I did with my writing (modified from *The Tongue Can Break Bones*).

Donghae Silvertown
Gangwon Province
April 30, 2023

A Dog Barking at the Moon

Cho Moo-Jung
(C. Bonaventure)

Book Lab
Seoul, Korea

401. Knowledge brings about troubling thoughts.
아는 것이 병이다.

This proverb mirrors another Korean proverb that was introduced earlier in Entry #102, "Ignorance is medicine (or bliss)." When we do not know what we do not know, everything is fine. Just like when we were infants or kindergarteners. There are very few matters we ought to worry about or struggle to acquire such as wealth and success. As we get older, we begin to go through schooling, start a family and guide our own children to stand on their own feet, retire from busy life, and finally sit back to reminisce what life is all about. We, or at least I, realize that the happiest years of our lives were indeed when we did not know anything at all. This is essentially what the proverb is alluding to. If innocence is a blessing, knowing is the source of troubling thoughts.

Beginning about three months ago, I have had sporadic episodes of low-grade headaches, rather sharp on the lefthand side of the back. It is different from other forms of the headache I have experienced in the past: it is not pulsating as I would expect from a bad hangover and unlike most headaches it is ADVIL-independent. It occurs every three to five days and each episode usually lasts about five hours. I was not able to associate the episode with any discernable cause, ranging from sleep apnea to a sedentary lifestyle. Soon I began to suspect a brain tumor or glioblastoma, an aggressive type of brain cancer. Although there was neither nausea nor persistent headache, I went ahead with a CT scan for the possible presence of a tumor, but the radiologist said all is normal. This could have been a false negative because of the low resolution of the scan and thus I was ready for further testing with MRI or even a biopsy.

A pessimistic hypochondria, I was for sure, but then my advanced age keeps telling me "What's the point?" Besides, albeit sharp, the pain was something I can live with and does not occur every moment of every day. So, I decided to ignore the whole incident, which has brought me peaceful sleep every night, a wise decision if I may say so.

Amyotrophic lateral sclerosis (ALS), commonly known as Lou Gehrig's disease, is a neurodegenerative disease that results in the progressive loss of motor neurons that control voluntary muscles. There is no known cure for ALS. In addition to Lou Gehrig, the great cosmologist Stephen Hawking died of the disease. In familial ALS, a young family member may find himself or herself in a quandary as to when they should test for the disease. Early diagnosis for positive results may be effectively a death sentence that will define the rest of their life from a different perspective. But, then, there is hope for a negative result, which will remove the anxiety of not knowing once and for all and will lead them to a life of a peaceful mindset.

We are constantly bombarded by a slew of news. Some of them are rather disturbing, to put it mildly. As of this writing, the Russian military has surrounded Ukraine for imminent invasion. Just yesterday, a policeman manhandled a black teenager with whom he was in a fistfight for a white. It was a real fight as the latter was not handcuffed. Then there was another winter storm going through the Midwest. In local news, a 29-year-old African American female pleaded guilty to having pushed a 74-year-old man off a bus to his death in 2019.

Not all news or stories are bad though. About a year ago, a 26-year veteran policewoman Kim Potter in Minneapolis accidentally killed a 20-year-old Black man during a routine traffic stop: she accidentally drew her gun instead of her taser. Yesterday, the judge gave her two-year jail time, which provoked a protest from the victim's family. They had wanted a maximum sentence. This was in spite of the tearful apology from Potter as well as the sincere plea from the judge. I, for one, it was an honest mistake on Potter's part and her agony for the killing was difficult to watch. Considering her 26 years of impeccable career for the safety of citizens, it was about the right sentence in my mind. For a change, my wife agreed with me also.

There are many stories and news that I wish I did not come across. They do not directly affect my life and yet interfere with my wish for a tranquil life. Admittedly, this is the selfish person in me speaking of course, but at this stage of advanced age, perhaps such a wish can be accommodated. A few top managers at CNN abruptly resigned a week ago because of love affairs within themselves. This was big breaking news but I just felt that I am looking at somebody's dirty underwear. Why do I need to hear about it? The possible Russian invasion of Ukraine is something I ought to follow closely for many reasons, one being respect for the sovereign rights of the people.

What I need is a mechanism that can filter the noise out there before they reach me. That being impossible, I may retort to the practice of "see no evil, hear no evil, speak no evil." (02/19/2022)

402. You can skip *daegam's* funeral but not that of his horse.
대감 죽은 데는 안 가도 대감 말 죽은 데는 간다.

An interesting Korean word here is *daegam* or 대감. A high government official in Joseon Dynasty (1392-1910) was referred to as *daegam*. It is perhaps equivalent to a cabinet minister of the US government. A Korean-English dictionary suggests "Your Excellency" but I just used the word, "boss." It is an old word that not many Koreans would use nowadays but one can refer to someone who is bragging about his government position as *daegam* just for fun in jest. I don't believe the word to be used with women.

Now that your boss has departed this world, there is no need to offer any further flattering gestures or unwarranted praise for him. But, the situation is different if and when he outlives his horse. By all means, you must attend the funeral service for his dead horse. It may be best if you bring a bundle of flowers and say a few words of consolation so that he can remember you in a favorable light. This is the crux of the above proverb, illustrating twisted advice on what is really important right at this moment.

Loyalty is one of the most important moral codes we live by along with other virtues such as honesty, courage, righteousness, compassion, etc. It involves two parties: the offeror and the object. The former is usually a person while the latter can be a cause, philosophy, religion, another person, group, nation, etc. What is offered, often without any calculus, are devotion, faith, trust, affection, respect, etc. Once developed, loyalty usually lasts one's lifetime. With this backdrop, we can safely say that only a person with shallow loyalty may follow the advice from the above proverb.

Loyalty is unconditional in that the person involved does not flatly ask for some kind of reciprocating reward. It is thus almost blind faith, although the "reward" is tactfully assumed among the parties involved. As such, some organizations cannot survive without the loyalty of their members. Gang members are often sworn in under an oath, and so is a military organization. Even a nation implicitly asks its citizen for their loyalty, called patriotism. Once such a norm is broken, the word betrayal, traitor, rat, or turncoat is assigned to one party by the other. Such accusation and blaming are the ugly sides of disloyalty, perhaps well depicted by the above proverb.

In the recently ended Beijing Winter Olympics, two Chinese-American female Olympians competed representing the Republic of China rather than the USA where they were born. Eighteen-year-old, San Francisco native, Stanford-bound Eileen Gu won two gold and one silver medal in freestyle skiing events. When asked by reporters why she represented China, a country notorious for its violation of human rights, she simply said that she was fulfilling the wish of her mother who was born in China. Since China does not honor dual citizenship, Gu must have given up her American citizenship to participate in the Olympics as a Chinese: however, she never offered a direct answer on the citizenship but said only: "I'm an American when I'm in the States while I'm a Chinese when I am in China."

The other one was a 20-year-old figure skater, Zhu Yi, born in Los Angeles. Zhu fell on her jump combination in the short program part, crashing into the boards of the rink. She also failed a planned triple loop. She was placed last, dragging down the Chinese team along with her. Afterward, she said that she was "upset and embarrassed" with her dismal performance. Later, in the free skate, Zhu fell twice and was again placed last. China ended with no medals in the team event. For the opportunity, Zhu changed her American name, Beverly, to a Chinese name, Yi, and she renounced her U.S. citizenship.

However one may look at the situation, both Gu and Zhu demonstrated a remarkable degree of loyalty to China. However, we witnessed a sharp contrast in their reception by Chinese social media. In the case of Gu, also known as Gu Ailing in China, Chinese netizens went nuts with her successful runs and she has been hailed as the "daughter of Beijing" and the "pride of China." She has been also well compensated financially as lucrative modeling opportunities are coming on her way. All of a sudden, she has become the perfect daughter of many Chinese parents.

On the other hand, Zhu drew considerable criticism on Chinese social media for her lackluster performance: her poor fluency in Mandarin and privileged background were typical complaints. Some also pointed out that she had stolen an opportunity for others to bring China a medal. They even told her to "go back to America."

I can understand but do not like the way the Chinese reciprocated their loyalty: the warm embrace of Gu and cold shoulders to Zhu. If the occasion truly reflects the essence of Chinese character, I am terribly disappointed with their "conditional" loyalty. And just see how we, Koreans, have been treating Chloe Kim, a Korean-American gold medalist. (02/22/2022)

403. Go to the countryside to learn the news in Seoul.
서울 소식은 시골 가서 들어라.

The bustling town of Seoul is too brimful with real news, fake news, misinformation, stories, rumors, gossip, and hearsay, to grasp the fact and truth straight. In addition, you cannot think clearly amidst all those noises and dust from people and cars and what-have-you. By the time these clatters get filtered and reach a rural area, only the news interesting and relevant to me would survive. It is like the clean water I would have after it percolates through multi-layers of sand.

Indeed the folks living far away are often much more knowledgeable about an event that happened right here. That is what the above proverb is saying. Here are some examples. My wife informs her friends in Korea of the whereabouts of the Korean entertainers, BTS. Everybody in town except the husband seems to know that his wife has been cheating. Why do the bystanders seem to see a better move in a chess game? A guy I thought I know pretty well made a beeline for the East Coast a few months ago, but I've just learned about his escapade from his ex-girlfriend. Everyone is laughing at a bewildering man with a Post-It note on his back stating, "I Don't Need Google, My Wife Knows Everything."

My wife and I usually do not follow local news and thus we get to hear about important happenings in this town, usually serious crimes, belatedly through national news. Son's misbehaviors or even good behaviors reach the mother's ear through the mothers of his friends or his teacher after she gets summoned. My immediate neighbor has been in hospital for appendicitis, which we learned from their friend at the church. About 50 years ago, I visited New York City for the first time and wanted to see the Empire State Building. A Korean friend of mine who had already lived in the city for several years still did not know how to get to the building.

In the above context, the proverb is similar to Entry #69, "A knife cannot carve its own handle," #109, "You cannot see your own eyebrow," and #141, "One feels a splinter under a fingernail, but not a troubled heart." We also have more famous lines like "Darkest is just below a candle (등잔 밑이 어둡다)," and "A monk cannot shave his own head (중이 제 머리를 못 깍는다)."

These all amount to a testament that the truth is frequently very close to each of us, just like an elephant in a room we do not see.

Figuratively speaking, the world has been rapidly shrinking in proportion to the advancing information technology. Upon clicking a fingertip on a cell phone, one can get access to any breaking news nowadays. Distance as implied in the proverb is no longer an important issue in communication. Gone is the built-in filtration mechanism referred to earlier. It is thus for each of us to determine what news is worth reading, digesting, and forming an opinion about. We will have to do all these in rapid succession because of the sheer volume and rapidity of breaking news. It is therefore not surprising to witness that bad, fake news begets further fake news. Such a situation mandates more careful scrutiny if the topic involved is global in nature, as it may require understanding the historic and cultural backdrop of other countries.

For many years beginning in 1992, I served as the faculty advisor for the Korean Student Association at the University of North Carolina at Chapel Hill. There were two rather independent cohorts. One consisted of bona fide Korean American kids who were either born here or immigrated to the States when they were a toddler. Most of them were in undergraduate programs. Some of them barely spoke Korean and essentially were American. And yet, they were eager to learn more about the country their parents left many years ago primarily for a better living.

The second group was largely graduate students who came to the States directly from Korea after they acquired a baccalaureate degree to obtain an advanced degree. They were more mature and had less time for socializing. However, it is this group who helped me raise the fund for starting a Korean language program at the University. In 2002, we were able to raise approximately $7,000 for the university primarily through donations from Korean churches in Carolinas. Of many helpers, I belatedly acknowledge the dedication of one particular "volunteer," Helen Shin (신혜린). In due time, the University formally offered a language course with a hired part-time instructor. It was the beginning of what has now become an academic program in the Korean Language and Culture Program.

As I look back now, it was a small but right step towards facilitating meaningful communication between people of different languages and cultures. One can now learn about Korea in Chapel Hill, North Carolina, without so much worrying about fake news. (02/26/2022)

⏰

404. Tears upon the first drink.
한 잔 술에 눈물 난다.

Two major functions of tears are lubricating the eyes and removing irritants. In addition, they serve as the first-line defense system as they contain some generic antibacterial enzymes as well as antibodies. They are formed and released from the lacrimal glands, which are located in the inner, upper corner of the eyes. Whenever the eyes blink, tears are spread in the space between the eyeball and the lids. They enter the drainage duct, called the nasolacrimal canal that runs along with the nose. They are eventually drained to the nasal cavity and discharged.

As far back as I can remember, I have been suffering from excess tears. The ophthalmologist whom I consulted earlier told me that the problem is from dry-eye syndrome. Their conventional explanation is that the excess tears are a response to irritation caused by the deficiency of tear film. This seemingly standard and convenient easy-way-out diagnosis appears to be their suspicion rather than based on some solid evidence. The diagnosis comes along with an impressive term also: keratoconjunctivitis sicca.

Regardless of their attempt to convince themselves, one conclusion that I had to agree with them is that the watery eyes are due to either excessive production of tears or inefficient drainage. For the former possibility, they have a long list of possible causes like allergic reactions. Since there are numerous potential allergens, it is nearly impossible to test the hypothesis.

On the other hand, testing the obstruction of the tear duct sounded like a simple task. I was thus subject to a procedure called "irrigation." In this treatment, a cannula is first inserted at the entrance of the drainage duct and a physician tries to force the passage of saline through the duct to the nasal cavity. If there exists a blockage, one will feel some back pressure.

It was done some 30 years ago, and hence I cannot remember the exact verdict, but apparently, there was some resistance when the plunger of a syringe was pushed forward. Thus, I was ordered to massage both sides of the nose bridge with hot potato wrapped in cloth for several minutes every night. The idea was that we can melt away fats that are blocking the passage. I tried the hot massage several times but there was no meaningful improvement in the state of my eyes. Truth be told, watching a ball game on TV was a more agreeable way to spend the precious evening hours.

I have been living with teary eyes for the past few decades. The ophthalmologist I was seeing most recently gave me a prescription for RESTASIS. The awfully expensive eye drop contains cyclosporin, a compound I used a lot in my lab before retirement. I didn't think it will work and, sure enough, it did not do anything. All I am doing nowadays is wiping the excess tears with Kleenex. Otherwise, tears can just overflow onto my face, a condition known as epiphora, without affecting my eyesight that much.

To make the matter even worse, I have become prone to producing more tears on an occasion that I would not have "cried" in the past. I have also noticed that I tend to produce more tears when I witness kindness and justice than sadness in a classical sense. Yesterday, I had teary eyes when I saw the defiant posture of Ukrainian citizens against invading Russian military forces. The patriotism displayed by both their previous and present presidents moved me to tears. This morning, I saw Mitt Romney, a publican senator and the opponent of Barrack Obama in the 2012 presidential candidate, who was praising Biden on some of the decisions Obama made against Vladimir Putin. Again, I was greatly impressed by what I witnessed and I was in tears. Blame my old age.

I am not as bad as my wife, but just like her, I "cry" a lot when I watch sad Korean TV dramas such as *Winter Sonata* (겨울 연가) or *My Mister* (나의 아저씨). This is a natural response of emotion but why in the world do I show tears when I watch Mitt Money saying what he was supposed to say? Am I hypersensitive to sentiment? I have a pair of warm hands and friends used to tell me that I, therefore, must have a cold heart and logical mind. What is wrong with me? Any act of kindness moves me to tears. Just yesterday, I learned that one of my favorite high school teachers, Lee Eu-rung (이어령), had just passed away. More tears.

Quite often I feel betrayed and become saddened by a friend or beloved one who casually uttered a few words without thinking that their words could offend me. I may quickly shed some tears without realizing that he or she did not mean to really hurt my feeling. The above proverb describes such a situation, where a seemingly trivial matter triggers teary eyes: as soon as a man swallows his first drink, he becomes emotional, producing tears. While the listener may be too sensitive but it is not a bad idea to go over beforehand what we are about to say to anyone. (02/28/2022)

⏰
405. Break fighting, offer mediation.
싸움은 말리고 흥정은 붙이랬다.

When I was a high school kid, I used to instigate pranks between two buddies of mine so that they could carry on further themselves. They were the victims of my plot but they didn't know any better. I just enjoyed their struggle to provoke more pain for each other. Both were surnamed Park and here I will call them Park 1 and Park 2. Don't get me wrong: all of us were bosom buddies. Park 2 passed away a long time ago, just after I left Korea. Inventing a feud between those two Parks was easy: I just tell Park 2 that it was Park 1 who removed the air plug on his bike tires after I did it myself. Park 2 then steals one of the arms of a wall clock in Park 1's room. In return Park 1 would steal Park 2's camera filters: Park 2 was an aspiring photographer then.

Park 1 had to do something in revenge, taking away Park 2's fencing weapon. If I remember, Park 2 used to have all sorts of interesting stuff like a bicycle, fencing, a camera, and even a pair of boxing gloves. His single mother dotted her only son without any limit, and Park 2 just kept asking for more. We were awestruck with envy by his array of toys. Park 1 wasn't exactly from a poor family either, but alas, he was just one son in an eight-sibling family.

What I was able to do with ease is opposite to what the above proverb promotes: try to break discords and try to provide mediation among the feuding parties. The word used, *heunng-jeong* (흥정) is closer to negotiation or bargaining: that is, the proverb advises us to become a mediator as a third party. Righteousness is overflowing from this proverb.

Empathy, in addition to the understanding of the procedural technicality involved, may offer a mediator the best approach to a mutual compromise or a bona fide mediation between disagreeing parties. Empathy would require the ability to place oneself in another person's position in a given situation. The ability or capacity of empathy must originate from one's own experience, both physical and emotional. A person with a linear life with a narrow "amplitude," compared with, say, an old well-read man with many adversities in the past, will have a hard time displaying genuine empathy.

Negotiation usually entails two parties with opposing interests. Since no third-party professional mediators are involved here, empathy could be even more important for a favorable outcome. If one party understands the weak point of the other party, they may enjoy a successful outcome. The 1975 movie, *Dog Day Afternoon* introduces a small-time crook named Sonny (played by Al Pacino) and his sidekick Sal (John Cazale) who were surrounded by police after a bungled bank heist in Brooklyn. They take a whole bunch of bank employees as hostages. Sonny and Sal were no match for a veteran detective and an FBI agent with their experienced team. The FBI has all leverage like Sonny's wife as well as his gay friend Leon. One can tell from the beginning that Sonny and Sal were doomed.

Just before the Russian army invaded Ukraine last week, French President Emmanuel Macron had met Vladimir Putin in an attempt to mediate the two parties involved but failed. Putin never gave it a chance. Just this morning CNN reported that in early February Chinese officials had requested Russian counterparts not to invade Ukraine till the Beijing Olympics is over. The news implied that Xi Jinping, when he met Putin at the Olympics opening ceremony, condoned, if not encouraged, the Russians to invade Ukraine. If we follow the advice of the above proverb, Macron was a good man while Xi is not.

On June 22, 2017, Bill Richardson published the following opinion column in Washington Post, just after his successful negotiation with North Korea for the release of Otto Warmbier. Richardson had served in various government positions, but he was more famous as a negotiator for the States in numerous global crises, especially with North Korea. Warmbier, a college student, entered North Korea as part of a guided tour group on December 29, 2015. Four days later, he was arrested at Pyongyang International Airport while awaiting departure and sentenced to 15 years of imprisonment for an attempt to steal a propaganda poster from his hotel.

I've helped rescue hostages from around the world and from North Korea, specifically..... To bring these cases to a resolution, we often work on three parallel tracks: identifying opportunities to create leverage; engaging directly with captors to ascertain what it might take to secure hostages' release; and working with the families of those taken hostage, who often find themselves in need of guidance. Working on all three tracks remains viable, but Otto Warmbier's case shows that it's time for a paradigm shift. (03/03/2022)

406. Explanation by a girl having a baby.
처녀가 애를 낳고도 할 말이 있다.

An unmarried teenager is about to give birth and offers an explanation as she is forced to. Given a choice, the girl wishes to avoid all inquiries but, alas, there is no way to hide her pregnancy. For a starter, she will have to tell everyone concerned about who the father of the baby is. If she cannot provide a definite answer, her explanation could be even longer. If she mumbles about the Holy Spirit and Virgin Mary, it is outright blasphemy. She may get stoned to death. However one may look at her situation, she is in a rabbit hole so to speak, a condition no one would envy.

As there will be many people who want to ask about her pregnancy, it may be a good idea for her to record a standard reply and play it whenever an occasion arises. Who would be interested in raising questions? Her parents and family may well be the first in line. Her current boyfriend may be the next. What about her friends, friends of her parents, her teachers, and her school counselor as well as the ones at her church? Even a stranger like her school bus driver may cast a quizzical glance at her swollen belly in the absence of any wedding ring.

What kind of questions would she be asked? For lack of any better approach, we will just follow the so-called *Five W's and an H* they teach aspiring reporters in Journalism 101. As to *who*, the identity of the baby's father is of utmost importance. Other subsequent questions may include his plan for the wedding and the support of their new family. The answer to *what* happened is so obvious, we will skip it altogether. *When* the conception took place may help pinpoint which boy would be responsible for her pregnancy if she has been promiscuous. The question will be followed by more concrete DNA testing. The questions of *where* and *why* are all intimately associated with *who*. Finally, one would ask how in the world she was not under birth control.

In the end, all those questions they ask are like water under a bridge, and everyone involved would pay attention to the future plan of the young parents involved. Not all is lost though if the teenage girl learns some valuable lesson from the accidental pregnancy. It may guide her to a more fulfilling and happier future.

30

The crux of the above prover is that even a person who made a big mistake has something to say, usually justification or excuse. These subjects were already covered in Entry #56, "Nose ring, earring." Just like all deaths have a cause as we saw in Entry #55, "No tomb is without a cause," every phenomenon we are experiencing has or should have an explanation. Some are rather routine or trivial so that we do not go through them all the time: for instance, "why does the sun rise in the east?" or "how did I flunk the college entrance exam in 1961?" As we see below, some other events are serious enough to seek an answer till the end of time.

On February 24, for no obvious justifiable reason, Russia invaded Ukraine in what appeared to be the largest conventional military attack in Europe since World War II. It was immediately met with widespread international condemnation and sanctions leading to a financial crisis. Anti-war protests in Russia were met with mass arrests. As of this writing, more than one million refugees fled to neighboring countries, in particular Poland. One day, they lived peacefully and the next day they had to leave their homes with an uncertain future. Most of the peace-abiding citizens on this planet were too flabbergasted to ask Vladimir Putin for a reasonable explanation for this outrageous action.

Since no one heard from Putin any acceptable justification, I am submitting my own perception here. Before the Soviet Union was dissolved in 1991 under political as well as economic failures, as many as 15 sovereign states including Ukraine formed the Union. All of them eventually seceded from the Union, declaring independence. Some of them expressed a desire to join NATO. Such a trend significantly reduced Russia's influence in the region, or "sphere of influence." Since Ukraine is the second largest, next to Russia, and well industrialized, the loss of Ukraine became a sour point in Putin's plan. This was particularly unacceptable when a citizen's revolution toppled a Russia-favoring government in 2013. It triggered Russia's annexation of Crimea in March 2014.

Ukraine has been continuously seeking closer ties with the West while fighting against Russia-backed their own separatists. For the lack of better expression, Putin has had enough and could not wait any longer for a new government that may favor Russia. He decided to annex Ukraine just like he did with Crimea. In essence, Putin implies that Ukraine was almost Russia's as late as 2013, and thus still is. Any explanation by a pregnant teen-aged girl would be more acceptable than Putin's. (03/05/2022)

31

407. Urinating onto frozen feet.
언 발에 오줌 누기.

Thanks to the location and the shape of the penis, man can control the trajectory of urination such that the warm liquid can thaw frozen feet, albeit momentarily. Then what, one may ask. If the ambient temperature is cold enough to freeze the feet, the heat of evaporation of the urine will withdraw more heat from the cold feet, if there were any heat left, making feet even colder in the blink of an eye. In essence, the above proverb says that a shoddy job is often worse than not having done it. A fundamental solution to a given problem often looks tedious and does not seem worth trying. This is particularly true in our contemporary society where a quick band-aid fix is in demand in a matter of time.

Half-cooked potatoes when one is in a hurry are not only terrible to eat because they have a hard texture and bitter flavor but also can cause headaches, nausea, diarrhea, and even death in extreme cases. This is because raw potato contains a poisonous, but heat-labile, compound called solanine. Weeds in an otherwise perfect lawn cannot be eliminated completely simply by being cut with a lawnmower. The only way I know how to get rid of them is by squatting down to the ground and pooling them out one by one in a complete entirety including intact roots. Spraying a weed killer leaves dead spots on the lawn. Besides, some commercial herbicides contain a presumably carcinogenic chemical.

Let us see how relevant the above proverb could be in juvenile development. The newly elected New York City mayor Eric Adams recently proposed that as young as 16-year-olds caught in possession of a gun be charged as adults if they do not disclose who supplied them with the weapon. Another State Assemblyman has gone one step further, introducing legislation that would permit the prosecution of 16-year-olds as adults when charged with possession of real or imitation guns. The proposal includes also those co-defendants possessing even imitation guns in a crime. This would expose them to the possibility of lengthy prison sentences and allow some of them to be jailed along with hard-core adults.

In 2010, 16-year-old Kalief Browder was jailed in New York's notorious Rikers Island, accused of stealing a backpack, a charge he consistently denied. Bail was set at $3,000, a sum his family could not afford. He spent the next three years there awaiting his day in court, including two years in solitary confinement. He suffered abuse from correction officers and inmates, and he attempted suicide. In 2013, the charges were dropped. Two years later, he committed suicide successfully this time.

When the mentality that tough laws can stop crimes is applied to "innocent" first-time juvenile offenders, as many ill-advised politicians and lawmakers tend to do, what happened to Browder is a typical result. Young adults in adult facilities are more frequently subject to sexual assault. A study reported that they were also five times as likely to kill themselves during juvenile detention. And they were significantly more likely to commit a violent crime after their release. Most alarmingly, trying more young people in adult courts is associated with more, not less, crime among young people. Even young adults tried in family courts do not fare well either: 16-year-olds charged in family court were found detained more frequently than youths of the same age charged in adult court (see Gladys Carrión and V. Schiraldi in the 03/10/2022 issue of *the New York Times*).

A recent Korean TV drama, titled *Juvenile Justice*, introduces a newly transferred female judge, Sim Eun-seok, and her junior judge, Cha Tae-ju, in a Juvenile Court. The former is a no-nonsense judge, as hard as a nail and fair and square, always following the book. Her nickname is "Judge Max." Judge Cha, on the other hand, treats every delinquent kid with the utmost compassion, working closely with counselors at detention centers. We may call them "bad cop-good-cop," who are trying their best to lead unfortunate young adults to a productive life. Their immediate boss, hot-tempered Judge Kang, is politically ambitious.

Each episode of the drama is full of contradicting interests of the people involved, but the major theme becomes clearer with each incident: we cannot and should not deal with juvenile delinquency in a mechanical mannerism of the law. The fundamental approach must be based on basic requirements in humanity as applied to young children. Solely relying on the court system in resolving a case after a case is like urinating onto frozen feet. It is a superficial maneuver of politicians to assure their constituents that they are doing something serious, much tougher than what their precedents did. Average citizens may go to sleep in peace with soothing words from politicians on local TV news. By the same token we, average citizens, should applaud those judges like Sim and Cha for their efforts. (03/31/2022)

408. Meant to draw a tiger, not a cat.
호랑이 그리려다가 고양이 그린다.

An ambitious painter had planned to illustrate a fearsome-looking tiger, perhaps inspired by the MGM film logo of the roaring lion head. Alas, his final product turned out to be a portrait of a rather docile kitten. We cannot tell from the way the proverb was written if such an unexpected outcome was due to his poor drawing skill or a change in plan in the middle of the drawing. Although the latter was implied, a standard interpretation is that one would ruin a venture if the person was too greedy or overambitious beyond his ability. It is then similar to Entry #6, "Sparrow tears legs racing against a stork." In the present essay, I would like to offer a slightly different take on the proverb.

As of today, Russia's unfathomable invasion of Ukraine has run its own course for more than six weeks, resulting in an embarrassing fiasco for the Russians and a biblical-scale tragedy for Ukrainians. Putin's imperial ambitions appear to be based on the "glorious" past of the Soviet Union before its dissolution in 1991 and possibly on longing for the romantic era of the Russian Empire prior to the Russian Revolution in 1917. Putin, during his tenure at KGB, was trained to view the West, particularly the US, as his enemy, and to see conspirators everywhere trying to weaken and humiliate Russia. Such paranoia must have also led him to the decision to grow his political and economic influence through the expansion of territory.

From the unsteady advance to the Ukraine territory and diminished value of the ruble, the whole world has now realized that Russia's military power has been over-rated and that their economy could be on the brink of total collapse. To add insult to Putin's pride, a Western alliance is now more unified than at any time since the worst tensions of the Cold War of the 1950s. Even many Asian nations like Japan, are offering humanitarian aid to Ukraine. These are all in addition to military aid from the European Union and the NATO nations. In effect, the whole world seems to be firmly unified by having Russia as a common foe. Putin must have been thinking of capturing a tiger but in the end, he may fail to catch even a cat.

The tiger is the largest cat species. It is recognized for its dark vertical stripes on orange fur with a white underside. It is territorial and a solitary predator commonly preying on boar and deer. The tiger appears frequently in mythology and folklore of many cultures, always in a positive context. The tiger is thus quite popular in coats of arms, flags, and names as well as mascots for sports teams. Indeed the tiger is the national animal of Korea.

Like a tiger, a cat has a strong flexible body, quick reflexes, sharp teeth, and retractable claws: all quite perfect for killing small prey. It is also territorial and solitary. Both tigers and cats communicate primarily via vocalization such as purring, trilling, hissing, growling, and grunting. In spite of these similarities, everybody can distinguish these two species. First of all, they are quite different in size and have little resemblance in their fur. Besides, the domestic cat is popular for a completely different reason from why we like tigers.

A problem would arise when a painter who has painted a cat-like tiger insists that it is in fact a tiger while most of the observers see a cat. Admittedly a painting is not some quantifiable scientific measure, but one can still distinguish a cat from a tiger. The difference in opinion or liking of a given painting, especially an abstract one, is a subjective judgmental call. Whose paint would you prefer, Pablo Picasso or Norman Rockwell?

Then there is an issue of perception and sensation in all other activities in our lives. Many years ago, two friends of mine decided to open a business together. This was just after we had graduated from college. One, call him A, brought in the capital, while the other friend B was in charge of the business end, which required a certain level of professional know-how. Friend A, being an investor, was not participating in any daily business. Once in a while, they had a regularly scheduled meeting to review the business progress. Sooner than later, A began to see that the profit was not as much as he had anticipated based on the plan that B had presented earlier.

By the end of the second year, their different reviews had become rather significant. For A, it was a disaster as the net income was much smaller than he had anticipated. Nonetheless, B maintained that they, after all, did not lose the principal although the total gain was minuscule. Here, unlike the above painting story, the discrepancy involved is an exact quantity, a number in the book. And yet, because they had projected different outcomes, they finally decided to end their collaboration. I heard second-handedly from other mutual friends that they no longer talk to each other. What they perceived, a cat or a tiger in the painting, or a half-empty or half-filled glass is what matters in practice. (04/01/2022)

⏰

409. Making others shed tears will make you bleed from your eyes.
남의 눈에 눈물 내면 제 눈에는 피가 난다.

This proverb says that if you cause someone to weep, your eyes will bleed, likely as punishment although this was not explicitly stated. There is a wide range of acts that can make others cry. If one cracks a great joke, people may laugh uncontrollably with eyes full of tears. Or one can shed tears of joy when a piece of happy news arrives unexpectedly at their doorstep. Sad movies will do the same. Moving, not necessarily sad, stories and videos can bring others to tears. Deeds of many modern-day Good Samaritans move people to tears of hopefulness in humanity. Ukraine President Zelensky's desperate pleas for help and Poland's generous responses find me in tears. Under some physiological conditions, one may suffer from excess tears: see more in Entry #404, "Tears upon the first drink." But these are not the type of tears that the above proverb is referring to.

Suppression of one's desire for happiness is one of the worst enemies of humanity. It is as bad as hanging a person in lynching. Shusaku Endo's novel *Silence* depicts 17th-century Japan, where Portuguese Jesuit priests are forced to witness their Japanese Christian brothers suffering from unimaginable cruelties that appear to test their own beliefs.

'I did pray. I kept on praying. But prayer did nothing to alleviate their suffering…. I have experienced that same suffering in my own body. Prayer does nothing to alleviate suffering'……. Then [Christ whispers] 'Trample! Trample! I more than anyone know of the pain in your feet. Trample! It was to be trampled on by men that I was born into this world. It was to share men's pain that I carried my cross.' The priest placed his foot on the [face of Christ]: Dawn broke. And far in the distance the cock crew.

Oppressing or rejecting people based on religion is another great enemy of humanity. It ranks way up high along with other causes such as skin color and sexual orientation. According to the above proverb, those who are responsible for depriving people of the fundamental premise of humanity should be punished and eventually will bleed from their eyes.

Of all types of tears, the tears from a young pregnant maiden who has just been abandoned by her ex-lover are agonizing not only to her but to the people around her. How is it possible for the man who she thought had been deeply in love with her to leave out of the blue? Regardless of the reason, the man has broken her heart. If we follow the proverb, his eyes will bleed from his act of betrayal in love.

Arirang (아리랑) is an old Korean folk song, estimated to be more than 600 years old. Its melody is well known throughout the world and is listed in the UNESCO Intangible Cultural Heritage. There are numerous variations and versions but all of them include a refrain, *Arirang, arirang, arariyo*, the first line in the score below. The first verse following the refrain reads as follows (here *ri*, or 리, is a measure of distance, approximately 0.4 km, hence 10 *ri* is only about 2.5 miles):

My love, if you leave me,
Your feet will be sore before you walk ten ri.

The girl's lament brings out the above words, not so much as a curse but as a prediction. Her still-lingering affection does not allow her to pray for bleeding eyes but merely for blistering feet. (04/08/2022)

410. A beggar is more miserable in an abundant year.
풍년 거지 더 서럽다.

This year happens to be a year of a very successful harvest and hence the sustenance is aplenty for everybody including the poorest among the poor. Nonetheless, here is a particular beggar who feels sad and depressed because others seem to be having a greater time than him in this year of abundance. The year of excellent harvest is Romanized here as *poong-nyun* (풍년), where *poong* and *nyun* mean plenty and year, respectively.

As I have been going about my life neither very poorly nor exceedingly well, witnessing how well others are doing is like watching a rapid stream passing by while I am standing still. In effect, I feel I am moving backward. When I am in a terrible situation, the last thing I want to see or hear about is how happy and successful other people are. Others may call it a bellyache from jealousy but it isn't the whole story. The narcissist in me has always kept me in the center and front of the world I live in and I have seldom lacked self-esteem. Besides, I am fully aware of the subjective nature of happiness. Yet, quite often I wish there are other people with whom I can share my misery, as in "misery loves company."

Would this uneasiness reflect the competitiveness in all of us? Is this an acquired trait or an instinct we were born with? No matter, it is unsettling.

As the Chinese have been prospering in recent years, Americans start to feel "threatened" economically as well as militarily. Extrapolating all recent relevant data seem to predict that it would be a matter of time before they will surpass the US on both counts. And think about the humongous size of their population that seems to be marching in lockstep forward under an autocratic government. If they have some social unrest, say, on the subject of LGBTQ, we do not hear about it through free presses in China. With this uneasy prospect, born was the so-called China Initiative in 2018 during the Trump era. It is being continued under President Joe Biden. This US Department of Justice program was designed to protect the top national security priority. The Initiative is to identify and prosecute those responsible for China's widespread theft of hundreds of billions of dollars a year in American trade secrets and intellectual property.

In December last year, the former Chair of the Chemistry Department at Harvard University, Charles Lieber, was convicted by a federal jury in connection with lying to federal authorities about his affiliation with the Wuhan University of Technology as well as failing to report the income he received from them. While his legal defense team maintained that they "will keep up the fight," no date has been set for sentencing.

In a similar incident, MIT professor Gang Chen was arrested at 6:30 AM in front of his family, handcuffed, described as loyal to China in public, and charged for having concealed seven Chinese affiliations in applications for $2.7 million in grants from the U.S. Energy Department. In the end, however, the charge was all dismissed because the prosecutors realized that Dr. Chen was not obliged to disclose those affiliations. "I am no longer the Gang Chen I was before," he said.

It was reported by CBS in January this year that there are still six China Initiative cases pending against researchers, three of whom are American citizens of Chinese ethnicity. One of these cases was the criminal trial of Feng Tao, a chemical engineering professor at the University of Kansas. It began on March 21 at a federal court in Kansas City. Tao was accused of lying about his ties to China and faced eight charges: six for wire fraud involving emails and electronic submissions of forms, and the other two for making false statements to the University and the US Department of Energy. Just two days ago, on April 7, a jury found him guilty of three counts of wire fraud and one count of making false statements. The verdict followed a two-week-long trial that had drawn the attention of civil rights activists. The latter group claimed the Initiative unfairly targeted Chinese Americans. Deliberation for sentencing has just begun.

I am now concerned about one of my previous colleagues and a friend, Leaf Huang at the University of North Carolina. He is also a Chinese American and has trained Chinese students, post-doctoral fellows, and visiting scholars. Just like the other three professors quoted above, he is also a world-renown scientist in our field of molecular pharmaceutics.

The US government's overly jealous scrutiny of research collaborations with China bothers me greatly. Is this trend a new form of McCarthyism in the academia of science and technology? Such sentiment will not go away so long as China remains prosperous and a "threat" to the US. Albeit somewhat tangent to the main topic, this is an unfortunate and sad analogy we can derive from the above proverb. (04/09/2022)

411. A *yangban* prefers drowning to dog-paddling.
양반은 물에 빠져도 개헤엄은 안 한다.

However you may look, dogs do not swim elegantly. They are just floating with four legs straight down into the water for paddling and their nose barely above the water. Thin legs do not offer any thrust of the body and thus move very slowly in what appears to be desperate efforts to save a dear life. They are far from the slick-body dolphins swimming.

If you were a *yangban* in old Korea, you would never adopt a dog paddle even when your life is on the line. Any *yangban* should have a certain level of dignity, or "face" in public. There is another similar proverb: even when you are freezing to death, *yangban* will not squeeze into a crowded gathering around an open fire, 양반은 얼어 죽어도 겻불은 안 쬔다. A man of high social status cannot mingle with *seomin* (서민) with fouling odor and in tattered clothes. Oh, no, never. They would prefer drowning to dog-paddling and stiff freezing death to sitting with crowded *seomin*.

The dignity assumed by *yangban* early in their lives becomes the dignity permanently embedded in them soon and lasts throughout their lives. They behaved as if they own the world with little regard for *seomin*. Such pretentious behaviors of *yangban* were a sure subject of mockery among *seomin*. I believe that's how the above proverb was spoken by *seomin* with tongue in cheek. "Those idiotic *yangbans* would give up their lives just to avoid the humiliation of becoming one of us." "They deserve their own fate, then!" These must be the words that *seomin* would murmur behind the *yangban's* back. See more in #367, "Even a flea has a face to carry around."

Throughout history, there always existed political, economic, and social classes. The rich would become richer at the expense of the poor, the ruling class always tried to maintain the status quo, and the intellectuals would look down upon average citizens.

When and if one class cannot endure more suppression from another, a revolution or a civil war would erupt. The recent centuries alone are quite rich in famous revolutions. Just to name a few, we have the American Independence War (1775-1783), the French Revolution (1789-1799), the Russian Revolution in 1917, the Chinese Revolution during the 1940s, the

Iranian Revolution in 1979, and the 4·19 Revolution in Korea in 1960. For the latter, see #247, "Silencing citizens is more than shutting my mouth up." Indeed, those revolutions constitute the bulk of human history. Per Carl Marx, class conflict is essentially human history.

I may be a bit too pessimistic but I must confess that I have been lately wondering if a revolution is imminent in the US, instigated by disgruntled citizens. Why do I entertain such a thought? Wherever I look, there appear to be too many fed-up citizens. They are people in poverty in spite of their sincere effort for survival, African Americans who may feel entitled to ill-defined something, disgruntled citizens of dubious political philosophy, ill-informed people under the influence of fake conspiracy theories, those who may feel alienated based on religious belief and race, people with a strong opinion on unfair tax, and other angry citizens for varying reasons.

Fortunately, right now, these unhappy people do not share a single common cause for their further disappointment. It keeps the critical mass needed for a revolution from materializing. I can't tell how long such a fortuitous situation would last.

Any seemingly trivial event can serve as a spark for the fully blown balloon of hydrogen gas to an abrupt burst. It can be voting suppression, transient inflation, the meltdown of financial institutes, some silly book-banning, any fiasco in immigration policy, an impotent remedial plan for climate change, unfair taxation, etc. We have been very fortunate, but you never know: some stupid politician makes an idiotic statement that will trigger a mass protest. In short, I feel as if we are walking on thin ice.

Well, there's always a class war going on. The United States, to an unusual extent, is a business-run society, more so than others. The business classes are very class-conscious — they're constantly fighting a bitter class war to improve their power and diminish opposition. Occasionally this is recognized... The enormous benefits given to the very wealthy, the privileges for the very wealthy here, are way beyond those of other comparable societies and are part of the ongoing class war. Take a look at CEO salaries.... (from Occupy: Class War, Rebellion and Solidarity by Noam Chomsky)

Does Chomsky happen to predict something similar to what was speculated above? (04/25/2022)

412. Turn around if the road ends.
막다른 골목이 되면 돌아선다.

In the spring of 2012, a good friend of mine, Doug Mendenhall, and I tracked a northbound 300-mile (approximately 500 km) Appalachian Trail starting at Daleville, VA, and ending at Harper's Ferry, WV. We came across a lot of rain, making the hiking miserable most of the time. One day - according to my journal it was May 23 - we were supposed to cover 13.1 miles from Pass Mtn Hut to Gravel Spring Hut. Throughout the day, the weather was perfect, the sun shining and the air crispy.

However, in the mid-morning, we came across a torrential creek, much swollen with the heavy rain of the previous night. Part of the trail on a big boulder was submerged in the water, but we could clearly see the continuation of the trail beyond several feet. On our left, the steep boulder continued further up seven or eight feet. At the top, there were bushes and trees. There were three options. First, we could have continuously walked on the trail just for a short distance although it was now under rapid water. The second option was that we somehow climbed over the stone face on the left and climbed down to the other side of the trail. The third choice was to turn around and backtrack a few miles.

We saw some young hikers taking chances with the first two options and succeeding. Both approaches were tempting but appeared too risky for this old man, especially with a 25-pound backpack and a pair of walking poles. We took the third option and survived to describe the experience now. It was certainly by default but was still a viable option. In this spirit, the above proverb seems to shed a positive light on what appears to be the least-appealing scenario, like the cup is half-full rather than half-empty.

Old Chinese warfare strategies are well recorded in 10 volumes, known as *Ten Military Classics*. Each volume deals with different aspects of warfare. Some of them are almost three-millennium old. The last strategy in Volume 10, known as "The 36th Tact," recommends, "Retreat now but plan for the future," if you are facing an almighty foe. It implies that fighting an insurmountable battle is plainly stupid. We should read the above proverb from this perspective. See more in Entry #128, "We sidestep feces because it is filthy not out of fear."

The proverb says that facing a high stone wall during your walk is not the end of everything in your life. You just turn around is what it suggests. This is easy to say but there would be always a lingering wish to overcome the wall, a real challenge. Here is an example from my own past.

All humans have in our blood circulating antibodies that recognize some specific molecular moiety expressed in animal tissues and organs. Call it an anti-gal antibody since the target of the antibody is rich in a carbohydrate molecule, galactose. This is the main reason we violently and swiftly reject any xenografts such as kidneys or the heart of an animal. If they are so efficient to attack and eliminate foreign tissue, why can't we use the system in eradicating cancers?

How can we then direct the ant-gal antibody to cancer? Compared to normal tissues in healthy people, ovarian cancer expresses a high level of the receptor for folic acid, one of the B vitamins. Our working hypothesis was that a chemical construct containing both folic acid and the galactosyl moiety, when introduced to the bloodstream, will mediate the strong attack of the antibody on ovarian cancer cells. Everybody, including my students and the National Cancer Institute of the National Institutes of Health, was quite enthusiastic about the project.

The chemical synthesis of the "matchmaker" conjugate containing both folic acid and the galactosyl compound proved extremely difficult even for my post-doctoral fellow with a PhD in organic chemistry. Experimental verification of the conjugate was another difficulty. We cannot use any simple animal model of human ovarian cancer because all their tissues express the galactosyl moiety and no animals have anti-gal antibodies in their circulation.

In a slightly different but somewhat related biomedical research field, there had been fierce competition among several biotech companies for developing genetically modified pigs that did not express galactosyl moiety in their tissues. In theory, these pigs can donate their organs to humans without any immune rejection. Only last year, the first human trial began with organs from such genetically altered pigs. It is very much like the human clones described in *Never Let Me Go*, a 2005 dystopian science fiction by the British author Kazuo Ishiguro.

Although my lab encountered many difficulties, I could not let the project simply fade away when I retired in 2013. I still wish I could go back to chemical synthesis from the beginning. (04/28/2022)

413. Hearing ten times is not as worthy as seeing once.
열 번 듣는 것이 한 번 보는 것만 못하다.

I do not enjoy travel as much as I thought I did in the past. By travel, I meant visiting esoteric and exotic places like Egypt, Mt. Kilimanjaro, or Silk Road. My standard explanation to myself is that I just want to avoid all associated hassles at this advanced age. Besides, we can learn about any interesting place via the internet at home with great leisure and comfort. Often experts also offer an explanation much greater in detail than the signboards at the sites. But I do admit that there is something one can experience only through physically being there, like they say, "Seeing is believing."

Almost 30 years ago, that is when I was young, my wife and I visited the mausoleum of Qin Shihuang, or 진시황 (259 – 210 BC), in Xian City, China. He was the first emperor of united ancient China. Beginning in 1974, approximately one mile east of the tomb, thousands of terracotta Chinese warriors, horses, and various bronze weapons were discovered about 16 ft deep underground. Except for one pit, which was to represent the commanding post, the other three are on average two square miles. When we visited, the site was under a huge roof and still being excavated.

The eyeballs, thin mustache, and facial expression of each soldier, the clothes they are wearing, the weapons they are carrying, or the spoke of bronze chariots can be indeed examined in greater detail from close-up pictures than watching from some distance away. However, its enormous dimension cannot be captured on a videotape for audiences in the living room. My wife and I had heard a lot about the place, but "seeing was indeed more than 10 times worthier" than we had studied in advance before the actual visit. We were simply awe-struck.

What struck me the most was the silence over the tomb of thousands of "alive" soldiers and horses. If there was tension anticipating invading armies and shouting orders, it must have been my imagination. So was the perceived smell of earth. Then, of course, sculptures: each portrait with its own vivid expression of more than 2,000 pottery figures could rival any masterpiece of Leonardo da Vinci (1452 – 1519), seemingly begging for proper recognition. Note that the mausoleum was built almost 17 centuries earlier than Leonardo da Vinci's era.

For some reason, of the five senses (hearing, seeing, smelling, touching, and tasting), seeing seems to offer the best long-lasting memory. Hearing and the other senses are short-lived in comparison and difficult to reproduce in the mind. As such, seeing is also the best form of verification as in "Doubting Thomas" or an eyewitness at a court hearing.

Thomas, one of the Twelve, was not with them when Jesus came. So the other disciples said to him, "We have seen the Lord." But he said to them, "Unless I see the mark of the nails in the hands and put my finger into the nail marks and put my hand into his side, I will not believe." Now a week later his disciples were again inside and Thomas was with them, Jesus came, although the doors were locked, and stood in their midst and said, "Peace be with you." Then he said to Thomas, "Put your finger here and see my hands, and bring your hand and put it into my side, and do not be unbelieving, but believe." Thomas answered and said to me, "My Lord and my God!" Jesus said to him, "Have you come to believe because you have seen me? Blessed are those who have not seen and have believed." [John 20: 24-29]

The court verdict in many criminal cases depends on the testimony of a key eyewitness, once again emphasizing the importance of "seeing." It is quite common for the guilty party to attempt to remove key witnesses before the trial. Thus, born was the witness protection program offered by the government. In some serious instances, such as organized crimes or matters involving national security, the protection of the witness goes beyond the conclusion of a trial. Often they are provided with a new identity and may have to live their lives under continuous protection from the government.

When a person accidentally witnesses a serious crime and the criminals know who the person is, his or her life becomes full of anxiety and fear, perhaps resonates with "see no evil," or Entry #102, "Ignorance is medicine." In the 1985 film, *Witness*, a young Amish boy is the sole witness to a murder. A police detective, played by Harrison Ford, tries to protect the boy but he himself becomes the target of ambush among his corrupt police colleagues and has to hide in the Amish country receiving care from the boy's widowed mother of a gunshot wound. The romantic feeling was mutual, but Harrison Ford leaves the community in the end. (04/30/2022)

414. An abscess on her back on her wedding day.
시집갈 날 등창이 난다.

I can only imagine what a maiden prepares, I mean, mentally, for the upcoming wedding. Most of the practical arrangements must have already been made in consultation with her mother, older sister, and friends, but when she is alone by herself like just before falling asleep what would she think about? In old Korea, the first day of their honeymoon will be the first time she will be exposed completely naked to her husband. Everything that will follow is something she has learned only through her mother and friends who have already married. They are rather sketchy at best.

Regardless of what she has heard or read about the first night, it would be her absolute determination to show her best to her husband to assure him that he is indeed a lucky man to have her as his wife. Then, alas, just the night before the wedding day, the bride-to-be noticed a blister forming on her back, a place she can feel but barely reach. It is an early stage of development and there won't be much pus even if she can and does squeeze the abscess.

Why now, of all 365 days of the year, she laments. Eventually, she resigns to the unavoidable conclusion that she would ask her one-day-old husband to deal with the problem. She just hopes that the abscess will grow quickly so that her husband can easily squeeze out the discharge tomorrow night. Still, she would much prefer not to have such an inconvenient incident during their first night together.

On the other hand, it may well be a blessing in disguise as it could define their life-long relationship in a positive and cooperative fashion. Is he faint-hearted or disgusted by the sight of pus oozing out of the blister on the otherwise beautiful skin of her back? Or would he be glad to be of help on Day One of their life? So many thoughts exhaust her into pretty fretting and shallow sleep throughout the night.

We came across a similar proverb describing an irritable incident happening on an important occasion. In Entry #17, "When it rains, it pours," I described a scholar who is looking forward to a tranquil time in a small village but finds the place he visits happens to be one of the busiest days of the year as they are having a noisy and crowded market day.

I do not know why it is such a case, but accidents tend to happen to me only Friday afternoon or evening after all the shops are closed for the weekend. The incidents with an injury, for instance, are usually not serious enough to visit the emergency room but uncomfortable enough to need some medical attention. One windy spring morning a sliver of mulch got into my eyes during yard work. Luckily I was able to find an eye doctor in a strip mall who opens his shop Saturday mornings.

Why do I always break dishes only after I clean them, or why does it rain after a car wash? Just after one bite, I drop the ice cream accidentally to the dirt. Am I unusually unlucky? The line I am standing on at the cashier is the shortest and yet it looks like I stay in the grocery store longer than anyone else. A beautiful lady sends a bright smile at a bar in my direction, but it is for another guy just behind me. I am about to park my car at an excellent spot, but a young kid gets in there faster than me.

Truth be told, such trivial but irritating and inconvenient episode happens all the time to anyone without discriminating between times or places. It just appears to happen only on a day of some significance. Coincidence is what it is but to those directly involved, it often seems to be an omen of something involving one's own fate.

Any rare coincidence is a matter of probability. If we cast a die many times, the odds of having each of the six numbers should be equal, or about 17%. If not, it would be fishy. Most gambling such as common card games and betting sports events award the highest for the outcome of the lowest probability. The return for the horse that is expected to win would be thus lowest for the given amount of betting while the horse that nobody projects to win provides a very generous return. So, we are more interested in the odds involved in a rare event, like getting struck by lightning or getting killed while driving a one-way street in the wrong direction.

As introduced in Entry #197, "None of the fingers is alike," the 2018 documentary *Three Identical Strangers* tells the story of three young men who discovered in 1980 that they were identical triplets, adopted by different families upon birth. The first two met through a fluke meeting on a college campus while the third joined them later via publicity on the media. What would be the odds of such a coincidence? I also discovered that the renowned British theoretical physicist Stephen Hawking died on Einstein's 139th birthday. Actually, this odd looks pale if we think about how long he lived, 76 years to be exact, with Lou Gehrig's disease. (05/02/2022)

415. People shared a meal fight in a court.
한 솥의 밥 먹고 송사 간다.

Although the original proverb in Korean appears to be very short, I had a hard time translating it into a short sentence in English. Let me try sort of a fundamental approach covering as many background materials as possible. First, *sot* or (솥): as described in detail in Entry #138, "Startled by a turtle and now by a cauldron lid," it is a cast-iron pot primarily used in fixing rice. Nowadays everybody prepares steamed rice using an electric cooker but even in the 1960s Koreans relied on heavy-duty *sot* for boiling rice. Those people who share steamed rice, or *bob*, out of a given *sot* must be closely related to one another, like family members. And yet they sue each other in a court of law for one reason or another.

Legal litigations among siblings are generally about inheritance: that is, financial interests. It is too common to address here. A married couple can sue each other especially when they go through a divorce. It can be quite nasty and ugly: as we speak now, the American actor Johnny Depp has just rested his case against ex-wife Amber Heard in his defamation trial. It all began with a 2018 Washington Post op-ed where Heard insinuated she had been the victim of domestic violence. Depp claims the article ruined his reputation and career. He is asking for $50 million in retribution. One time, their lives as a married couple must have been as close to each other as can be, or "shared rice from the same pot" so to speak.

The following story is from an article by John Mbati in the 12/03/2021 issue of *kenyans.co.ke*, "Father sues son, demands 20% of his monthly salary." The crux of the story told by a 73-year-old Kenyan is a sentiment that will resonate well with many old Korean parents. As presented in Entry #99, "All fields are fertile to diligent farmers," Korean parents are notorious for their obsession with their children's education and would sacrifice nearly anything. Parents seem to justify their sacrifice for the prospect that their children can now receive the type of education that they never had and as a result, will enjoy a comfortable life that has somehow evaded them. What is not said openly is of course their anticipation that their children will take care of them later when they age.

The papers filed at a Kenyan court by the old man stated that his son was absorbed by city life and left him to fend for himself. He argued that he deserves to be well catered for after toiling to provide a better life for his son and complained that he sold his parcels of land to educate the son. He also gave the son his share of the inheritance, a quarter of an acre of land, and blessed the son prior to his marriage. The court papers added that the old man further paid a dowry, which comprised an undisclosed amount of money, four cows, and other items. The aggrieved old man thus wants upkeep as compensation for his sacrifice.

He outlined that the son was employed by a government agency in Nairobi and solely enjoyed his salary, allowances, bonuses, and insurance. The young man was also in line for a pension upon retirement. "I used all the resources I had to enable him to be in a good position so that he can help our family. I request 20 percent of his salary to be given to me as the father." The father of four added that the family was dependent on the son who allegedly cut connections with them after landing the city job. Efforts to solve the matter amicably were fruitless as the son was unreachable.

"I have tried several times for years to seek assistance from my son, but all in vain. He is the only one, out of my four children, who is gainfully employed," he told the court. Since he cannot afford a lawyer, he filed the case and represented himself in court.

I do not know how the court decision turned out, but I wish him well. Just think about the mental agony the father had gone through before he was forced to file a formal complaint against his own son. By the same token, I cannot stop condemning his son for the "betrayal."

We, Koreans in both North and South Korea, inherited the same heritage in history, culture, religion, and most importantly language from our ancestors up to the end of the Second World War in 1945. That is, we used to share bowls of "rice from the same pot." Then, different political ideologies invaded the land along with the remnant imperialism from the 19th century carried by Russia and the US. This inevitably divided the same people into two nations.

How much I resent the way this part of modern Korean history has developed now become a moot point and we come to resign that two Koreas are here to stay for many generations to come. I am certain that we will not be able to unify in my lifetime. The only thing I can do now is to oppose a similar development in other parts of this planet. (05/04/2022)

416. Even a dog comes to you when called.
이웃집 개도 부르면 온다.

The status of dogs has dramatically enhanced in modern Korea. First of all, in the old days, we seldom kept a dog inside the house. My parents always had a dog as far as I can remember, but we spent a little time with them playing together. Our dogs were more or less for alerting us when a stranger showed up.   Sometimes our dog would bite an innocent kid in the neighborhood for no obvious reason. Then we used to shave off some hair - I remember we would collect the hair from the bottom side of the tail - and burn the hair. The resulting tar was smeared over the site of the bite on the victim. To this day, I still don't know if there is some scientific reason for the treatment or if it was just a superstitious ritual.

Our neighbors' dogs recognized us and left us alone. When we called them on a rare occasion, they would trot to us with their tails wiggling. This is about the extent of my interaction with their dog. The above proverb implicitly asks why you cannot respond when I call you. Even a dog does when I call them. A timely response would be particularly critical when someone in a dire situation asks you for help.

We can find a case of the point from the Korean War. But for the military intervention from the United Nations, spearheaded by the US, the democratic South Korean government would not have survived the War. We are "eternally" grateful for the timely help. Summarized below is what was happening in the later part of 1950.

North Korean military forces invaded South Korea on Sunday, June 25, 1950. Just after the first two months, the South Korean Army and American forces hastily dispatched to Korea were on the brink of defeat, retreating to a small area behind the Nakdong River, known as the Busan Perimeter. It was a matter of days before South Korea would completely disappear from the map. In September, the commander-in-chief of the UN Command, General MacArthur, launched a risky amphibious UN counteroffensive at Incheon, a port city just west of Seoul, cutting off North Korean troops and supply lines. Those who escaped envelopment were forced back north. Shortly after the successful landing, Seoul was recaptured. This was undoubtedly the turning point of the War.

The UN Security Council was able to establish the UN Command consisting of 21 countries headed by the US. It was possible because the Soviet Union was boycotting the UN for recognizing Taiwan as China, and also because mainland China was then not recognized by the UN. That is, neither of them was present at the Security Council meeting to help their ally, North Korea. This situation was a significant difference in the role, or lack of role, of the UN in the current Ukraine-Russia war.

The Ukraine-Russia War has just entered its third month. This time, the UN has been impotent in terms of military aid since Russia is sitting in the Security Council with veto power. Instead, once again, the US took the initiative for developing a joint condemnation with European allies against Russia's invasion. This reaction of the European Union is more than just out of fear that someday they will be also invaded by Russia. There has been a higher calling for humanity in preserving democracy as well as for compassion toward the needy among the Ukrainian refugees, as exemplified by the Polish government and their people.

While we hear many heart-warming stories involved in humanitarian aid to Ukrainian refugees, particularly in Poland, we have also recently witnessed a different type of response to the needy. The story is from China. The official policy of the Chinese government toward the COVID-19 pandemic amounts to, for the lack of better expression, a prison system.

In the past several weeks, Shanghai, the financial capital of China and a city of more than 26 million residents, has been on lockdown and its citizens were subject to the most stringent measures including isolation during mass testing and extended quarantine periods.

Some video footage showed healthcare staff wearing special suits, much like the ones that astronomers may wear, wrestling residents to the ground and leading them away toward a white van. Other similar videos have shown people protesting the lockdowns, and fighting for food and medicines. Babies sometimes were separated from their parents. It was so surreal that I thought I was watching some futuristic movie dealing with a dystopian society.

While as many as 23 Chinese cities were said to have implemented either full or partial lockdowns, the Chinese government has refused to review the Zero COVID policy that President Xi Jinping had implemented. Although he claims he can minimize the losses, the chaotic situation in Shanghai suggests things got out of his control. (05/04/2022)

417. Kick a jagged rock to pain the foot.
돌부리를 차면 발부리만 아프다.

If you kick a jagged rock protruding from the ground, you would feel a sharp pain in the foot: the harder you kick, the more pain you will have. Here, the words "rock" and "foot" were translated from the Korean words *dolburi* (돌부리) and *balburi* (발부리), respectively. Note the presence of rhyme, which was lost in the translation. Now, a relevant question would be why one would do that. Is it because you hate rock very much? Or was it just a habit you developed at a very young age? Or are you trying to dig it out? Or is it because you kick the rock out of quick anger or frustration?

The expression of anger or deep frustration can take various forms. For a given person, it would depend on the occasion. It can range from simple shrugging to the catharsis of foul language and smashing furniture like kicking a rock firmly embedded in the ground. To a man of pride ad wealth, for instance, losing money from the stock trade may not be as bad as when he is verbally insulted in public.

Likewise, it also varies from one person to another in a given situation. On a sinking ship, some may pray or others may curse. Invariably though, when mad, people would overreact with exaggerated irrational behaviors, as we have seen in similar proverbs: Entry #124, "Burning a house down to get rid of bedbugs," and #376, "Pull a sword out to fight a mosquito." Overreactions out of a short temper, when looked back many years later, are often a source of embarrassment, especially when the cause of anger was trivial or based on some simple misunderstanding. It is the surviving memory of the pain in the "foot."

I still do not know how other professors made their graduate students work hard in the lab but all I remember now is how frustrating it was. Truth is that I did not know how to inspire or prod them. The "carrot-and-stick" approach of appeasement along with a threat to remove them from the program can do only so much. Such occasions of tense conversation always made me feel awful afterward. Have I gone too far? Did I personally insult the student when I said this and that? Would he visit the department chair? But how can I renew the grant with such a dismal pace of project progress?

One particular student, a quite intelligent young man, did not work as hard as one would expect from a man whose livelihood at that time was from my research grant. Much cajoling bore no meaningful results. With firm determination, I confronted him one last time with an ultimatum that he had to find another mentor in the program. Both he and I knew it would be impossible without any good reference from me.

Without any preliminary warning, he confessed that he had been suffering from migraine headaches for many years and that lab work could be outright dangerous physically. I withdrew the ultimatum and he agreed to continuously work with me with a new level of commitment. Again, at home, I did not feel good at all not so much about the outcome but about my immature conclusion that he was simply one of those lazy students. It was like kicking a rock on the ground and I felt a sharp pain in my foot. (As a footnote, later I learned that it was not him but his live-in girlfriend who had been suffering from the chronic headache but that I kicked the rock at that time remains an unshakable memory.)

In early 2014, Russia invaded and subsequently annexed the Crimean Peninsula from Ukraine. There were tremendous outcries throughout the world, especially from the US and nations of the European Union. Since Russia is a permanent member of the UN Security Council, the UN was impotent in terms of enforceable punishment. In short, the Russian bullying act on the global stage has remained noticeably intact.

Emboldened with their fruitful tactics with Crimean annexation, in February this year, the Russians invaded Ukraine with the hope of a similar outcome. How wrong they were. Unlike what they had anticipated, there was no uprising of pro-Russia Ukrainian separatists. The condemnation of the invasion was unequivocal throughout the world. Even those nations with close ties with Russia on oil imports were outraged this time. Most importantly, the military aid from the US and the rest of the NATO members have made Ukrainian forces quite formidable. Beginning a few days ago, pundits have been talking about the possible win by Ukraine in the war.

Today is the 77th anniversary of European and Russian victory over the Nazis. Traditionally, it is one of the most celebrated days in Russia with all that fanfare. However, this year, speaking at the Victory Day parade, Vladimir Putin described the war in Ukraine as an unavoidable response to Western policies. Nothing new here but most noticeable was his subdued body language. He seems to feel a "sharp pain in his foot." (05/09/2022).

418. One bushel returned on one gallon lent.
되로 주고 말로 받는다.

Imagine a neighbor who ran out of potable water during a terrible drought. Being a good Samaritan, you give them a gallon, or one *doe* (되), of water. Later you receive from them a bushel, or one *mal* (말), in return. The proverb uses two old Korean units of volume, where a *mal* is ten times bigger than a *doe*, implying that a kind act is compensated quite generously later. What is exchanged can really be any kind of deed.

According to the 2019 report from APAC (Asia-Pacific), since 2008, South Korea has provided more food and other donations to the UN aid program for North Korea than any other nation. In 2019 alone, South Korea provided $4.5 million to the UN World Food Program along with 50,000 tons of rice. It was the largest donation from South Korea to the UN Program. It should be able to support 1.5 to 2 million children, pregnant women, and nursing mothers in North Korea.

Just yesterday, BBC News reported that more than a million people have now been sickened by what Pyongyang is calling a "fever." Some 50 people have died, but it's not clear how many of those cases tested positive for COVID-19. Since North Korea has only limited testing capacity, few cases are confirmed. In the meantime, their leader Kim Jong-un has lambasted health officials and ordered the army to help distribute medicine as a wave of the pandemic sweeps through the country.

Upon learning of such a dire situation in North Korea, newly elected South Korean President Yoon Suk-yeol offered on May 13 to supply North Korea with COVID-19 vaccines and medical equipment. In order to help the neighboring country curb the spread of the disease, South Korea intends to hold talks with North Korea in the next few weeks to discuss COVID-19 relief measures. Considering Yoon was inaugurated as president only a week ago, what is truly remarkable is the prompt shift in the gesture of humanitarian aid with no strings attached.

What does the South receive in return for their kindness? On May 12, North Korea fired another three short-range ballistic missiles toward the East Sea of Korea. This was just two days after President Yoon Suk-yeol was sworn in and five days after the North fired a ballistic missile from a submarine. It was also the 16th missile launch this year alone. It is hard to believe but South Korea is like being bitten by a dog they have been feeding all along. We have come across similar proverbs in Entry #174, "My ax injures my foot," and #189, "Lend the money and lose a friend."

When one curses or harasses someone, would they receive a "bushel" of the same? They should, in my own sense of fairness and justice: what one gives is what one receives, or "eye for an eye." More than three months ago, the Russian army invaded Ukraine without any justifiable excuse. Putin might have thought that they could shake some weaker countries loose from their alliance with the West but it really backfired. Not only did their move strengthen the bonding of the European Union but also render Finland and Sweden to consider joining NATO.

We are supposed to see good deeds returning in abundance for good deeds offered. However, it did not work out that way in the above example involving North Korea. The South instead received a "bushel" of outrageous and horrific responses. If one carries out a bad intention upon others, they are to receive a "bushel" of the same. Indeed, Russia was universally condemned for the invasion of Ukraine.

Another case may involve a situation in which a person treats another person in the meanest manner one can think of, and yet the victim comes back with forgiveness. Upon hearing the question from Peter about how many times to forgive a brother who sins against him, Jesus says Peter should forgive the person 70 times seven [Matthew 18:22]. If you recall, Peter originally asks if forgiving seven times is sufficient and appropriate.

We can find in history and fiction many courageous people of principle, conviction, loyalty, faith, trust, and love. Socrates spent his last day in prison, and so did Galileo Galilei and Yoo Gwan-soon, a Korean version of Joan of Arc: see Entry #215, "Stealing the doorknob of a police station." The Portuguese Jesuit priests appearing in Shusaku Endo's novel *Silence* amply demonstrate mental fortitude over the physical pain: see Entry # 409, "Making others shed tears will make you bleed from your eyes."

These and other heroes of mine, whom I cannot go through all with limited space and time, have set the course for humanity at the highest level one can imagine. For what they did individually in a given field and collectively for society, they have received and will continuously receive a "bushel" of unending admiration throughout history. (05/15/2022)

419. The life of a fly is what we have.
파리 목숨 같다.

The female housefly lays eggs on decaying organic matter such as food waste, injured animal tissue, or feces. They hatch into maggots, which further develop into pupae about 3/8 inch long. Adult flies feed on a variety of liquid or semi-liquid substances including human waste. They carry pathogens, contaminate food, and contribute to the transfer of food-borne diseases. Besides, they are physically annoying. For these reasons, they are considered pests. Adults normally have a short lifespan: two to four weeks.

From birth to death, they are intimately surrounded by what humans consider filthy and offer more harm than anything else. When I was a child, I used to ask myself why God created such a pest: sometimes I naively thought it a good proof that God does not exist. And mosquitos, spiders, and leeches. Why do they exist? I still cannot answer the question.

In literature, their short lifespan was also not unnoticed and was often compared with the life of a human being. The above proverb laments the same point: our lives are ephemeral and vain, just like the life of houseflies. We may now live as long as 100 years but relatively speaking it can be as short as three weeks of a fly's lifespan. In the end, one can ask, "What is the true meaning of life?" While preparing this essay, I came across William Blake's 1794 poem *The Fly*. It speaks of the brevity of life as well as mortality subject to uncontrollable circumstances, the same as the above proverb.

Little Fly,
Thy summers play
My thoughtless hand
Has brushed away.

Am not I
A fly like thee?
Or art not thou
A man like me?

For I dance
And drink & sing,

Till some blind hand
Shall brush my wing.

If thought is life
And strength & breath:
And the want
Of thought is death,

Then am I
A happy fly,
If I live,
Or if I die.

The above poem is certainly kinder to flies than I am. The fly will be the last creature I would have had in my mind if I wanted to reflect on the fragile nature of human life. Fragile? Our lives could be fragile in a physical sense, but one's spirit and belief can survive generations through what he or she has left behind in their art and writings.

Just nine days ago, on May 8, one of the most prominent Korean poets, Kim Ji-ha, passed away at the age of 81. He was not only prolific in poetry but also famous for his unending protest against any form of political suppression of democratic movements. His anti-establishment, especially against those involved in corruption, touched the nerve of many people and served as an inconvenient and irritating thorn to them. Famous was his dislike of the "five bandits (오적)," which are comprised of chaebol, national assemblymen, high-ranking government officials, military brass, and secretary members of government. One common denominator of all these is corruption.

Of numerous jail times, his death sentence in 1974 was the most dramatic and troublesome among his friends and readers. Korean CIA, under the iron fist of the Park Jung-hee regime, conspired to develop a fraudulent scenario to suppress any political movement of college students for democracy. Kim was accused of being one of the leaders according to the concocted scheme by the CIA. Thanks to concerted efforts by his contemporaries, he was released. However, he was arrested again when he exposed the truth behind his original death sentence.

One of our contemporary poets, Chu Kwang-il, dedicated the following poem to Kim Ji-Ha's passing.

온 산에/봄꽃들/모두 졌다네. (Gone from all over the hill/Are the Spring flowers). 신록 짙어가는 계절에/ 김지하 시인도 먼 길을 떠났다네. (In this season of lush green/Kim Ji-ha has also departed for a long road). 읽을 때마다/내 눈시울을 뜨겁게 만들던/그의 시만 남았네. (Only left behind are his poems/That always brings me to tears).

Flowers are indeed a much better representation of human life. As in humans, there is a period of promise, prosperity, maturity, recollection, and an irreversible ending. Once gone, its memory lingers for a while but then the memory of memories disappears in due time. (05/17/2022)

⏰

420. Can't taste boiling soup.
끓는 국에 맛을 모른다.

I suppose that the ideal temperature for serving a given dish must depend on who is eating. However, one can generalize without worrying too much about committing an embarrassing error. A Korean cold noodle dish called *naeng-myun* (냉면) must be served with blocks of ice floating. The waitress in Korean restaurants brings out various pot stews, or *jji-ge* (찌개), such as stew of seafood or tofu, in a dark-brown porcelain bowl while they are still bubbling. They are hot in taste also. Several Korean dishes whose names end with *tang* (탕) such as *gom-tang* (곰탕), *galbi-tang*, (갈비탕), and *seolung-tang* (설렁탕) are best served when they are warm.

Similarly, one can generalize the ideal temperature for drinks, realizing that the taste of each beverage at different temperatures would be different. I drink red wine at room temperature while white wine and champagne while cold. Beer is always kept in a refrigerator. "Whiskey on the rock" is of course with a chunk of ice. I drink other liquor or spirits at room temperature. I drink Macallan single malt scotch following the procedure I learned from my wealthy hairdresser back in Chapel Hill, North Carolina: a dash of water to a couple of fingers and stir vigorously. Then, drink "through the nose," all at ambient temperature.

They say that coffee must be brewed when it is most fragrant, at about 95°C (203°F), and served at 85°C (185°F). But we also drink iced coffee, just like tea, hot tea as well as iced tea in the summer.

When one is in a hurry and hungry, they may try the boiling soup at the risk of burning their palate. What can they taste? Probably nothing because they are so startled by its temperature that there won't be any other instinct capacity or ability at that moment. So, the above proverb says that one cannot truly understand the nature of a given task or cannot devise a solution to a problem at hand if they are in hurry. It implies the importance of mindfulness and focusing. See, Entry #3, "Thread through the eye of a needle, not around the body." It is also similar to "Haste makes waste," or "more haste, less speed."

Except for modern times, the Korean Peninsula was frequently invaded by neighboring nations. Of the few invasions by Japan, *imjin waeran* (임진왜란) was the most consequential. The seven-year war started in 1592 with the invasion by the army of Toyotomi Hideyoshi after he had unified Japan. Although Hideyoshi was powerful enough to conquer all feudal Japanese samurai factions, he lacked the shogun background, an essential requirement of the ruler of Japan during that period. Perhaps to compensate for this weak point, he sought military power to legitimize his rule and to become less dependent on the imperial family.

Two years earlier, the Kingdom of Joseon sent two emissaries, Hwang and Kim, to Kyoto to probe Hideyoshi's true intentions. They were treated badly by Hideyoshi. When Hwang and Kim finally delivered a letter from King Seon-jo (선조) of Joseon after an unwarranted delay, arrogant self-made Hideyoshi assumed that the Koreans had come to pay a tributary homage to Japan. In the end, the Korean ambassadors asked Hideyoshi for a reply to King Seon-Jo back at home. It took 20 days for Hideyoshi to respond to the request. The letter was too discourteous and thus Korean emissaries politely asked again Hideyoshi to redraft it.

Ambitious he was, Hideyoshi invited Joseon to submit to Japan and join in a war against China. It was the essence of his letter. He was fully aware that this invitation was never accepted by Joseon. It just served as a perfect excuse for the invasion of Korea.

When Hwang and Kim returned, the Joseon court held serious discussions on the letter from Hideyoshi. While Hwang maintained that a war was imminent, Kim claimed that the letter from Japan was nothing but a bluff. Earlier King Seon-jo and his court had been informed that Japan was in turmoil with various clan armies fighting each other, but it was an old story before Hideyoshi had completed the unification. The bottom line was that Joseon had substantially underestimated the combined strength and abilities of many Japanese armies at that critical time.

Joseon was also very keen on how the Ming Dynasty of China might think of their loyalty. Many, including King Seon-jo, believed that Ming should be informed upfront lest they suspect Joseon's allegiance. The final outcome of the lengthy discussion was to wait further, hoping Hideyoshi's threats of invasions were just another Japanese pirate raid. Such unjustifiable procrastination, which was based on conflicting reports from emissaries, was like trying to avoid any soup at all costs. (05/19/2022)

421. A ghost's wailing.
귀신이 곡할 노릇이다.

The concept of *gui-shin* (귀신), or ghost, in Korea is certainly frightening, especially among children, but it is far from that of Satan. In fact, it often appears in an affectionate context. Regardless of where the ghost may appear, one thing is certain: they are almighty powerful and thus can do anything in their power, good or bad, silly or clever. See more in Entry # 191, "The very ghost at your home will carry you away."

It is thus surprising to see the above proverb describing a ghost wailing, most likely out of frustration. Is there something or some phenomena that even a ghost cannot fathom? It must be an exceptionally rare situation like "The sun rose from the west this morning," or "A 50-year-old virgin gave birth." If and when something extraordinary happens that I cannot explain within my wits, I might as well say, while scratching my head, "This is like a ghost wailing!" Older people with shorter memories like the present me are prone to such occasions more often. I had the car key in my pocket a few minutes ago, but now I cannot find it. Where are my glasses, for God's sake? Why did I enter this room? See also Entry #334, "Even a ghost won't understand you if you are quiet."

One of the few events that I was not able to understand even with deep empathy was when someone makes an incredible mistake. This is the type of person we do not expect to make such an embarrassing error. This is a story of "Wrong-way Marshall" and anybody who witnessed must have uttered "What in the world...," or "a ghost wailing!"

During a football game against the San Francisco 49ers in 1964, Jim Marshall, a member of the notoriously intimidating defense team of the Minnesota Vikings, recovered the ball after a fumble and ran an impressive 66 yards into the end zone. He immediately spiked the ball onto the ground in celebration of a six-point touchdown. But it was the wrong end zone, giving up two points to the 49ers as a safety play. What was he thinking? Or what was eating him on that day? Since then, the episode has been referred to as "Wrong-way Marshall." As a footnote, despite the mistake, the Minnesota Vikings were still able to win the game 27-22. Lucky him.

Many strange phenomena happen in nature. In most instances. possible explanations advanced by expert scientists still remain a hypothesis awaiting water-proof verification. Death Valley National Park, located on the border between California and southern Nevada, is one of the hottest places on earth. Here, across the dried lake, heavy rocks are moving all by themselves leaving behind distinct trails. These rocks, some estimated to weigh 700 lbs (320 kg), are collectively called Sailing Sones, Sliding Rocks, or Rolling Stones. The apparent movement of rock, which nobody actually witnessed, has been attributed to everything including aliens from outer space. In some cases, a rock moved over a 250-meter distance.

One theory is that the rocks "float" on the ice formed in the muddy bottom of Racetrack Playa and move around due to occasional strong wind that whips across the vast lakebed, leaving a trail on the mud. In summary, no one has established a verifiable reason for how and why the stones are moved from one place to another. Our ghost must be scratching his head and lamenting his own inability.

A couple of weeks ago, on May 10, a newly elected Korean President, Yoon Suk-yeol, swore his oath. The ceremony, held in front of the Korean National Assembly Hall with more than forty-thousands attending, was quite an occasion with many hopes for its citizens. Several friends, who have been rather frustrated by the previous Moon's administration, sent me snapshots of a strange sight of a "rainbow" right in the middle of the sunny daytime of the inauguration ceremony. The first few pictures I received just showed an isolated, ill-defined rainbow.

Then there was a video taken by an amateur that showed a circular rainbow around what appeared to be the sun. This together with the above bona fide rainbow was interpreted as a hopeful sign and promising omen for the new president and his administration. It was indeed remarkable the rainbows happened to appear just during Mr. Yoon's swearing-in. I hoped there would be more stories in the news media on this incredible coincidence, but not much further was available online.

Then I came across a phenomenon called parhelia, or sundogs. It is an optical phenomenon that consists of a bright spot on one or both sides of the Sun. Two sun dogs often flank the Sun within the so-called 22° halo. I am wondering loudly if this is what happened on May 10 during Mr. Yoon's swearing-in. Either way, I'd like to believe it was a good omen for his career and his administration in the future of Korea. (05/23/2022)

422. Heading for Seoul leaving eyebrows behind.
서울 가는 놈이 눈썹 빼고 간다.

You may wonder why someone who is about to take a long trip to Seoul wishes to shave off his eyebrows. Why on earth would one do that? For some cosmetic reason? Otherwise, would the sophisticated people in Seoul laugh at his thick and bush hairs of eyebrows? Without eyebrows, he may look like a leper. Would it be his intention? If so, why?

The long trip on foot he is embarking on would be physically demanding in addition to planning numerous pragmatic issues such as where to stay for sleep, what and how to acquire sustenance, how many clothes and extra straw sandals to carry, what to wear every day, etc. In the end, the planning would all boil down to how much his luggage should weigh. He will place all essential items on a square fabric and tie two opposite corners to become his backpack. Most likely he will somehow tie the bag on one end of a wooden staff so that he can carry it on his shoulder, balanced with an extended arm. Alternatively, he may carry the bundle on his back.

Since his pack will be severely limited in volume as well as weight, he must carry only essential items. To him, the eyebrow isn't essential! How much does the eyebrow weigh? Very little, but that is the point. To reduce weight, he has to cut down on nearly everything.

Modern-day travelers know how to pack only needed items. Their motto is travel light. It will give you freedom and flexibility. One can move quickly through airports and public transport. Besides, you can easily keep track of your luggage and thus not lose it. Briefly, use a lightweight case, carry no more than two pairs of shoes, and consolidate all sorts of entertainment options into one gadget, most likely a cell phone with a pair of earbuds. But, most of all, we have to remember that we can buy almost everything out there. This is one of the most contentious points I always have argued with my wife. Just carry money. Her counterpoint is that it will be awfully expensive. My counter-counterargument is that we shouldn't leave home if we cannot afford the trip.

"Travel light" is also most relevant in a backpacking venture. In preparation for the backpacking on Appalachian Trail (AT) many years ago, I read many "how-to" books on the AT. All of them discussed how to reduce the weight of the backpack without jeopardizing our lives. One even suggested that we cut the toothbrush in half to cut the total weight. I did not do it but the crux of advice served me well throughout the 600-mile tracking. All foods were in a dehydrated state like Korean cup ramen, beef jerky, dried banana, scrambled egg, soups, etc. The pouch containing dried beef stroganoff with noodles from Mountain House was my favorite.

"Travel light" has been also a good pointer in my life. As I mentioned earlier somewhere, I am an unapologetic minimalist. As they say, we were all born with empty hands and will depart this world with empty hands. Then why bother accumulating things? I suppose we need the "stuff" to live a comfortable life but, even here, one could say there must be a limit, right? How can one close eyes voluntarily at the moment of last breath if they are so very much attached to the "stuff" they accumulated during their lives?

My minimalistic lifestyle has been most noticeable when, for instance, I compared it with my wife in using kitchen utensils. I use one spoon not only to stir the soup while I am preparing it but also to eat it. Often, especially when I eat alone, one bowl serves many purposes, perhaps steamed rice plus soup, and side dishes often directly from their original container. In short, I subscribe to the wisdom of the so-called TV dinner. I have only a few dishes to clean whereas the aftermath of my wife's cooking is like a battlefield.

In Entry #218, "A needle beats an ax," I introduced the mid-19th century Korean poet named Kim Saat-gat. He took a life-long journey as a perpetual traveler until he died in 1863 at the age of 56. His open-ended journey, mainly on foot, from one village to another, was accompanied by poems that often tried to define a life. His eccentricity is likened to Don Quixote and his simple life represented the best of a minimalist. I used to envy his "romantic" lifestyle when I was a young college kid. But, alas, where am I now?

Catholic and Buddhist priests and their female counterparts, nuns, do not have anybody to leave their possessions to except close relatives such as nephews and nieces. What would be their possessions? Perhaps old family pictures, journals, a pair of glasses, shoes, garments worn till their death, books, rosaries, and a bank account with a few dollars in the balance. One could pack all of these in a small cardboard box and carry it away, not unlike their ashes. They do not have any incentives to save as they do not have anybody who would inherit their "wealth." Is their simple life why I like priests so much? In comparison, how much spiritual guidance they have offered me contributed to my affinity with them? (05/25/2022)

423. The trumpeter at the end of a parade.
행차 뒤에 나팔

Imagine the July 4th parade in a small town: a fire truck or two, the high school marching band, one or two flat-bed flower trucks with some kind of queen with a big smile, rows of old veterans, and kids of course. There seem to be more participants in the parade than bystanders. Just like other parades, the beginning is of greater fanfare while the end is like the tail of a snake, not much of a hooray. Then, who wants to be the last trumpeter at the end of a village parade? They are the insignificant participant whom people may not pay much attention to or the ones who could be the laughingstock after the parade. But there has to be an end and someone has to be there.

For more than a decade, I lived on a small but deep lake called Gull Lake in Richland, Michigan. Every winter, it froze completely and won't thaw till March or so. It was cold with winds from the north sweeping across the lake, rattling the windows on the second floor quite mercilessly. The cracking noise I would hear during the dark and cold nights from the expanding ice was quite eerie, to say the least. Each time, I wish there is no north side. The guy who is taking care of the end of a parade may wish the same: why can we not have the end or north? The truth is that we will have to live with the dual nature of things around us. See Entry #65, "Even shoes come in pairs."

Once we accept the unavoidable existence of both beginning and end in a parade, we can ask a question ourselves about where we want to be at. Of course, everyone wishes to lead the parade rather than take care of the end. We have seen a similar case found in another proverb. See Entry #166, "The head of a rooster is preferred to the tail of a dragon." What was not discussed though was the fundamental question as to the origin of such desire in humans and possibly throughout the animal kingdom. Why does everyone want to become a leader rather than a follower? By definition, the probability to become a leader is smaller than a follower, defining the competitive nature of humanity throughout history.

Both competition and cooperation are ultimately for gain: for the former, the gain is more on the individual level whereas the latter is a result of a collective effort. We usually try to avoid conflict and competition if we can in pursuing our gain. At some point, however, the cooperative efforts turn into a situation where one or a few try to gain more than others in competition with one-time collaborators. Once their intention becomes known to others, competition begins in earnest as almost everyone wants the same. At this stage, conflict may appear.

Cynics may thus subscribe to the notion that people are fundamentally individualistic, selfish, and competitive, driven just to get ahead by any means necessary. In contrast, the Chines philosopher Mencius (맹자, 373 - 289 BC) maintained that we are born with righteousness and goodness. I like this line of thought. He believed that it is the society that guides us into bad-moral characters. Indeed, the current capitalism we live in appears to reward selfishness, greed, bottomless ambition, and winning by any means. Although I am rather pessimistic about this, I sure hope that these traits stop or at least slow down a bit in the future for our next generations.

So, what is wrong with becoming the caretaker at the tail end of a big parade? A short answer would be nothing. It's just a matter of perception. Someone may point out the lowly status of that position, but as I said earlier, someone will be at the end of the parade. This antonymic nature of many matters we face was already discussed earlier but trying to avoid such a position may simply reflect one's inferiority complex or lack of self-confidence. See Entry #98, "Handsome people necessitate ugly ones."

Presented below is another, perhaps the standard, interpretation of the above proverb. The word, dwe-e (뒤에), was translated as "at the end," which has led to the above writeup. The word can also mean "after," which would lead to a somewhat different meaning. Thus, the proverb asks us why to blow a horn after the parade has all passed by. Isn't it too anti-climax? It is the same as Entry #373, "Fixing the barn after the cow escapes." A blare of trumpeters carries little significance after the main event is over.

On May 24, an 18-year-old gunman entered an elementary school in the small town of Uvalde, Texas, killing 19 fourth graders along with two teachers. The victims were either nine or 10 years old, at the pinnacle of their youth, all excited about the upcoming summer break. The gunman entered the classroom and presumably the carnage began soon. The town policemen and other state officials arrive at the school shortly later but entered the classroom to kill the assailant only after a long 78-minute wait. People started to speculate that many lives could have been saved had they confronted the gunman much earlier. It is still a developing story, but they behaved like "the trumpeter after the parade." (05/29/2022)

424. Monk's comb.
중의 빗.

The Buddhist monk shaves their head, a practice also known as tonsure. It is a symbolic gesture for rejecting the common ego. When a boy or a girl becomes a monk or a nun, shaving hair serves as the first step of official ordination. Once done, it is the monk's duty to keep their head always cleanly shaven. They may need a razor. What they will not miss is a comb.

The comb or hairbrush is an essential item for most of us, especially women, but is of little use for Buddhist monks and nuns, known as *biguni* (비구니). The comb to a monk is much more useless than "a square peg in a round hole." If one develops a list of stuff that is worthless to a given cohort, a comb to a monk may be at the top of the list.

- comb for monks
- masterpiece paintings for the blind
- a penny for a billionaire
- denture for a newborn baby
- ten-dollar bills for a vending machine
- lightening for golfers
- cake in a picture for a hungry man
- cow to chicken or vice versa
- high-heel shoes for nuns
- ice block to an Alaskan
- an umbrella in Las Vegas
- a slide rule to an engineer
- a humidifier in the summer
- a Democrat in the Republican convention
- calculus for an artist
- compassion for a merchant
- a girlfriend for a Jesuit priest
- *bulgogi* for a vegetarian
- front pant fly for women
- Buddha statue for Christians

So, the above proverb unequivocally states that what is valuable to me may not be so to other people. When an old widow is compelled to downsize her possessions, how can she give up things that she has developed so much emotional attachment to throughout her life? Do they become "a comb to a monk" all of a sudden? She may shed some tears looking at some old pictures or maybe not, smiling with sweet memories. Either way, she would be fully aware that all becomes a moot point when death comes along. Before that realization, she might have acquired the wisdom laid under the above adage, how a comb becomes of little use to a monk.

Changing a gear a bit, let us take this opportunity to examine what tonsure means, besides rendering comb useless, from a larger scheme of things in religions. As said earlier, it signifies the rejection of the ego on an individual level but may collectively reflect how inclusive Buddhism is, say, in comparison with Christianity and Islam.

In August last year, British author Salman Rushdie, 75, was stabbed several times before his scheduled lecture at the Chautauqua Institution in New York. The attack by a 24-year-old Muslim from New Jersey was in response to the fatwa calling for Rushdie's death. It was declared just after Rushdie's *The Satanic Verses* was published in 1991. He lost his sight in one eye and one of his hands was incapacitated following the attack.

The book introduces two Indian expatriates in contemporary England. Early in the novel, both are subject to dramatic transformation upon surviving a plane crash. Their subsequent struggle with self-identity in England is the main theme of the novel. To me, it was a great novel written in magic realism, but it was blasphemy to Muslims.

The Islam-Christianity conflict goes back to the Crusades era of the 11th through the 13th century. Moving fast forward, we still face some serious issues involving, for instance, the Middle East. The apparent immiscibility of the two major religions on this planet has created inter-continental conflicts for many centuries. Even within Christianity, there appears to exist subtle tension between Catholicism and Protestants. Exclusivity displayed by these religions causes mutual distrust if not outright hatred.

In contrast, of the six major religions - Protestantism, Judaism, Hinduism, Catholicism, and Buddhism - we seldom hear of any violent conflicts involving Buddhism. The observation makes me wonder why it is the case. Tonsure makes a comb useless to a monk but it certainly shows that ego has no place in humanity. (05/31/2022, updated 03/28/2023)

425. Even crabs know their place.
게도 제 구멍이 아니면 들어가지 않는다.

The crayfish or the crab in shallow freshwater or rocky seashores, once disturbed, scurries only to their own burrow to hide. They do not enter a crevice or cave that belongs to somebody else is what the above proverb is telling us. An implication is that one should not enter somebody's premises, as a thief might do in the dead of night, or a nation should not invade another weaker but peaceful sovereign country by force, as Russians are doing with Ukraine as we speak now.

How a nation approaches another nation for whatever intention takes various forms and shapes. Unlike military invasions, peaceful exchange occurs rather naturally for language, culture, fashion, religion, art, sports, education, political ideologies, civil rights, entertainment, etc. They are often actively imported or welcomed by the host country. This spontaneous process does not entail any formality such as going through a custom house. In fact, no governmental attempt to control, for instance, the international cultural flow has been successful.

The failure results not because the government has not tried hard but because people's wish overpowers any control by a third party. André Malraux, the French Minister of Culture during the post-Second World War period, tried to stop American English words from contaminating their "pure" language. I don't think they were very successful. Jack Valenti, one-time head of the Motion Picture Association in Hollywood, might have been right when he stated that culture is like chewing gum, a product like any other.

Anything can come and go depending on the will of the consumer or people. See Entry #83, "A drizzle still can wet your clothes." If this isn't the fundamental right of humanity, what is?

The influence of foreign languages especially English would leave a long-lasting impact on Korea. As we can trace the root of many Korean words to Chinese, centuries later the Korean linguist will find that many Korean words we are using now are from American English. It would be analogous to the origin of many English words traced back to Latin and Greek words. See more in Entry #58, "Frogs don't remember they were once tadpoles."

We have, for instance, a perfect word for "law school," or 사법대학, and yet Koreans have adopted "law school" in bastardized Korean pronunciation and write in Korean, 로스쿨: see also Entry #173, "Listen to the elder, rice cake will come to you." As a footnote, the word, *sabob daehak* (사법대학) itself originated from Chinese characters. The trend of such changes began to appear in the past three decades or so.

Anglicization is defined as the practice of modifying foreign words, names, and phrases to make them easier to spell, pronounce, or understand in English. An example would be "*sabob daehak*" for 사법대학, or law school. I do not know if there is an English word that defines the opposite of Anglicization: that is, write in Korean an English word. If there is, I am not aware of it. Perhaps Koreanization? In the above paragraph, I just said, "bastardized Korean pronunciation and write in Korean" and presented "로스쿨" for "law school" as an example. This is where many Koreans get in trouble or encounter some embarrassing situation.

The Korean word for egg is 달걀 (*dal-gyal*). It is an authentic Korean word as far as I can tell and has been used for centuries. However, nowadays many "sophisticated" Koreans use the Korean pronunciation of egg, or 에그 (pronounced as *egeu*). I heard that a Korean living in the States had a hard time asking for eggs at a corner dime store pronouncing *egeu*. Had the Korean not learned the bastardized word for egg, he could have eventually learned the correct pronunciation of the word, egg. In retrospect, perhaps writing 엑, instead of 에그, could have been a bit better. No matter.

Like English, various forms of entertainment and sports constantly invade Korea. Remember the Beatles in the 1960s? What about American films? Nowadays, foreign actors routinely visit Korea with a new release. Tom Cruise, for instance, was in Korea last June to promote his new film, *Top Gun: Maverick*. I cannot tell exactly how baseball became our national sport along with soccer, but it may come via Japan after World War II. This type of cultural flow has been so spontaneous that we don't monitor their arrival every day. It is as if they have resided in Korea all along.

In contrast, Christianity arrived in Korea not without initial suppression from the late Joseon Dynasty. But for those martyrs of Catholic Jesuit priests, the new religion on the Korean Peninsula would not have survived. Just look around to see how many churches we have now. (06/03/2022)

426. You can have meals at different places but sleep in one place.
밥은 열 곳에 가 먹어도 잠은 한 곳에서 자랬다.

When I was growing up in Korea, dinner is one meal our family would share together almost every evening. There was no mandate for the tradition, written or spoken, but it was just the way it was. If someone is late, my mother used to keep a separate meal for the sibling. It was never a fest to today's standard, but it was an occasion everyone talked about their opinion on certain matters happening on that day. It can vary from a topic in politics to bona fide gossip. Being the youngest in the family, I was more or less a listener rather than a talker, and what I learned from such a dinner table turned out to be immeasurable. It won't be an overstatement if I say my taste in art, music, and literature was formed through those occasions.

Recently, however, we eat wherever pleases us or whenever an occasion calls for. This was particularly true in this family of two with somewhat different professional demands. So, the first part of the above proverb is in agreement with our situation prior to retirement. It doesn't matter where you take care of your meals, either alone, with colleagues, or with the family altogether. You may have ten different places where you can have a meal. But the second part of the proverb says that you ought to sleep in one place no matter what. Why?

When we are children, except for occasional sleepovers at a friend's place, we sleep at home. As a college student away from home, you just stay in a dorm or share a rented house with housemates. As an independent adult with a secure job, one can stay anywhere depending on financial circumstances. This is the period when young people would be most active in seeking a spouse. Once labeled as promiscuous in the small world of dating and hookups, the reputation can travel fast and widely, often hampering the prospect of marrying up. At least such was the case during my youth, especially for unmarried maidens. It was a double standard as we see now, but a promiscuous woman was more harshly looked down upon than a womanizer. The proverb is thus saying that one has to be careful where to "perch" for the night for this cohort of young people.

Once married with a family to raise, it is absolutely mandatory to stay at home every night with the family. There shouldn't be any other way. But, once in a while, we hear someone succumbs to curiosity and gets off the rail to eventually ruin their marriage. While promiscuity is frowned upon among humans in any civilized society, there is a species of apes that shows extreme promiscuity presumably for sexual pleasure. They are bonobos.

Unlike most of the current human society where male dominance has been a norm, female bonobos appear to play a central, perhaps even dominant, role in their social life. Besides pleasure, they seem to avoid unnecessary aggression with promiscuous sexual behaviors. Bonobos engage in sex in virtually every partner combination, an exception being the case of incestuous relations. The above proverb is patently not applicable to the bonobo society.

In *The Great Switcheroo* by British writer Roald Dahl, the husbands of two young couples successfully deceive their spouses so that each can sleep with the wife of his friend: thus the word *Switcheroo* is in the title. Vic Hammond lusts after Samantha Rainbow. Vic devises a plan that would allow him and Jerry Rainbow to switch wives for a night without the women knowing it. They meet several times to go over every detail of the plan. This includes describing the sexual routines they adopt when making love to their wives.

Naturally, both men regard the other's approach to making love with disdain and insist that his own procedure is much superior to the other guy's. Vic, who is very proud of his own procedure and sexual technique with his wife, is particularly outraged when Jerry criticizes his routine.

On the planned night, each is able to sneak into the other's bedrooms without incident. But in the middle of having sex with Samantha, in total darkness as necessitated, Vic realizes that in the heat of lovemaking, he has forgotten all about Jerry's technique. Samantha at first tenses up, but then responds with gusto. Both are quite satisfied in the end.

The men return home, once again without any problem and full of pride in their own cleverness and performance. For Vic, however, the satisfaction lasts only overnight as his wife Mary admits that she has never really enjoyed sex with him until the night before. In the end, two things become quite clear: One, Vic has been a terrible lover to his wife Mary all along in spite of boasting about his approach. Two, Jerry also forgot to copy and use Vic's technique. Either way, both men look quite pathetic. That is the price they pay for not having slept at home. (06/05/2022)

427. The tongue cannot touch the bottom of the heart.
혀가 깊(길)어도 마음속까지는 닿지 않는다.

The tongue, with its ability to form the sound of words, constructs *maal* (말), or spoken words in Korean. If you hold your tongue, you cannot speak: it is that simple. The above proverb says that, even with a silver tongue, you cannot fully express in words a deep emotion you have in your heart. A direct translation could be, "Even an extended tongue still cannot touch the bottom of your heart."

Professor Richard L. Schowen at the University of Kansas taught us bio-organic chemistry that dealt with the reaction mechanism of enzymatic reactions. It was a tough course, especially for those students with so-so chemistry backgrounds like me. His lectures were so smooth that all of us perfectly understood what he was delivering in class. A few hours later, however, when I went over my own note, nothing was concrete anymore. I could not even recognize my own writing as if I had been hypnotized earlier for an hour. It wasn't just me: all of my fellow students were the same way and many years later we all shared the same sentiment with hearty chuckles and sweet memories.

I have only fond memories of Professor Schowen. He was the only smooth talker I had admired, a rare exception. I have treated all other fluent speakers invariably with a skeptical eye. This is particularly the result of constant exposure to nonsensical utterances from politicians, both in Korea and the States. The following story may illustrate my pessimistic view of many hypocritic gun lovers with silver tongues.

On May 14, an 18-year-old, who has been supporting white supremacy, killed 10 African Americans at a supermarket in Buffalo, New York with an AR-15 semi-automatic rifle. On May 24, another 18-year-old opened fire at an elementary school in Uvalde, Texas, killing 19 students, all nine to 10 years old, and two teachers. As if these are not enough to shock the nation, at least 17 people were killed and 54 injured this weekend, over the deadliest this year, all over the country: in Philadelphia; Chattanooga, Tennessee; Saginaw, Michigan; Omaha, Nebraska; Summerton, South Carolina; Macon, Georgia; Mesa, Arizona; and other towns and cities.

The Gun Violence Archive, an unaffiliated non-profit research group, has reported 246 mass shootings in the US so far in 2022. More than 18,700 people have lost their lives due to gun violence in 2022, according to the Archive. This is one of the most absurd statistics that I have ever encountered during my long lifetime. Now, the spate of these recent shootings has pushed guns to the front and center of a national conversation as leaders reckon with how to curb the alarming rate of violence.

The standard soundbite from the gun-lobbying group has been, "Guns don't kill people, people kill people," or firearms controls could have no effect on homicide rates because "human nature being what it is." Then "Freedom is identified with the right to self-defense and the latter is identified with possession of a firearm." It all legitimates "good guys with guns" and concludes that the answer to gun violence is more guns.

The Second Amendment of the US Constitution reads: "A well-regulated Militia being necessary to the security of a free State, the right of the people to keep and bear Arms shall not be infringed." This constitutional right has been the mantra of many politicians and even legal scholars. As far as I am concerned, these "silver tongues" are speaking nonsense having lost sight of the big mountain at the expense of a few trees they see just in front of them. These folks, who are fully aware that the Second Amendment has outlived its usefulness, simply lack "common sense." I am neither a connoisseur of the Constitution nor do I want to be one. Then, all I have been hearing sounds like typical BS, albeit well-spoken by smooth talkers.

According to the above proverb, a well-delivered elegant speech or a well-written novel still may not be able to properly reflect the true feeling kept deep at the bottom of the heart even when the intention was honest. This is a matter of the ability of the speaker or the writer. More importantly, it all depends on how the audience or reader accepts them. After all, that is how a given literary work is reviewed, criticized, and receives a score.

I tried several times, each time with a great deal of determination, to complete *Infinite Jest*, all 1079 pages, by David Foster Wallace. A screwball comedy it was, and yet I invariably find, entering a few paragraphs into the first chapter, myself wondering what I would have for dinner. This is in spite of all the high acclaim by literary critics. I've just begun *Crying in H Mart* by Michelle Zauner, a Korean American, who longs for her deceased mother through Korean food. The story resonates so well with what I have gone through that I finished the book in no time at all. (06/07/2022)

428. A bigger thief catches the smaller ones.
큰 도둑이 작은 도둑을 잡는다.

In the world of gangsters, the hierarchy seems to be in proportion to cruelty in dealing with members of other rivals: the more violent act a guy can display, the more respect he seems to garner. In *God Father*, a Hollywood studio head refuses to offer a role in a movie to the godson of Vito Corleone (Marlon Brando) and wakes up in bed to find the severed head of his prized stallion. During open warfare among the gangster families, Michael (Al Pacino) is sent to Sicily for his safety, but Michael loses his wife-to-be in a car bomb intended for his life. This type of gruesome story travels fast among the feuding families, resulting in awe and respect among them. With time, the seemingly weaker family without any legendary violence to boast about or display is eventually swallowed up by a stronger family.

The above proverb can be used in the above context, in analogy with the phenomenon known as Ostwald Ripening in physical chemistry: see Entry #317, "Beating the boulder with an egg." It is a natural phenomenon in which small particles suspended in liquid spontaneously fuse into bigger particles. This well-established theory adequately describes the disappearance of dime stores and the appearance of Amazon, Walmart, Costco, etc. See also Entry # 354, "A wealthy family at the expense of three villages."

A nuanced interpretation of the above proverb is that thieves can control themselves, a stronger one serving as an internal regulator or governor. In some instances, this underground rule may be more practically meaningful than the surveillance and control by law enforcers. The most powerful clan may behave as if they were the one that other families should really reckon with, although to the third party, like law-abiding citizens, they are all the same, thieves. See Entry #26, "No need to rank thieves: they are all thieves."

Ironically it is the underground kingmaker who cries foul when they see small-time criminals commit fraud. It is typical hypocrisy, but who is going to challenge the big boss? We do not need to look too far into the past to find some incidents that could reflect the crux of the proverb. What former President Donald Trump asked his cronies to do to reverse the election he lost is illegal but more importantly the way he treated those who refused to follow his wish was like asking them to join him in a sinking ship.

Tomorrow, June 9, 2022, I will begin to watch the much-awaited House Select Committee hearings investigating the Jan. 6 insurrection. To everyone, it was one of the gravest assaults on the democracy of this nation. The attack on the US Capitol was carried out by supporters of Donald Trump, who falsely claimed that the 2020 election was somehow rigged. That he not only encouraged the rioters but also did not stop them from attacking the Capitol is a crime of paramount significance. The hearings will shed more light on the attack for many days to come.

In addition, Trump committed two other "crimes." First, he begged Georgia State Secretary Raffensperger for 11,800 votes so that the election result from the State can be reversed. Raffensperger did not oblige. Now local legal officials are looking into a possible criminal prosecution of Trump's move. Secondly, on Jan. 5, Trump called on Vice President Pence to reject Biden's win and send the results back to the states. Pence, who was to formally preside over the joint session to certify Biden's victory, issued a statement that he had no authority to do what Trump was asking him to.

Since then, both Raffensperger and Pence have become the target of ridicule from Trump and his allies: i.e., the mainstream Republicans. This series of events involving the former president likens a situation where a big boss in a crime syndicate tries to lure more innocent followers to become his pawns and showed anger when they refuse to become his soldiers. As it turned out later, there were other people who decided to keep some distance from Trump, his daughter Ivanka and her husband Jared Kushner. They appeared to be the only adults present in the thick of the unfolding saga.

Long before Biden was declared as the new president, this power couple, perhaps closest to Trump than others, decided to leave the White House for Miami. No matter how vigorously Trump claimed otherwise, neither Kushner nor Ivanka Trump believed that the election had been stolen. "While the president spent hours and days after the polls closed complaining about imagined fraud in battleground states and plotting a strategy to hold on to power, his daughter and son-in-law were already washing their hands of the Trump presidency. Kushner's decision to withdraw from the most consequential moment of the Trump presidency left few effective counterweights to the plotters seeking to subvert the will of the voters to hang on to power." (from the June 8, 2022 issue of *The New York Times*) History will be kind to this couple as well as Raffensperger and Pence. (06/08/2022)

429. A hungry tiger devours even a eunuch.
호랑이가 굶으면 환관도 먹는다.

Let us go over the Korean word, *hwan guan* (환관) or *nae sie* (내시). Both nouns, which originated from Chinese, mean a man without testicles and/or a penis. In the case of *nae sie*, more common in old Korea, a boy loses his testicles via castration becoming a eunuch. The *hwan guan* loses both penis and testicles as in emasculation. This used to be more common in China. Here, a boy while being held down, a sharp knife severs his penis and testicles in one swift movement. A plug is inserted into the wound to stop full closure and leave an aperture for the passage of urine. Technically the *nae sie* can perform sex, but the *hwan guan* cannot. An important commonality is that neither can have their own children and that they are not distracted by lust or sexual matters.

The eunuch performed various functions in different cultures: most notably they would serve as guardians of women or harem servants. As they are less threatening and cannot perform sexual acts, eunuchs are perfect for servants of a royal court where many maids live a lonely life. Eunuchs in a palace may also perform domestic functions for the ruler, such as fixing his bed, bathing him cutting hair, relaying messages, etc. In some instances, they become "the ruler's ear," yielding invisible power.

Although their job was generally modest, their essential functions were such that their employers would compensate them rather generously. Many poor parents in old Korea would seriously entertain the thought of having one in the family. Although the lives of *nae si* were rather comfortable, their social status was invariably at the bottom of the totem pole. Many people would prefer doing nothing to do with this rare and strange breed of people. According to the above proverb, tigers also wish to keep some distance from eunuchs unless they are terribly hungry, that is.

What a eunuch is to a tiger with a full stomach could well be what the LGBTQ cohort is to ordinary people. Talking about LGBTQ (lesbian-gay-bisexual-transgender-queer) is certainly not a fond exercise during family dinners. Thinking about the topic alone already causes a tingling sensation on the belly button. It is just an inconvenient subject that older generations try to avoid with their children until one of their children informs them he or she is gay. A typical story may develop as follows.

Before a couple marries in a conservative Christian community, they have grown up vaguely believing homosexuality was a sin against their values. The topic has never entered their daily life. Then, out of nowhere their son who has been active in the church youth group tells his parents he is gay during the spring break from his college. Immediately the parents ask the son not to tell anyone, repeatedly ask him how sure he is, recite Bible passages, and finally put him through conversion therapy.

After every effort fails, they are now forced to resolve the in-house dilemma and quickly realize it is nearly impossible. As the timid first step for seeking outside helps, they may first meet the "friend" of their son, invite other gay Christians to dinner, and finally begin to meet other parents in the same situation. This slow but inevitable transformation parallels a shift in public opinion in recent years. As recently as 2004, 60 percent of Americans opposed same-sex marriage, however now it is completely reversed, encompassing nearly all demographic groups. A record number of LGBT candidates have been elected to various positions in the US and state governments as well as many celebrities: Chicago mayor Lori Lightfoot, an openly gay Democratic candidate for president Pete Buttigieg, a gay governor in Colorado Jared Polis, comedian Ellen DeGeneres, et al.

In the end, those parents who are initially shocked come to realize that they have to resolve the issue: "disown a child or change their attitude." Senator Rob Portman from Ohio and former Vice President Dick Cheney have been speaking in favor of gay rights after their children came out as gay.

For a tiger, in a normal state of satiety, eunuchs would be as appealing as a kitchen sink. However, once awfully hungry, a tiger would devour anything including a eunuch, implying that a man in hunger or serious despair would do anything. This line of thought is another way to interpret the proverb. An English version may well be: "A drowning man will grab at a straw." Steve McQueen, the "King of Cool" with his antihero persona, was dying of mesothelioma, cancer associated with asbestos exposure for which there is no known cure. He went to Mexico for unconventional treatment after his US doctors told him they could do nothing to prolong his life. Much controversy followed without much success. He died in a small clinic where the doctors and staff were unaware of his actual identity. He was only 50 years old. (06/11/2022)

430. At best, a flea's jump.
뛰어야 벼룩.

Adult fleas are only about three 3 mm (1/8 inch) long. They do not have wings, but with strong hind legs, they can jump and leap a distance of some 50 times their body length, a remarkable feat in itself. And yet, the proverb is mocking, "So?" Even though they can leap more than a foot, it isn't a big deal to human eyes, possibly meaning that one can run away from a crime scene but they can't go far enough to completely hide. Or, one can deceive people for only so long. In this sense, this proverb is a derivative of Entry #100, "A long tail gets stamped," or "꼬리가 길면 밟힌다."

In crime movies, bank robbers or thieves of expensive jewelry divide their loot after a successful raid and each retires to a hiding place in an isolated, obscure island in the Caribbean Sea or some such place. After the movie is over, I am generally left with a skeptical thought that they will eventually get caught more easily than hiding in a crowded, bustling place like New York City or Los Angeles. A stranger, seemingly with a lot of spending money in cash, on a sparsely populated island would be a good target for suspicious eyes. That is to say, there seldom is a perfect crime. Or is it?

In January, $6.8 million worth of jewelry disappeared from a luxurious seven-story department store in Berlin widely known as KaDeWe. The store is as famous as Berlin landmarks like Victory Column or the Brandenburg Gate. Three masked, gloved thieves were caught on surveillance cameras sliding down ropes from the outside windows, successfully evading its sophisticated security system.

They got away without any hitch, but they did leave DNA evidence in a drop of sweat on a latex glove discarded next to a rope ladder used to reach the ground floor. Police ran the material through the German crime database. And they got a hit, two in fact. The computer identified Lebanese-born unemployed 27-year-old identical twins. They had lived in northern Germany since age one but still had only permanent residency, not citizenship. They have criminal records for theft and fraud.

Police arrested the brothers in February at a gambling arcade. Both were charged with burglary, an offense that carries a potential 10-year prison sentence. But in March, just before the case went to trial, they were released. The authorities had no choice since the court ruled: "From the evidence we have, we can deduce that at least one of the brothers took part in the crime, but it has not been possible to determine which one." Identical twins share 99.99% of their genetic information. The law does not allow the authorities to detain someone indefinitely just because he is just suspected of a crime.

Disagreeing with the general sentiment that "the mills of justice grind slowly and often not very finely." the twins said, "We are very proud of the German legal system and grateful." Apparently, an identical twin can often walk away from jail time. In 2004 in Boston, a suspected rapist blamed his identical twin when confronted with matching DNA. Although he was already serving a sentence for a rape conviction, the jury could not agree on a verdict. These cases involving identical twins are not truly perfect crimes. They are the beneficiary of the limit in genetics in forensics.

The raid on the compound in Abbottabad, Pakistan, where Osama bin Laden had been hiding, took place in May 2011. The CIA-coordinated operation was carried out by US Navy SEALs with various support teams. It took almost 10 years subsequent to the 9·11 Attack, successfully ending the long-lasted search for bin Laden. This 10-year wait pales when one hears the following story, the oldest murder case resolved in American history.

In the early evening of December 1957, a seven-year-old girl Maria Ridulph was playing with her next-door friend Kathy just in front of her home in Sycamore, Illinois. Then, a young man whom they did not know very well approached them. Kathy momentarily went home to get a pair of mittens to fight off the cold hand. When she came out again, they had disappeared into the dark and cold night. It took 54 years for Illinois State to hunt down and convict this man. The story unfolded as follows.

In 1993, Janet Tessier learned from her dying mother that her older brother John Tessier was the one who murdered Maria. At that time the Tessiers lived only a block and a half from the Ridulphs. Janet struggled with this shocking deathbed confession from her mother until 2008 when she informed the police via email. Three years later, in 2011, the Illinois State Police detective was able to find John Tessier in a retirement community close to Seattle, Washington. When arrested, John was 73 years old. However one may look at the outcome, it certainly supports the notion from the above proverb: albeit a flea can leap long, about 50 times its body length, it will be eventually captured. (06/12/2022)

431. The pine looks greener during the wintertime.
겨울이 다 되어야 솔이 푸른 줄 안다.

The pine is evergreen but we don't see them clearly as such during the warm weather when other greener deciduous plants flourish. Their adult leaves are needles of rather dull green, which doesn't help them be noticed either. Only when the annuals are gone in the winter, they do proudly emerge. We appreciate their snow-covered green needles in the crisp winter air of the forest: just like we appreciate the sun only after a long period of rainy days or pouring rain after a long drought in Las Vegas.

What are those we miss most only after they disappear? For me, at the top of the list would be my mother. As I wrote in Essay #66, "I have few invites, but many places to visit," when I thought I was ready to take good care of her as my finance and time were dramatically improved, she wasn't around any longer. I had put off nearly everything when I was a student, including visiting my mother in Korea. Admittedly there were no simple financial means to make the visit, still, it sounds like an excuse deep in my mind. It will remain one major regret I will depart the world with.

A dear friend of mine who lives in Dallas has just come back home after a long visit with her 94-year-old mother and sister in Michigan, wrote me about how wonderful her visit was. I couldn't envy her more when she indicated that she and her husband may move to the small town to be with her mother as soon as her husband is ready. Since she has a grown-up daughter with her own children and since she is showing what a thoughtful and dedicated daughter she has been, they are all learning through "osmosis" what they will do after my friend becomes really old. Very wise she is, not that she has been "calculating" the return of her devotion to her own mother.

When we have too many options to choose one decision from, the sheer overwhelming number itself can blur our judgment, like "chasing two rabbits at a time." Late in the spring or at the peak of summer, there are so many greens around us that the pine with needle leaves fails to lure our attention. After all, it is the season of full-blown flowers of many colors, accompanied by butterflies and songbirds. But these colorful plants often with sharp thorns are short-lived to give an impression of cantankerous prima donna opera singers. Think about beautiful red roses, for example.

We, Korean youths, were taught to respect and cherish resilience over 15-minute fame and cultivate long-lasting affection, if not owe, steady loyalty. We were to look down upon any efforts for instant glorification. Those are too cheap for our self-esteem. We were taught to spot a destination far from here and follow the straight line to the location without much whining. If adversities arise along the way, we were to confront and resolve them rather than circumvent them. What could be a better representation of such teaching than the pine? How could one forget the fragrance from the pine forest just after drizzles along with the sound of chant from a Buddhist temple deep in a mountain?

When we lived in North Carolina, the house was sitting on high ground with a sizable bank down to a small street from the rest of our neighbors. Every spring I spread the slope with either double-ground hardwood or pine straw. Each has pros and cons. Both would look great, especially just after done. Mulch fades its dark reddish color and aromas more quickly than pine needles. And spreading mulch is much more labor-intensive: from a pile after the delivery I have to transfer it to a wheelbarrow with a pitchfork. Then I pour them on the ground with some distances between the pile. Finally, using a dirt rake, I evenly spread them. Often I see blood in my urine afterward.

Needless to say, my preference was pine straw. I just drop them off from my left armpit to the ground with my right hand continuously shaking. I don't need any tools and even have to bend my back. I stopped the pine straw when my neighbor told me it would be a fire hazard.

Up to this point, I have interpreted the above proverb from a positive angle. Then I came across a different explanation. The pine is hiding, as a backdrop, behind all those greens during the warm weather months. Now that every green is gone, the pine has to reveal itself. Here, it is similar to Entry #100, "A long tail gets stamped." or "꼬리가 길면 밟힌다." I might have told this story before but here it is again.

During the Second World War, a German spy was caught in London by his simple habit. British counter-espionage team had been monitoring and gathering evidence from their suspect but the spy was quite clever and thus elusive. One day, as he was crossing a street, he was looking left first. It was the final piece of evidence that the spy was not a Briton but an authentic German. People drove cars differently in the two countries. If we follow the second hidden meaning of the proverb, it can be said that no one can hide indefinitely. (06/16/2020)

432. A silly dog barking in a field.
개 못 된 것은 들에 가 짖는다.

A well-trained guard dog would bark at a stranger on a deserted street or attack an intruder at home. That was the justification for their existence in our household back then and they were well compensated by my parents for their work. In contrast, here is a stupid dog that keeps barking at a wide-open field for no obvious reason. Probably, this type of dog wags its tail to strangers and even follows them till the dog gets lost.

This silly dog personifies a man who cannot or does not do what he is supposed to do but goes around bragging about himself as if he has done the most important things in the world. We have come across such people in our lives. It is just a matter of probability: out of eight billion on this planet, there must be some outliers. In many communities like a workplace, they are not only dispensable employees but also in many instances should not be there, as they can do more harm to the organization. This is in contrast to those who are absolutely needed as they offer valuable contributions.

In the case of Rudy Giuliani, a mysterious and extraordinary transition took place from the latter category to the first. He served as the United States Attorney for the Southern District of New York from 1983 to 1989, one of the most powerful and prestigious positions sought after by any prosecutor. At that time he was in the age of early 40s. Then he was elected as the Mayor of New York City from 1994 to 2001. For his leadership after the September 11 attacks in 2001, he was called "America's mayor," and named Person of the Year by *Time* magazine. He was given an honorary knighthood in 2002 by Queen Elizabeth II of the UK.

Between 2002 and April 2018 when he joined President Donald Trump's personal legal team, he dabbled in various ventures ranging from a security consulting business to political activities for Republican Party. During that period, something profound must have happened to him to begin a precipitous downfall to the point where he was barred to practice law in the State of New York in 2021. For instance, he was one of the central figures in the Trump–Ukraine scandal, which led to Trump's first impeachment in December 2019. After the 2020 presidential election, he represented Trump filing many lawsuits in attempts to overturn the election results, making false and debunked allegations about rigged voting machines, polling place fraud, and an international communist conspiracy.

As of today, May 6, we have had three hearings in the U.S. Congress on the Jan. 6, 2021, assault on the Capitol by former President Donald Trump's supporters, including Giuliani. He was at the rally, inciting the rioters in a public speech, along with other yes-men including the original schemer of a plan to have the election result reversed. As I see it, Giuliani is the perfect example of the dog appearing in the above proverb.

At the dawn of the 20th century, the Korean Peninsula with its antiquated society was the target of many imperialistic nations for potential annexation. The Joseon Dynasty (1392- 1910), well behind other nations in the industrial revolution and thus too weak to be truly independent and fledgling in modernization, was on the brink of permanent collapse. The parties interested in Korean Peninsula included Japan, Russia, and the United States. In the end, it was Japan that was successful in securing the Japan–Korea Annexation Treaty in 1910.

At this critical juncture of Korean history, the prime minister who facilitated the power transfer to Japan was Yi Wan-yong, the number-one public enemy of the nation. On December 22, 1909, Yi was on his way back to his office riding his personal rickshaw from some official function in Myung-Dong Cathedral. It was stopped by a street vendor on a wheel of roasted chestnut that came out rather abruptly from a side street. During the wintertime, chestnuts roasted over an open charcoal fire are one of the most favorite snacks and such vendors were still in fashion when I was a kid.

The chestnut seller was in fact an assassin of Yi. After taking care of the rickshaw puller or Yi's security detail with force, the assassin was able to push his dagger deep into Yi's shoulder. Yi was fleeing from the scene while bleeding. The assassin followed Yi and was able to attack further on the abdomen. Yi collapsed on the ground profusely bleeding. To every witness, he was dead right there on the cold ground.

The name of the assassin, the national hero number-one, was Yi Jae-myung. He was a physician from the States. He returned to Korea upon learning what tragic events Korea was undergoing. The patriot in him brought him to do something for his beloved nation. Now that he achieved his goal he surrendered himself to the police after shouting, "Independent Korea!" Unfortunately, the traitor survived and outlived the patriot for another 17 years. Here, one Yi was the dog in the proverb. (06/17/2022)

433. A dog from the seashore is not afraid of the tiger.
바닷가 개는 호랑이 무서운 줄 모른다.

When I am facing what is unknown to me, for example, death, I may have some apprehension but not necessarily fear. I am a law-abiding citizen, then why shall I fear a policeman? If a dog has never encountered a tiger, the dog may not feel threatened by a tiger. After all, this dog was born and lived his whole life by the sea. What tiger? What is a tiger, anyway? The dog might have witnessed fishermen processing a huge whale or many fish in the seafood market but never met a tiger. So says the proverb. It is similar to Entry #102, "Ignorance is medicine," # 114, "A one-day puppy isn't afraid of a tiger," # 338, "Tadpoles in a well," or plainly "No brain, no pain."

If a man has lived all his life where he was born and has never ventured outside his locale, his experience-based knowledge or wisdom must be quite limited. This is particularly true in the old days when there was neither Google nor Naver. And yet he could be boastful in his own belief that he knows a lot about many subject matters. After all, he is a learned man. This misguided self-esteem is not only dangerous to himself but more importantly to the people he was elected to lead. People with closed minds tend to be "my way or no way." On the other hand, wise people are aware of their limited knowledge: thus, they are open to the notion that "they know what they do not know" and continuously try to understand the nature of everything.

Human history has benefited from so many open-minded leaders who were more than willing to accommodate any reasonable new philosophies and science. Sejong the Great (1397 – 1450), the fourth ruler of the Jo-Seon Dynasty of Korea, was one such king. He is the inventor of hangul, the Korean alphabet. A bronze statue of King Sejong, 9.5-m (31 ft) high, is presently sitting in the Gwang-hwa-mun Square, right at the center of Seoul, in front of the Sejong Center for the Performing Arts and above an underground museum. It was dedicated to Hangul Day in celebration of the 563rd anniversary of the birth of the hangul.

Sejong was the last of King Taejong's three sons but was the king's favorite. He was only 21 years old when Taejong abdicated. Although his father continuously influenced his governance, young Sejong developed a particular fondness for science. In an attempt to help farmers, he issued a farmer's manual introducing various farming techniques. The scientists in his court developed new water clocks, armillary spheres, a standardized rain gauge, a printing press, and sundials. His administration also attempted to replace the old barter system in commerce with a national currency.

Above all these advancements is his creation and introduction of hangul, the native phonetic writing system for the Korean language. All historic records indicate that it was Sejong himself who singlehandedly invented hangul. What is most impressive is the fact that this set of novel alphabets seems to be quite independent of the Chinese system. A Chinese character corresponds to a single syllable that is also a morpheme each with meaning, or a word, whereas hangul is a phonetic system. Because of the large number of characters involved in the Chinese language, ordinary Korean folks were not able to easily communicate with each other in writing. Hangul has 14 consonants and 10 vowels. One can write an infinite number of pronunciations including English words.

Sejong's ultimate goal behind the effort was to enable all classes of Koreans to read and write. People not familiar with hangul can typically pronounce Korean script accurately after only a few hours of study. In spite of, or because of, the noble purpose he laid out and the simplicity involved in mastering it, Sejong faced backlash from the high society of the rigid caste system prevailing at that time. Hangul was often treated with contempt by those in power and the elite class known as the *yangban* families. They continued to use Chinese hanja as a token of their social status. Even in my generation, using hanja was considered desirable as it reflects higher education. Hangul slowly but surely gained popularity, especially among women and fiction writers. Its importance in national character was well illustrated by the fact that it was outlawed by the Japanese during the annexation from 1910 till 1945.

On the opposite end from Sejong in the spectrum of the population are those people with active ignorance: see Entry # 114, "A one-day puppy isn't afraid of a tiger." Sometimes these noisy people can win all arguments on all subjects simply by the stubborn refusal of truth: see Entry #199, "Speak louder, win the argument." A few minutes ago, I came across the following story in *the New York Times*: The Republican Party in Texas made a series of far-right declarations as part of its official party platform over the weekend, claiming that President Biden was not legitimately elected, and referring to homosexuality as "an abnormal lifestyle choice." (06/20/2022)

434. Becoming kimchi of green onion.
파김치가 되다.

As pointed out in Entry #182, "Having kimchi juice before the rice cake is served," kimchi is the main side dish in any Korean meal. I don't think there is anybody who would dispute this assertion. Kimchi would be equivalent to the apple pie on July 4th in this country. It is basically salted vegetables such as cabbage and radish fermented with various seasonings including chili powder, scallions, garlic, ginger, and sometimes pickled krill or other small fish. Because kimchi contains a large quantity of garlic and is fermented for a while in preparation, it gives off a unique pungent smell quite notorious among those who know anything about Korea. And yet, many foreigners can get "addicted" to kimchi.

Typically Napa cabbage is first soaked in a generous amount of salt for a few days. Because of the high salt concentration, the water flows out of the cabbage, rendering the cabbage shrink and producing much liquid. The phenomenon is similar to the so-called crenation of red blood cells in a hypertonic solution. To this, added are various condiments like crushed red pepper, minced garlic, and green onion.

There could be hundreds of different types of kimchi made with different vegetables as the main ingredients. Cabbages and radishes are the most commonly used vegetables. Other kimchi vegetables may include cucumber, eggplant, scallions, spinach, etc. The above proverb is specifically concerned with the kimchi of green anions. During the marination step with salt, green onions lose all their water to really shrink to paper-thin without any strength, They behave like long-dead straw from a pond, simulating a state of dead tired, worn-out, or dog-tired.

Just the other day, June 19, an 18-year-old Korean pianist, Lim Yunchan, won the first prize in Van Cliburn Concoures. He was the youngest pianist who won the competition in the 16-year history and Koreans back at home as well as the Korean expatriates in this country not only celebrated but also felt great pride in his performance. During the early stage of the competition, he played Mozart and Beethoven.

In the final round, he played Rachmaninoff piano concerto No.3, which is, according to Wikipedia, often considered one of the most technically challenging piano concertos in the standard classical piano repertoire.

Owing to its difficulty, the concerto is respected, even feared, by many pianists. One particular pianist lamented he had not learned this concerto as a student when he was "still too young to know fear." The finale is quick and quite vigorous and Lim was frequently jumping out of his chair for a triumphant and passionate conclusion in the third movement.

My wife and I immediately went through YouTube looking for his past performances. In one, he was playing a short keyboard concert by J.S. Bach and sweating profusely: sweat dripping from his nose onto the keyboard! After such mentally as well as physically demanding performance, one is bound to become the "kimchi of green onion."

On Memorial Day, we traditionally have two important car races: one is the Indy 500 at Indianapolis Motor Speedway in the early afternoon and the other is the Coca-Cola 600 in the evening at the Charlotte Motor Speedway in North Carolina. It is hard to believe that there have been a few drivers who attempted to enter both races of a total of 1,100 miles with two completely different types of cars. The legendary racer John Andretti was the first one who attempted it in 1994. It is quite understandable that these drivers lose several pounds with the events and they would be an outstanding example of the kimchi of green onion in appearance.

As I approach 80 years of age, I often feel like the kimchi of green onion. My skin is no longer without any blemish, my eyes are drooped with bags underneath, my hair is getting thinner every day, my walk has lost the bouncing gait, have to wear a shoulder brace for the bad posture, and have to endure headaches from so-called occipital neuralgia. But most alarming is this sentiment of abandonment and questioning the legitimacy of my daily routines. Many things now appear of little purpose, a clear sign of the fast-approaching end of life.

As mentioned, when green onions are soaked in a highly concentrated salt solution, the water inside the green onion exits to the outside resulting in shriveled skins behind in the kimchi. Formally, one says the water outflux is due to the higher concentration, or thermodynamic activity, of water inside. Then, what would cause me to become the kimchi of green onion? What is departing from our body and mind as we age? What is the equivalent of water in the case of the kimchi of green onion? One can say it is the desire for living that is leaving aged people. But it is just another way of saying we are getting old. See, for more, Entry # 88, "No warrior can stop aging." (06/22/2022)

435. Loud snores from the ledger.
곁방살이 코 곤다.

This man who is renting a room snores more loudly than the owner of the house. With this proverb, a case can be made where the tenant behaves as if he owns the house. Such a situation can develop if the owner is too passive or the renter is quite aggressive. The combination of both may cause the transfer of the house deed and the owner may become the ledger.

The parasite lives on or inside the host causing harm or even death to its host. It can feed on the host for an extended period of time or share the food of the host as in the case of intestinal parasites. They are usually smaller than the host but reproduce much faster than the host. In due time, the parasite is no longer a ledger but becomes the landlord.

In a similar vein, any sneaky behaviors of a person who is about to take advantage of the naivety and kindness of others would be like the loud snoring of the ledger in the above proverb. For instance, in a romance scam, one feigns romantic intentions toward a victim, gaining the victim's affection and trust, to eventually extort money. This type of fraud has become quite common online, especially targeting lonely widows. It can further develop into bona fide blackmailing like sextortion.

Here is a typical example I have constructed. A teen-aged girl is lured by an online "friend" into exposing her breasts to him on her webcam. Obviously, the instigator has been very good at such sweet talk to innocent girls. Over the following several months, she becomes blackmailed while he sends the screenshots to people she knows. It results in agonizing hours for the girl and she eventually commits suicide at the age of 15.

On a global stage, between the late 16th and early 18th centuries, at the peak of their prowess, British Empire ruled as much as 20% of the total area of Earth, thus the nickname, "the empire on which the sun never sets." They achieved this feat with military power backed by the industrial revolution and cunning commercial practices. But more curious is how they maintained their colonies and territories without much biblical-scale bloodshed. They started ruling other nations as a guest but ultimately became the governing body. That is my perception, reflecting the above proverb.

The military and commercial dominance in India in the mid-18th century slowly morphed into educational, social, and cultural reform. I believe this was the key to their successful "stay" in India for more than 200 years until India became independent in 1947. The same can be said for their stay in Hong Kong till 1997. And it was the script that Japan was following after the forceful annexation of Korea in 1910. As I see now, however, a big difference was that we Koreans were not as docile and submissive as Indians or Hong Kong residents. The anti-Japan and independence movement is something all Koreans can still be proud of.

The arrival of a foreign religion and replacing the original religion of the natives follow a similar scenario. A case of the point would be the beginning of Christianity in the Joseon Dynasty, a nation deeply imbued in Buddhism and Confucianism. Catholicism was first introduced to Korean Confucian scholars visiting China at the dawn of the 17th century.

During the subsequent years, Joseon officially outlawed Catholicism, and thousands of followers were persecuted including several French Jesuit priests. It was then reintroduced with an official blessing around 1790. Protestantism arrived in Korea later via primarily American missionaries. At present, Christianity is the main religion, with approximately 8.6 million and 5.8 million Protestantism and Catholicism, respectively. This is a remarkable phenomenon considering how rapidly Christianity has declined in Europe.

Christian missionaries played a pivotal role in the Westernization of Korean society and the modernization of Korean education: they started over 300 schools and 40 universities including a few top universities. They also helped our independence movements during the Japanese occupation. We, Koreans are most grateful for their contribution to Korea's modernization.

It has, however, resulted in the current dilemma, a somewhat blurred separation of church and state. It is not uncommon for church leaders including Catholic Bishops to speak out about certain political views in public. If they do not, the followers seem to urge them to do so. As one may expect from such rapidly flourishing expansion, there have been some corruption scandals in Protestantism involving church leadership.

In summary, Christianity remains a major religion in Korea for the middle class, youth, intellectuals, and urbanites. Nowadays, we see a church on almost every block in Seoul. One time it was a guest, like the ledger in the proverb, but Korea has now become a nation of Christianity as it assumes the role of the landlord. (06/23/2022)

436. A gourd dipper for avoiding thunder.
쪽박 쓰고 벼락 피한다.

The hard skin of gourds, especially those with an elongated end, can be made into an excellent dipper of water for drinking. Just split it into two halves. One can drill a small hole at the narrow end for a leather strip to pass through. It will be helpful for hanging or attaching to a backpack. The resulting product is light but sturdy and shiny outside. The dipper is usually small, about 6" at most. See more in Entry #74, "A leaky dipper at home leaks also in the field." Here in this proverb, one tries to protect himself from thunder with a gourd dipper, a nonsensical and laughable scene. It describes poor preparedness or ineffective means for a given adversity.

When we come across a sudden catastrophic accident, the last thing we do before we lose conscience is close our eyes. This response is not so much for protecting our eyes but simply an intuitive response without any analysis of the situation, just as small children usually close their eyes when they get injections. We close our eyes as if not seeing can mitigate the expected pain. The small dipper can serve as a blind but it is just a band-aid avoidance of reality rather than a fundamental solution.

Modern medical practice is largely based on the treatment of symptoms by means of medicine rather than the elimination of the pathological source, like the surgical removal of, let's say, a malignant tumor. Even when a physician makes a correct diagnosis, what they prescribe are usually pills for reducing discomfort. People of my age will take several medicines daily: medicines for lowering blood pressure, low-density lipoprotein (LDL), carbohydrates, and controlling urination. Basic solutions for these problems are all based on physical interventions such as diet or exercise.

These contemporary approaches to general health, which we may call gourd dippers, appear to be still working well as noticed by the extended life expectancy in recent decades. Per Wikipedia, in China, Russia, and the US, it has increased to 77, 73, and 78 in 2020 from 44 (!), 66, and 70 in 1960, respectively. Now that the traditional causes of death such as cardiovascular diseases and diabetes-related problems are under control, the life span is dictated by other causes such as cancer. For cancerous diseases, the gourd dipper has not been working very well.

When one nation decides to invade another nation or declare war, they would carefully prepare for the war based on a thorough "scouting report" in advance. In 1982, the so-called Falklands War began when the Argentine forces invaded the Falkland Islands which had been under the rule of the British government. After the two-month occupation, the Argentine forces surrendered, an embarrassing outcome on a global stage. See Entry #399, "A mayfly attacking the fire."

Almost four months ago, Russia invaded Ukraine but now they seem to get stuck in a stalemate, just causing more human casualties. In what appears to be a proxy war for the US against Russia, Ukrainian forces have thus far demonstrated unexpectedly strong resistance against Russian advances. The current status of a seesaw in itself is considered a Russian defeat and many diplomats in the West may have to devise a means of a dignified exit for Putin. We should not forget that he is a man of pride.

In both the Falklands War and the invasion of Ukraine, the instigators might have underestimated the military strength and resoluteness of their enemy. Likewise, even the almighty Imperial Japan miscalculated the strength and resilience of the United States before they embarked on the Second World War. In the hindsight 20:20, we can easily point out the flaws involved in preparation for war, but no one can develop a water-tight plan. As they say we just "prepare for the worst, and hope for the best."

So, we can ask ourselves again if it is worth using a gourd dipper to protect ourselves as the thundering lightning is approaching quite rapidly. Most likely we will be crouching with both arms wrapping the back of the head, possibly with one hand holding the dipper. Our question is similar to "Why is a drowning man clutching a straw?" Chances are quite slim that the gourd dipper or a straw saves one's life. Nonetheless, the chance is a finite number. Compare it with the absolutely zero probability if one doesn't. As mentioned earlier, these behaviors are intuitive, if not instinctive. If so, does our intuition has a built-in calculus?

We acquire intuition through experience and use them without conscious reasoning. It is unconscious knowledge and offers us the ability to understand something instinctively. It is a concept discussed in the realm of psychology rather than in hard science like physics. And yet, the paucity of fundamental understanding of intuition at a "molecular level" has not discouraged researchers in the field of artificial intelligence to develop a tool in machine learning of intuition. (06/25/2022)

437. No power lasts 10 years, no flower lasts 10 days.
십 년 세도 없고, 열흘 붉은 꽃 없다.

The power and (red) flowers referred to in this proverb stand for everything that almost all ordinary people are striving for in their lives. The list can be long but the important ones are wealth, fame, glory, prosperity, happiness, adoration, respect, health, family, etc. The Korean word for these is simply *se*, or 세. My Korean-to-English dictionary translates the word into influence, might, power, and strength. None of these, according to the proverb, would last 10 years just like a beautiful red flower won't last more than 10 days.

It simply says that nothing lasts forever and everything must end eventually. This may include the ever-expanding universe as well as the mayfly with a lifespan of a few days. It is hard to visualize the end of the universe but not having witnessed it does not necessarily establish that it will go on forever. A corollary to the proverb is that everything must have a beginning. In our church this morning we had a baptismal celebration for two beautiful baby girls, each about nine months, with their proud parents. They are saying "hello" to us and I am about to say "bye" to them.

The birth-to-death is far from linear. As pointed out in Entry #2, "Sunny spots and shade change places," the ebbs and flows of fortune always follow one's life, and time changes everything as we know now: see Entry #48, "A decade can change rivers and mountains." Life equated to vanity has been a very popular topic in Korean proverbs: #55, "No tomb is without a cause;" #71, "Getting old but not dying is sad;" #88, "No warrior can stop aging;" #117, "There is no field free of any weeds;" #129, "No fish survives in distilled water;" #147, "Old tigers go home to die;" #160, "Plan an acorn to build a pavilion;" #245, "A Buddhist disciple *na-han* eats dirt;" #323, "The catacomb is just outside the front gate;" #338, "Tadpoles in a well;" and #393, "Good times pass fast."

Let us briefly survey how fame comes and goes in one's life. More importantly, we will look at how fame affected the lives of people. It would be fair and satisfactory to them if they benefit from fame during their life. In a sense, posthumous fame is useless (see more below). The contemporary writer John Grisham, for instance, has just come up with a new novella collection in addition to the 28 consecutive number-one fiction bestsellers. Along the way, he has become a millionaire, just like J. K. Rowling, the author of the Harry Potter series.

I read all of Stieg Larsson's trilogy, *The Girl with the Dragon Tattoo*, *The Girl Who Played with Fire*, and *The Girl Who Kicked the Hornets' Nest*. All of them are page-turners. However, all of them were published after his death in 2004, and thus he did not have a chance to enjoy what the book's loyalty could have afforded. In fact, I remember hearing some "noise" among his family members and live-in partner as to his income from the books. The point is that this brilliant writer, who confessed he was never confident of his "ability to put his thoughts into words," never enjoyed the fortune from his titles. Sad and shameful.

The American philosopher Henry David Thoreau (1817-1862) lived a simple life, always close to nature. He was never understood or fully appreciated by people. Only after his death, did his ideas and work influence many people. His famous line relevant to the current subject may well be, "What you get by achieving your goals is not as important as what you become by achieving your goals." So, he chose not to seek fame per se. The Pythagorean Theorem was named after the Greek philosopher Pythagoras, born around 570 BC. This, one of the most famous mathematical equations, has since received more than 370 (!) proofs. All records show that his life was quite simple, just like Thoreau's several millennia later.

Most of the famous Impressionist painters lived a miserable life. Just to name a few, we have Vincent van Gogh (1853-1890), Paul Gauguin (1848-1903), and Paul Cézanne (1839-1906). Unlike Claude Monet (1814-1926), who was frequently exhibited and somewhat successful during his lifetime, these poor painters barely survived. In particular, the life of van Gogh was particularly painful as he also suffered from mental depression in addition to his constant poor finance. Upon breaking up his friendship with Gauguin he severed a part of his own left ear with a razor.

The posthumous fame of these artists brought about the skyrocketing price of their works. A single piece of their work is now commanding tens, if not hundreds, of millions of dollars in open auctions. A tiny fraction of these monetary compensations could have altered their miserable lives to more comfortable ones. In hindsight, this was outrageously unfair. It is sad and even resentful. My lament and sympathy may be why I like their paintings more. (06/26/2022)

438. An awl in the pocket.
주머니에 들어간 송곳이라.

Imagine an awl or a several-inch-long drill bit in the side pocket of your pants. Whenever you move, it doesn't stay standing and falls sideways, like a screwdriver in the back pocket. It will stick outward for everyone to see in broad daylight. So, this proverb says there is a certain thing you cannot hide in your pocket or keep secret from other people. The more you try to hide, the more apparent it would become.

We all carry a set of criteria when it comes down to what to hide. Any criminal record would top the list and any embarrassing episode would follow. Even for the former, there will be individual differences. Some may not care if their speed ticket becomes public but they may invariably try to hide the prison term they received for some fraudulent activities. Embarrassment would be certainly subjective: some may feel embarrassed when falling down a slippery icy road while others (like me) may boast about visiting the women's room in a drunken stupor at a bar.

At the root of the criteria would be a basic sense of civility, ethics, morality, goodness, honesty, truth, and even beauty. This is to say that it really reflects a given person as a whole at a given point in their life, defying any further generalization. Such variety also exists as to how one keeps something secret for an extended period of time if not forever. The Southwest of the country has suffered a severe drought in recent years and Lake Mead began to show its bottom. Last month, they discovered human remains in a barrel that has surfaced on the dry land.

Then, there are people who brazenly committed a crime and yet behave as if nothing has happened and meet the public with a thick-skinned face. Often we do not know if they committed the crime unwittingly or knowingly. During the months of June and July, the House Select Committee is having a series of hearings to investigate the Jan. 6 attack on the US Capitol. Many pundits speak of what former President Trump did or did not do prior to and during the riot in the context of Nixon's Watergate scandal of 1973. One thing they failed to emphasize is the significant (at least to me) difference between the two presidents: Nixon tried to hide his dishonesty while Trump is bragging about his shameless acts. I do not know which is worse.

Nixon's attempt to deny everything that he was hiding clearly showed that at least he shared with the nation a common set of criteria on what constitutes a crime according to the law of the land. In the end, he was caught red-handedly. President Ford made the right decision to pardon him so that he could avoid jail time. Trump, on the other hand, does not have any shame for what he was conspiring. He does not seem to have any moral compass that will guide him to steer the nation. Perhaps he was born and raised that way and now he is beyond repair. Obviously, his aides and millions of his supporters did not understand the crux of the above proverb: you cannot hide an awl in the pocket. Sooner or later the truth will be exposed to the public. Duh....

Money, especially money earned in a rather dubious manner, would be difficult to hide from IRS, neighbors, and friends. Winning a lottery is public knowledge and thus you do not need to hide or announce it, except maybe from dubious charity organizations. Otherwise, how can you explain a brand new Porsche suddenly sitting on your driveway or new pieces of appliances being constantly delivered?

Prudent use of the sudden fortune requires discipline and raises the question of why you have gone through all those hassles to have money that you cannot use freely. Financially savvy thieves would know how to set up a secret bank account in foreign lands such as the Cayman Islands or Gibraltar, they may be beyond the reach of small-time offenders.

Love affairs would be another matter that the parties involved would keep secret from their spouse. Considering how much effort is required to do so and forever lasting guilt towards their spouse, one often comes forward confessing the "crime" and asking forgiveness once and for all. Sometimes it does not work as often "advertised." Here is a story from the 6/23/2022 issue of *The New York Times*.

My wife and I have been married for eight years. We're in our 30s and have two children. I love her; she's my best friend. Unfortunately, I made a big mistake: I got drunk at a conference last month and slept with another woman. I swear it was a one-time thing and meant nothing to me! When I got home, I decided the right thing to do was to tell my wife what had happened, apologize and promise it would never happen again. I knew there might be fallout, but I had no idea she would be so upset. She has practically stopped talking to me and threatened to throw me out. I've apologized so many times. This is killing me! What more can I do? (06/28/2022)

439. A beggar receiving a horse.
거지가 말 얻은 격.

This poor man, who is barely making ends meet all the time, is given a horse with no charge at all. Who gave away the horse is not important, but how he is going to keep the horse is. Right off the bat, where is he going to keep the horse and how can he afford to purchase the feed? He himself doesn't have a place to sleep or money to buy his own meals. He could sell the animal but maybe it is prohibited by some sort of contract when he received the horse. Why horse of all things? I don't have any foggiest idea, but its size as well as how much a horse eats must be considered in the proverb.

At first glance, a free horse sounds like good fortune, but he quickly realizes that it is a burden to the sorry state of his affairs. In fact, a horse would be the last thing he needs or wishes to have right now. What about some cash or even a loaf of bread? In short, the proverb implies bad things piling up on top of the bad situation a person is already in. We have already seen similar proverbs: see, for example, Entry # 17, "When it rains, it pours," and #36, "An unlucky man breaks his nose even when falling backward." One thing unique about the Koreans of yore appears to be the paucity of lucky breaks in addition to constant misfortunes.

We read the following short story by O. Henry, real name William Sydney Porter (1862 – 1910), in our high school English class. *The Gift of the Magi* introduces a young couple Della and Jim, each with little money trying to buy Christmas gifts for each other. Della buys a gold chain for Jim's pocket watch with the money she receives after she sells her long, beautiful hair. On Christmas Eve when Jim comes home from work, Della tells him that she sold her hair to buy him the chain.

Jim gives Della her present, a set of ornamental combs. He tells her that he sold the watch to buy the combs. In the end, they realize their Christmas gifts are of little use at present, just like a horse of the beggar, but their actions show how invaluable their love truly is.

In one of Aesop's fables, *The Fox and the Crane*, a fox invites a crane to eat with him and offers soup in a bowl. The fox can lap up easily, while the crane cannot with its beak. The crane then invites the fox to a meal, which is served in a narrow-necked vessel. It is easy for the stork to access but impossible for the fox. The meals offered to the invitee were like a delicious-looking cake in a framed painting.

Quite often I would have many valuable things in abundance that are useless in a given situation. For instance, what good is my credit card or paper currency for a vending machine that accepts coins only? What shall I do with those unused toners for the printer that has just quit? In my desk drawer, there are many mismatched locks and keys. What am supposed to do with them? I have already had a headache just thinking about what to do with the stuff we now have when we move to Korea for good. Most likely we will live in a small place and where can we keep the "horse?" What shall I do with books that will become just dead weight in the end?

If there is one thing that has never been excessive for most of us, it is money. I've never met anyone who complains about too much money they have. On the contrary, everybody seems to be able to find a suitable place or cause for spending money. The more money one has, the more things we can find that can use the money.

Time may be another matter that we will never have too much, especially when we are getting older. The future is getting shorter compared with the past. With this pressure, I find more things I would like to try but my ambition is severely curtailed by physical stamina and mental decline. Nonetheless, I can generalize prevailing sentiments by listing the following items. Each of them could be equivalent to the horse given to the beggar. See also Entry #424, "Monk's comb."

- Dead son's penis
- A man on deathbed hitting the jackpot
- Old weather forecast
- Old boyfriend of the mother
- Feast for a full stomach
- Typewriter
- Bread in a picture
- Fund-raising among the poor
- Donald Trump for Democrats
- Ice in Alaska
- Blazing sun during Nevada summer

(06/29/2022)

440. No sleep, no dreams.
잠을 자야 꿈을 꾸지.

This is such an obvious statement that it does not need any further elaboration, except to say that a cause always leads to a consequence or consequence prerequisites a cause. The cause-and-effect was the subject of Entry #62, "A pear drops to the ground as a crow takes off."

The word dream often means an aspiration. Here, dream prerequisites desire. Its fulfillment also requires effort. This sequence is part of ambition, especially for young people for a professional career. For retired old people, what constitutes their dream must vary depending on the philosophical outlook of their existence and the spiritual and religious world they are in.

We all know what a dream is but scientists do not understand how it happens and what physiological purpose it serves. Dreams occur mainly during the so-called rapid eye movement, or REM, stage of sleep. Here, the brain is active enough to register what we dream and record it as a kind of shaky memory. This is all an observation, a descriptive science at most. Now anyone can ask "So, what's next?"

The mysterious nature of the dream has encouraged its interpretation as a tool for Western psychoanalysis or as an omen in Korea and other cultures. Both Sigmund Freud and Carl Jung were big with dream analysis, although there is no reliable evidence that understanding dreams is of any value in assessing one's mental well-being. Our ancestors also believed in the significance of dreams. Typically, dreaming of a pig, a dragon, or even a large snake was thought to bring fortune, and one was discouraged to share what one saw in a good dream with others.

The positive association between a pig in a dream and good luck might have been established by a kind of positive feedback loop. Someone must have dreamt of a pig and he found a fortune. He might have told others of such. The listener forgot the story until one day they experienced the same. Starting with this coincidence, such an association began to spread widely. Then any same coincidence feeds more convincing anecdotes to others. Many centuries later it would become a firm correlation.

My dreams are usually scary in the dark grey background, like falling down into deep water, getting lost in a strange town, being chased by some nasty enemy, or flying to unknown places. But I like dreams for what it's worth. First, dreams offer me some adventure during sleep. Otherwise, the sleep could be totally black-out time. Besides, once in a while, I get to see old friends even a few deceased ones. And finally, there are sweet and romantic dreams that you wish to last forever. Even in a very frightening dream, I am often conscious enough to remind myself it is just a dream. This assurance of safety turns the scary dream into a rather pleasant experience as if I were on a nasty battlefield with the assurance that I won't get killed.

Dreams as an aspiration do not occur during sleep. They are part of one's ambition and destination far in the future. It helps develop a roadmap so that one can follow it with minimal distraction. Everybody has dreams but how well they are defined and how much effort one invests in the goal depends on the individual. As I look back on my life, I did not start my youth with any burning desire to become something, not to mention a chemist. Somehow along with my life, I must have taught myself to love what I do. All I look back on now, it has turned out okay.

Efforts or willpower in achieving a dream must be "sleep" as referred to in the above proverb. Dreams without this determination are called daydreams. We all have daydreams. Along with real dreams, it constantly helps us recalculate the roadmap. My hunch is that most people follow such an ordinary path to their destination.

Collective dreams are often a guiding principle for a cohort, community, society, nation, or even the world. Let us hear what Martin Luther King had to say in 1963 on the step of the Lincoln Memorial.

"…. even though we face the difficulties of today and tomorrow, I still have a dream. It is a dream deeply rooted in the American dream. I have a dream that one day this nation will rise up, live out the true meaning of its creed: "We hold these truths to be self-evident, that
all men are created equal.

I have a dream that one day on the red hills of Georgia sons of former slaves and the sons of former slave-owners will be able to sit down together at the table of brotherhood. I have a dream that one day even the state of Mississippi, a state sweltering …." (07/01/2022)

441. Lending is easier than collecting.
앉아 주고 서서 받는다.

A direct translation would be: "You lend the money while sitting comfortably but you collect the debt while standing," meaning that getting your money back is much more difficult than you thought when you lent the money. The difficulty of collecting debt is indeed the very reason for the existence of debt collection agencies. They are third parties that creditors often bring in if their efforts to collect payment fail. If you have to rely on their service, you are already in bad shape with the borrower.

If the sum of the money involved is small and the borrower is a friend, it would be a particularly awkward situation. This is what Mark Twain had to say: "The holy passion of friendship is so sweet and steady and loyal and enduring in nature that it will last through a whole lifetime, if not asked to lend money." See more in Entry #189, "Lend the money and lose a friend." Likewise, the American writer Richard Armour (1906 – 1989) said: "That money talks, I'll not deny, I heard it once: It said, 'Goodbye'."

Borrowing money is as difficult as, if not more difficult than, collecting a debt owed to you. Per Benjamin Franklin, "If you would know the value of money, go and try to borrow some." Self-esteem and pride often get in the way such that asking for money can be felt like outright begging although the borrower honestly promises, himself as well as the benefactor, to pay it back in full plus interest. See also Entry #273, "Avoid autumn drizzles under an in-law's whiskers."

Most of all, we do not have many choices from whom we can borrow money: parents, in-laws, or friends. One can formally try a loan from banks with a lien on a car or house. If it becomes unsuccessful, people may visit a pawnshop with a much higher interest rate. Either way, if the borrower fails to pay it back, he may lose his house. Here are the lyrics of *This Old House* by Crosby, Stills, Nash & Young in 1988.

Midnight, that old clock keeps ticking,
The kids are all asleep and I'm walking the floor.
Darlin' I can see that you're dreaming,
And I don't wanna wake you up
When I close the door.

This old house of ours is built on dreams
And a businessman don't know what that means.
There's a garden outside she works in every day
And tomorrow morning a man from the bank's
Gonna come and take it all away.

Lately, I've been thinking 'bout daddy,
And how he always made things work, when the chips were down,
And I know I've got something inside me
There's always a light there to guide me
To what can't be found.

This old house of ours is built on dreams
And a businessman don't know what that means.
There's a swing outside the kids play on every day
And tomorrow morning a man from the bank's
Gonna come and take it all away.

Take it all away, take it all away, take it all away.
Take it all away, take it all away, take it all away.

Remember how we first came here together?
Standing on an empty lot, holding hands.
Later, we came back in the moonlight
And made love right where the kitchen is,
Then we made our plans.

This old house of ours is built on dreams
And a businessman don't know what that means.
There's a garden outside she works in every day
And tomorrow morning a man from the bank's
Gonna come and take it all away.

Take it all away, take it all away, take it all away.
Take it all away, take it all away, take it all away.

However one may look, lending and borrowing money are not something one can casually take up whenever deemed convenient. (07/04/2022)

442. A hut is burnt down, so are bedbugs.
삼간초가 다 타도 빈대 죽어 좋다.

In the proverb, a small hut of about 20 ft by 20 ft with a thatched roof is referred to as 삼간 초가, *samgan-choga*. Here, *sam* and *gan* mean three and a measure of length, approximately 6 ft, respectively, while *choga* means a thatched cottage. Up until about a century ago, the roof of residential homes in the rural area of old Korea was all made of a thick layer of straw. The wall was invariably built with mud breaks and doors and windows commonly used rice paper. They can burn easily. Small but it is somebody's home and unfortunately it gets burnt down. But, also killed are house bedbugs.

That the bedbugs are gone is certainly a silver lining of the unfortunate event, albeit nothing to boast about. The proverb seems to suggest that there is always something positive in all adversities if one really looks for them. It is equivalent to: "The glass is half full not half empty." An optimist sees the light at the end of the tunnel while others may see a dark tunnel. In hell, optimists are said to enjoy the dry heat. The optimist believes that the future will work out for the best, reflecting resilience in the face of stress.

We all know an optimist when we see one. But who is the beholder of such positive outlooks? What made them an optimist? A standard answer seems to indicate it is heritable implying biological origin to some extent. It is also influenced by environmental factors, including the family environment. Good health appears to be a desired condition but not a necessary one. I have never considered myself an optimist but always admired one. I am not sure if I can train myself to become one.

A cursory survey of the web-based sources offers me a wide range of suggestions, one being "be optimistic!" I am asking myself how to become optimistic and the first answer is to be optimistic. Some other suggestions are not bad: practice compassion, be grateful, remember your prior successes, know your triggers, practice forgiveness, etc. Of these, I like the suggestion with the memory of my own successes in the past. Indeed, I'd like to regurgitate some in my long life but I don't seem to be able to find any outstanding successes that I can revisit with glee. What a shame.

Some others are tough to practice every day: always forgive? I have just learned that someone started to shoot people celebrating in the July Fourth parade in a Chicago suburb killing at least six. I am not sure if I can forgive such a criminal. In short, I guess I will live out my life as I have been. After all, that is what others say: an old dog never learns a new trick.

As said earlier, any tragic events, when scrutinized carefully, are accompanied by a silver lining. Sometimes it can be minuscule as all bugs get killed in a house fire but in some other instances, it can be quite significant. The modernization of Korea and its becoming one of the economic powerhouses in the world are often attributed to the two wars we were deeply involved in, Korean War and Vietnam War. History tells us that wars have stimulated the organization of society in addition to economic prosperity. Some would go far as to declare that war is a necessary evil.

When a person totals a car in an accident, he or she would get a new car. It will certainly cost some money but a new car is a new car. Otherwise, the person could have driven the car more than 100,000 miles. The COVID-19 pandemic, however miserable it might have been, offered to validate the approach with an mRNA vaccine. The concept has been there in the field for many years and yet no one was ready to invest in the practice side of the approach until 2020. This will be remembered as a historic breakthrough in vaccinology. They say that failure is the mother of success, which may well epitomize best for the hidden meaning of the above probe.

What would be the silver lining of the current dysfunctional world particularly in terms of climate change? A few days ago, the Supreme Court of the US (SCOTUS) made one of the worst rulings in my memory. They deprive the Environmental Protection Agency (EPA) of most tools they have in controlling pollution that has been accelerating global warming. I was so disappointed that I had to do something. Below is what I wrote for the 07/01/2022 issue of *the New York Times*. I guess my anger and frustration from this new trend of SCOTUS and subsequent letter writing was the silver lining of the disappointing court rulings.

Conservative justices must have left their "common sense" at home when they came to the court that has dealt with gun control, Roe vs Wade, and very recently EPA. They lost sight of the mountain as they were too busy counting trees. The former reads as people while the latter as their dogma. My lament. (07/04/2022)

443. A sleepy daughter-in-law to a dozing family.
조는 집에 자는 며느리 들어온다.

Among friends, this particular family is well known for their laidback, not necessarily lazy, style of living. In fact, people call them a "dozing family." Now, their son has just gotten married and his wife turns out to be even more relaxed and optimistic than anybody else and is thus known as the "sleepy daughter-in-law." This is the gist of the above proverb, equivalent to "Birds of a feather flock together," or "The apple doesn't fall far from the tree." In Korean, one can say, "그 애비에 그 자식," or "the very son of his father."

One may ask, why "like likes like?" Would there be any genetic code for such an inclination? Or is it completely environmental in origin? A 2012 study from the University of Edinburgh found that genetics were more influential in shaping key traits than a person's home environment and surroundings ("Character traits determined genetically? Genes may hold the key to a life of success, study suggests." *ScienceDaily*, 16 May 2012). The researchers, employing more than 800 sets of twins, found that identical twins, whose DNA is exactly the same, were twice as likely to share personal characteristic traits compared with non-identical twins.

The experimental evidence is quite convincing for their conclusions and questions the long-held notion that family and the environment around the home are most influential on a person's psychological well-being. Indeed their study results support the common trait of being laidback found in the above "dozing family." Then, how can we explain their son found an equally "sleepy" wife who does not share any genes? Or does she?

A more recent collaborative study from several countries concluded that self-regulatory personality traits are strongly influenced by organized interactions among more than 700 genes despite variable cultures and environments. (The study subjects were from Finland, Korea, and Germany.) These sets of genes modulate specific molecular processes in the brain for specific traits. See I. Zwir et al., "Uncovering the complex genetics of human character," *Molecular Psychiatry* 25: 2295–2312 (2020). Following this study, we could conclude that the "sleepy daughter-in-law" must carry the same clusters of genes also found in her husband.

Finding the same gene clusters in both the son and the daughter-in-law is "after-the-fact" and does not answer how they met each other in the first place. They might have met each other at a bar that is usually frequented by laidback people. Or they might have met at a party and noticed each other right away as neither was particularly talkative and hyper. Or a mutual friend believes that they should meet because the friend thought both of them are equally laidback in handling themselves. But, in the end, they must have fallen in love because they feel quite comfortable in the presence of each other. This point might be particularly important for people who find it too much work to constantly gauge the mood of the other person.

Would pessimists show affection to one another? I doubt it although they may share some similar gene clusters. What are they going to do when and if they get together at all? In contrast, optimists seem to get together quite often. Last month, for instance, there was the Optimist International Convention in Reno, Nevada. No matter what kind of official agenda they might have, I can easily visualize the fun they could enjoy together off the schedule. Indeed the gambling town Reno and nearby Lake Tahoe would be good places for them to meet and have fun together.

Besides being comfortable with others, having common interests would facilitate bonding. When we were kids, the goal was to have fun together. Later it could be a hobby like sports, music, literature, etc. Thus we form or participate in various club activities. Once we become active members of society, making money and finding a spouse become the immediate and most urgent goals of our lives. Unfortunately, these activities are rather competitive and we do not socialize with the same mindset we used to have when we were much younger.

Inter-species interactions including symbiotic relationships may give an impression that they are rather passive and reactive rather than proactive as if their relationship is in response to a common enemy. We have seen such a case in Entry #116, "The crayfish sides with crabs." In essence, it is said that "an enemy of my enemy is a friend." When I was single, I had both a cat and a basset hound. They didn't particularly like each other. My hunch was that the cat thought the dog was just too stupid to be a play partner, which I concurred with to some extent. When we walked the neighborhood, the cat had never been on a leash but the dog had to be. In this particular instance, their cool treatment of each other was based on apathy, which could have come from mutual disregard. (07/06/2022)

444. Wild strawberries in dead winter.
동지 때 개딸기.

It is impossible to find wild strawberries on the day of the winter solstice, *dong-ji* (동지) as said above, or plainly during the dead winter. Thus, the above expression stands for something one cannot obtain easily. A corollary is that, if you find the strawberry, it will be extraordinary, like catching a flying arrow with a bare hand or hole-in-one on the golf course. The following story we learned yesterday may illustrate such an occasion. First, given below is some background material.

Every year, the Nobel Foundation selects one or a few Nobel Laureates in each of the following categories: physics, chemistry, physiology and medicine, literature, peace, and economics. Notably missing is an award in the field of mathematics. Many historians of science have postulated several plausible reasons for the conspicuous omission. I like the following speculation best as it is the most interesting humanistic explanation.

Alfred Nobel (1833 – 1896) was a chemist who established in 1900 the Foundation with the wealth from the invention of dynamite and other businesses like armaments manufacturing. He remained unmarried, although he had at least three lovers. One of the three women apparently cheated on Nobel with a famous Swedish mathematician, Gosta Mittag-Leffler. It made Nobel hate the man and mathematics, the subject Mittag-Leffler was associated with. It was simply his personal slight and resentment.

Then, what award would be equivalent to the Nobel Prize in math? It is the Fields Medal, established in 1936. The name was coined after the Canadian mathematician John Charles Fields who was instrumental in establishing the award. But unlike the Nobels, the Fields Medal is awarded only to a mathematician aged 40 or younger, and only once every four years by International Mathematical Union (IMU). The prize includes a monetary award but the sum is less than that of any Nobel Award.

Now, here is the main story. The day before yesterday, on July 5, the IMU announced that a Korean-American professor at Princeton University, Huh June (허준이), won this year's Fields Medal along with other three other mathematicians from the UK, Sweden, and France. I have never thought that a Korean scholar would win in my lifetime a prize of such caliber in basic science such as theoretical physics or math. This rather pessimistic view was from my firm belief that the educational system in Korea fails to inspire young people for originality or creativity: see Entry #64, "A new antler is more prominent." Now I stand for correction: Korean can produce "strawberries in the dead winter!" A more interesting story is how he has become such an outstanding mathematician.

Huh was born in 1983 when his parents were studying here in the US but he was educated in Korea. His dream was to become a poet but eventually got his high school equivalency diploma. While he was majoring in physics at Seoul National University (SNU), he discovered his passion for math when the renowned Japanese mathematician Heisuke Hironaka taught at SNU for a year as a visiting professor. Hironaka won the Fields Medal in 1970. At Hironaka's urging Huh obtained a Master's degree from SNU, while frequently traveling to Japan with Hironaka and acting as his personal assistant. Finally, he went on to the US to study for his doctoral degree.

Because of his poor academic scores during his undergraduate education, almost all graduate programs he applied for admission to turned him down. This was in spite of Hironaka's recommendation letter. He managed to enter the PhD program at the University of Michigan via another school and it was then in 2009, while a PhD candidate, he offered proof of the so-called Read-Hoggar conjecture which had been unresolved for more than 40 years. The rest was history as they say. Prior to the Fields Medal, Huh had received a string of prestigious awards: to name a few, the 2019 New Horizons Prize for Early-Career Achievement in Mathematics, the Blavatnik Award for Young Scientists, and the Samsung Ho-Am Prize in Science.

Other Korean "wild strawberries on the day of winter solstice" may include the 1988 Summer Olympics in Seoul. It was the Korean version of the 1964 Tokyo Olympics, a rite of passage for the flourishing Korean economy and re-introduction of Korea to the world that might have some second thoughts on the democracy in Korea under Park Chung-hee's authoritarian regime. Korea was only the second Asian nation to host the Olympics and ranked fourth in the medal count.

I was then in the States but I was quite proud of the symbolic event of the "coming-out party" by the "new Korea." Since then, Korea has never looked back, wrapping up in what has become known as the "Miracle on the Han River." (07/07/2022)

445. A dagger in the smile.
웃음 속에 칼이 있다.

There are at least two categories of enemies. In the first category, your foe is upfront in expressing his or her disgust for you to make sure that you know they don't like you for one reason or another. They are always lurking over you with any excuse for striking you first. Mutual animosity is no secret to anybody who knows both you and your foe. The second category consists of pseudo-friends who are always nice to you and pretend that they are your friends. In truth, they are exactly the opposite. They are ultimate betrayers. If you were to choose one over the other, which foe would you prefer?

My choice would certainly be the first category, hands down, any time any place! Although they are my adversaries, at least I can respect their honesty. They do not sneak around behind your back spreading false rumors against you. They don't have to as everyone knows. Some of my friends would also know how I feel about the given relationship. It is all in the public domain, which serves as a sort of security guard also. In case something happens, either I or my foe would be the primary suspect.

The motive of the pretenders in the second category varies depending on the circumstance. Maybe they need something from me, like money or a reference letter. Here, flattery is the key element. They will say anything to obtain what they want: how nice my pair of shoes are, my 30-dollar wristwatch must have cost a fortune, how young I look this morning, etc. They are on the borderline of being bona fide a liar.

Some of these pseudo-friends can go one step further trying to harm me not merely stealing something. That is really what the above proverb meant to say by a dagger hidden in a smiling face. They would say, "I come in peace," and at the same time try to stab me in the back. They are the worst kind of humans in my dictionary, cowards who basically cheat themselves. Such an episode of betrayal seems to be most common among politicians who become blind in the pursuit of power and hegemony. Human political history is very rich on this point. Here is one example.

Chen Boda (1904 – 1989) and Lin Bao (1907 – 1971) were the two pillars during the first 20 years of Mao's People's Republic of China. Chen was the brain of their doctrine while Lin was his counterpart in military affairs. Chen drafted most of Mao's speeches and provided the main frame of their propaganda. Most notably, he was the architect of the infamous Cultural Revolution, which started in 1966. Lin played a pivotal role during the Chinese Civil War against Chiang Kai-shek's Kuomintang forces. He led the Manchurian Field Army to victory and led the People's Liberation Army into Beijing expelling Chiang's army. Although their fields of expertise were quite different, Chen and Lin maintained a close and harmonious relationship.

Once Chiang's government and army retreated to Taiwan in 1949, there began internal tension between Mao and Chen-Lin alliance. According to Song Jae-yoon, a Korean historian of modern China, Mao started to feel uneasy about the combined power that Chen and Lin could exert and their possible insurgency. Mao thus began to conspire to eliminate both of them from their power structure.

From 1966 until 1969, Chen played an important role in the Cultural Revolution. However, his ultra-radical line and close ties with Lin Biao eventually led to his downfall in 1970. Note that the so-called Little Red Book, a textbook guiding the Revolution, was coauthored by Chen and Lin. In addition, Chen opposed Zhou Enlai's attempt to de-escalate the Cultural Revolution and refocus on consolidating the Party. The upshot was his downfall along with curtailed fever of the Cultural Revolution. In 1973 he was condemned as a "revisionist secret agent" for his associations with Lin Biao. He was tried and sentenced to 18 years in prison but was released due to his poor health. He died in 1989 at the age of 85.

Lin was the longest-serving Minister of the National Defense of the People's Republic of China and was instrumental in establishing Mao's cult of personality in the early 1960s. He was named Mao's designated successor although he just planned to survive the Cultural Revolution alive and well. However, in 1971, Lin died in a mysterious "Lin Biao Incident" when a small plane that was carrying him and his family crashed in Mongolia. The official explanation was that he and his family attempted to flee following a botched coup against Mao. Most likely, they fled out of fear they would be purged.

It is hard to believe that both Lin and Chen, who devoted their whole lives to Mao's political ambition, were in the end treated as if they were public enemy number one by Mao and his successors. Lin's devotion to Mao was such that to the public Lin was "Mao's best student," to which Lin responded by stating, "I don't have any talent. What I know, I learned from Mao." In the end, Mao showed a smile while hiding a dagger. (07/09/2020)

446. Mountain to hunt pheasants, sea to catch fish.
산에 가야 꿩을 잡고, 바다에 가야 고기를 잡는다.

When one contemplates opening a new retail store of any kind, everyone tells them there are three prerequisites that he or she has to pay the utmost attention to. The first consideration is location. The second is location. And the third one is location. I couldn't agree more with the advice. A pizza place or a bar could be close to a college. It is not a bad idea to open a car dealer or a furniture store where there are a lot of them aggregated together. Eateries and clothes shops might be the same. An area concentrated on a given business will be remembered by ordinary citizens and offers the consumer a variety of choices.

The above proverb says the same with obvious advice: where you are heading must be consistent with what you wish to obtain. A seemingly trivial deviation from the right direction at an initial stage can become a serious departure from the original direction, like a scissor's gap. In the end, you may not recognize where you are. In trekking a remote trail, you usually have one footpath but once in a while, you may meet a crossroads. Taking the wrong path can be quite costly in time as well as physical exhaustion.

After I graduated from Seoul National University College of Pharmacy, I worked for a pharmaceutical firm for one year as a research scientist. Albeit brief, that period was an opportunity to go through some soul-searching as to the future. I could almost see my life all laid out. It wasn't pretty. The circumstance was a good reason to leave Korea for further opportunities. In addition to this "repelling" force, there was a magnetic attraction to graduate studies in the States. Both forces were working in a concerted manner of pushing and pulling. I was 24 years old.

Fast forward, now at the age of 79, I plan to go back to Korea and complete my life there. In this case, my recent disappointment with the collective trend and decision on climate change, gun violence, deeply divided political landscape, and other societal issues seem to push me out of the country where I have lived for more than 50 years. I have to confess that this "repulsive" force is much more than the attractive pull from Korea, a country that has become almost foreign to me by now. Traveling back and forth between the two countries appears to be the only other option. It is a scenario that I am not that crazy about.

If we introduce another dimension to the proverb, that would be time. We now have four possible combinations. The right place at the right time can be when one goes to the seashore at a perfect time as a school of hungry fish has just arrived and hence they caught an abundant amount of fish. A person can go to the wrong place at the wrong time. This would be the worst combination of the four. This idiotic man brought all hunting gears to the sea for pheasant hunting and met a heavy downpour. Cold and hungry he came home empty.

An amateur fisherman goes to the seashore with a great deal of excitement of hope, but alas, it was the time of ebb. There is no way he can walk over the grey, slimy, and gooey ground to access the seawater. It is just like the silt of ashes. He does have a pair of rubber boots, however, the actual shoreline seems to stretch miles away. Besides, it feels like quicksand and could swallow the fisherman alive. This would be an example of the right place but at the wrong time.

The final combination of the wrong place at the right time can be tricky in that the "right time" depends on one's viewpoint. Let's say that a robber goes to the wrong target store, which happens to be well equipped with security measures, and gets arrested quickly by the police who were immediately alerted through a secret communication system. According to his plan, it was the right time since only one keeper was manning the store. It turned out to be the wrong time for the attempted robbery but the right time for the police squad and ultimately society.

One early evening in February 2019, Chicago police officers raided the apartment where the 49-year-old Black social worker Anjanette Young lived alone. She was enjoying a quiet night when officers barged into her place, yelling at her to put her hands up. When she complied, the only cloth she was wearing fell out of her hands. She was handcuffed while she was still naked. The raid was successful on time but the officers went to the wrong address. Three years later, the Chicago City Council unanimously approved a $2.9 million dollar settlement for Anjanette Young.

Reviewing what I wrote above, I realize that getting to the wrong place seems to be a more serious error than arriving at the wrong time. This may well be the reason why the above Korean proverb did not say anything about timing. (07/11/2022)

447. Say tomorrow what you want to say now.
하고 싶은 말은 내일 하렸다.

If you really wish to blurt out right now some resentment, disappointment, displeasure, or complaint, you'd better hold your tongue till tomorrow so that you can think it over tonight. You may have a second thought. The proverb is essentially the same as: "Think ten times, say once" or "Count backward from ten before yelling." It is a lot easier to talk about than to practice controlling emotions. However, this proverb is a part of our ancestor's broad advice on *maal*, or spoken words. Listed below are the proverbs on the topic that we have already gone through.

- Be careful what you say, even inside a coffin.
  관속에 들어가도 막말은 말라. (#1)
- An empty wheelbarrow makes more noise.
  빈 수레가 더 요란하다. (#10)
- The tongue can break bones.
  사람의 혀는 뼈가 없어도 사람의 뼈를 부순다. (#15)
- Say something kind and nice to expect the same.
  가는 말이 고와야 오는 말도 곱다. (#23)
- Straight words from tilted mouth.
  입은 비뚤어져도 말은 바로 해라. (#180)
- Speak louder, win the argument.
  남대문 본 놈과 안 본 놈이 다투면, 안 본 놈이 이긴다. (#199)
- A full water bottle makes no noise even when shaken.
  병에 가득 찬 물은 저어도 소리가 안 난다. (#209)
- Words shared with a cow, but not with a wife, are safe.
  소더러 한 말은 안 나도, 처더러 한 말은 난다. (#250)
- For gossip, even a guy on a double crutch comes forth.
  남의 말이라면 쌍지팡이 짚고 나선다. (#275)
- Three-inch togue ruins a five-foot body.
  세 치 혀가 다섯 자 몸 망친다. (#357)

I do not know exactly why controlling *maal*, specifically when to speak what and how became such an important issue in Korean culture in the past, but earlier in Entry #357 I attributed it to the Chinese influence. It was an easy way to avoid serious analysis. Let me try to crack at it one more time.

One of the most profound properties of *maal* is that once spoken it disappears into thin air. There is no way to get them back: it goes out one way irreversibly. The speaker can be proud of or ashamed of what he or she has just said. From the measurement of brain waves, scientists estimate the time interval of 0.6 seconds between the thought in the brain and forming *maal* using the vocal cord. They said it is as fast as eye movement as the vocal system is so close to the brain, much faster than the communication between the brain and the rest of the body.

Because *maal* is formed so fast that speakers often unintentionally reveal many aspects of themselves such as where they are from (through accent), physical state (e.g., the vigor of speech), psychological state (emotions or moods), education and experience (words they use), etc.

From these two observations, i.e., irreversible loss of *maal* and exposure of themselves through *maal*, our ancestors must have asked themselves what they would gain by talking, especially with and among strangers. Their answer must have been, "Not much." Conversely, they must have also realized that they do not lose anything when they do not talk. Most likely the latter sentiment must have prevailed as they might have been in a state of paranoia quite often because of often-prevailing social or political unrest.

From this backdrop, we can see why it would be more liable and dangerous if one shouts in the catharsis of despair. As a youth, I used to have a short fuse. Whenever I received a bad review of my research manuscript for publication or a grant application for research support, I would be so mad that I just couldn't hold anything inside me. I would share their critique with a few seasoned postdoctoral fellows to release my complaints. Then I would sit down and start to write a letter of protest to the editor or the funding agents. Invariably, the letter would contain many nasty words, essentially claiming that the reviewers are plainly ill-qualified for the job.

My anger and frustration calmed down somewhat by the time the letter was complete. Sometimes I showed the letter to my senior staff in the lab. Some of them were courageous enough to advise me to sit on the letter overnight and advised me to read it again the next day. More often than not, I would not send the letter. (07/12/2022)

448. Even a rabbit digs three burrows.
토끼도 세 굴을 판다.

Rabbits are the main prey of cats, foxes, weasels, badgers, coyotes, and birds of prey. When threatened, they flee to their burrows with extensive tunnels, or "warrens." That is where rabbits rest, sleep, and raise bunnies. They are very good at digging into the ground and building an underground structure built for maximal security, resulting in the above proverb. It says "three" burrows, in which the number three means "as many as" three. If rabbits build such elaborate warrens with sophisticated structures for safety, can we humans do the same?

Everything we do, professionally or domestically, requires a prior consideration of security and safety. We develop an appropriate measure of insurance upon assessing the risk involved. It ranges from a lightning rod to auto insurance. It would be foolish to live in a house without a lightning rod or to drive a car without any auto insurance.

The British violinist, Oliver Lewis, broke the world record in playing *Flight of the Bumblebee* by Russian composer Nikolai Rimsky-Korsakov (1844-1908) in mere 63 seconds, a Guinness World Record. In 2011, Lewis unofficially broke his own record on Ellen DeGeneres's show, clocking in at 47 seconds. Since then he has been known as a musician who has the fastest fingers.

Many musicians insure individual body parts in order to protect their livelihood. For instance, Keith Richards of The Rolling Stones is said to have insured his hands for $2 million. Lewis' hands are insured by the insurance company Hencilla Canworth Limited for $1 million, or $100,000 per finger. The monthly premium is $3,500. Although he admits that the insurance makes him a bit more tempted to take risks, he still avoids any potentially risky activities like skiing, extreme sports, playing with sharp knives, etc. He said, "I won't go chopping up coconuts with a machete."

In my "previous life," I was a professor in pharmaceutical chemistry at one of the major universities. When we submit a research grant proposal, in my case to NIH (National Institutes of Health), we voluntarily reveal weak parts in the application more or less to preempt critiques. That is an attempt to say that we have already thought about the shaky part of the grant. More importantly, we also outline what we can do in case a proposed experiment fails. This is in accordance with what the above proverb suggests: prepare for the worst and hope for the best.

Below, I am reproducing what I wrote in a grant application that I submitted in May 1999 to NIH, titled *Second-Generation Long-Circulating Liposomes.* I introduce this segment not so much for expecting readers to follow the content but for demonstrating how much preparations go into grant writing. Incidentally, this particular proposal was not funded.

> ***D. 11. Anticipated Difficulties and Alternative Approaches:*** *Our major concern centers around the synthesis of the MSA (Membrane Spanning Anchor)/Peptide conjugate, (compound)* ***16*** *on p. 30. As pointed out on p. 30, the solid-phase synthesis of the second peptide library after attaching MSA to the first library may not proceed smoothly. It will be especially critical as the number of coupling increases. When cleaved from the resin, an asymmetric product, asymmetric in peptide size, may result (e.g., 30-mer in the first and on average 20-mer in the second library). If MALDI-TOF (Matrix-Assisted Laser Desorption/Ionization – Time of Flight) data support such a case, we will try an approach with fragment condensation. Here, we will prepare a large batch of 10-mer libraries first and repeat the coupling reaction with these 10-mer fragments. If all fails, we will not have an opportunity to evaluate how the presence of polymer inside the liposome (i.e., configuration* ***Ic*** *in* ***Fig. 1*** *on p. 17) affects the association of the polymer on the outer surface. We predict that, even without the polymer inside (i.e., with* ***Ib*** *in* ***Fig. 1****), MSA will be superior to those with DSPE (Distearoyl Phosphatidylethanolamine). This is because its inner anchor still carries a zwitterionic polar glyceryl PE head group.*

I submit an apology if I have bothered the readers with the above highly specialized field of scientific research write-up. The point I wish to relay is that we are supposed to consider all potential risks and be prepared for them with possible solutions when we are facing an important task. As stated above, even with the best of my effort, the grant was not funded. The failure to secure the grant was a disappointment but did not cause much regret knowing that I had done my best. (07/15/2022)

449. An impatient man pays for drinks in advance.
성급한 놈 술값 먼저 낸다.

Who in the world would pay for drinks at a bar in advance? Who is this idiot? Is he out of his mind or does he have so much money that he doesn't care what follows what? How does he know how much he is going to drink? For Pete's sake, this isn't a gas station that asks you to pay upfront for an exact gallon of gas. Well, the answer is that this man is simply impatient or quick-tempered. In the long run, his impetuous behavior will cost him dearly.

This morning at the Mass we listened to the following Gospel of Luke, *Jesus at the home of Martha and Mary* [10:38-42].

> *As Jesus and his disciples were on their way, he came to a village where a woman named Martha opened her home to him. She had a sister called Mary, who sat at the Lord's feet listening to what he said. But Martha was distracted by all the preparations that had to be made. She came to him and asked, "Lord, don't you care that my sister has left me to do the work by myself? Tell her to help me!"*
>
> *"Martha, Martha," the Lord answered, "you are worried and upset about many things, but few things are needed—or indeed only one. Mary has chosen what is better, and it will not be taken away from her."*

Father Bill's homily interpreted Martha and Mary as presenting action and contemplation, respectively, and that we should balance between these two extremes. Too many activities without thoughts may well reflect the crux of the above proverb, while too much contemplation without much action could be just laziness. Jesus seems to side with Mary by telling Martha that all we need is only one thing, listening to the teachings of Jesus. From this interpretation, one can go further and deeper, dealing with spiritual values versus material business.

An interesting word used in this proverb is 놈, or *nom*. As I explained in Entry # 118, "A thirsty man digs a well," or 목마른 놈이 우물 판다, the word could simply mean a man or a guy. Under some circumstances, it could be used as derogatory, like a son of a bitch. Here, our ancestors used it jokingly for wit and humor.

A rash decision is often part of a passionate dispute like a heated quarrel between married couples. Here, emotion overrides rationale, and controlling emotion is easier said than done. Still paying a bill at a bar in advance is not a crime of passion but a reflection of a person's character, as hot-tempered people tend to let circumstance dictate actions. I still consider myself having a short fuse but what makes me think before acting nowadays is the feeling of the irrelevance of getting upset. What is the point of winning an argument or even gaining a few dollars in investment? I think old age seems to do such a trick as the desire for living the rest of my life in peace is much more desirable than anything else.

When I was in high school, I used to play a board game called go a lot with friends, older brothers, in-laws, or even a stranger at a game parlor. The board, made of very thick wood with four short legs, shows a grid of 19 lines running in both directions. Each player is given white or black pebbles and places one at each move on the crossline. The aim is to build more territory than the opponent. Just like chess, it requires some serious strategies, immediate as well as long-term, before making a move but we rarely paid due elaboration for two primary reasons.

One of the most basic rules of the game is that you cannot change your mind and redo it once you place your stone on the board. But strangely enough, as soon as I place my piece, I would realize it was a bad move and I see a far better one and try to take it back. Thus, as soon as my opponent makes a move, I would place my stone immediately so that he cannot change his mind. That is when most of our quarrels would start. Once my opponent allows my plea of changing my mind, I am to be as generous as to allow him to take his stone back also. Otherwise, he will cry it is unfair.

The second reason I would make a premature move quickly is that I do not want him to have sufficient time to discover my bad move and change his mind. That is to say, my immediate move without really examining what he did is in fact to cover my mistake before he does. I know this is exactly what happens to his thinking also. No wonder why our game ends very fast and why most of my opponents and I turned out to be very poor go players.

As I see now, those rash moves in the go game did not offer sufficient time to help us be aware of why our skill has never improved. That may well be the reason we all eventually abandoned the hobby. (07/17/2022)

450. Would a hungry tiger not devour a *yangban*?
배고픈 호랑이가 원님을 알랴?

As pointed out in Entry #372, "Old sayings are without flaws," many Korean proverbs are asking a question, goading listeners to their own answers. This proverb is also a rhetorical question with a resounding answer that a hungry tiger will not distinguish its potential meal, a nobleman from the average citizen or a billionaire from homeless people. Here, The former is referred to as *won-nim*, 원님, in the original but I just used *yangban*, a Korean word that the readers are more familiar with by now. As to *won-nim*, see Entry #396, "Get to blow a trumpet thanks to the boss."

When one is hungry, all one can see and think about would be food: gone will be any pretense based on familial pedigree or social status. How can one blame them in such a dire state? It is a matter of survival that is directly linked to human instinct. Under some harsh conditions, people as a last resort practice cannibalism. Two famous examples would be the ill-fated Donner Party (1846–47) and the following story.

On October 13, 1972, a chartered flight from Montevideo, Uruguay to Santiago, Chile, crashed in the Andes mountains. The plane, Uruguayan Air Force Flight 571, was carrying a rugby team and its supporters. The wreck was located at an elevation of almost 12,000 ft (3,570 m) in the remote Andes, just east of the border with Chile. Miraculously, as many as 18 survived extreme hardships for 72 days, including exposure to cold weather, starvation, and avalanche. They resorted to cannibalism.

As the weather improved, two brave survivors climbed over a mountain peak of over 15,000 ft (4,600 m) for 10 days in Chile to seek help. They traveled about 40 miles (64 km) for 10 days without any gear to speak of. On 23 December 1972, the last of the 16 survivors were rescued. The news of their miraculous survival became sensational headline news throughout the world and led to a 1993 film, *Alive*. The crash eventually became known as the Andes Flight Disaster as well as the Miracle of the Andes. This is not simply a hungry tiger devouring a man but men eating human flesh just because they were suffering extreme famine. What more relevant examples would be there for the above proverb?

Hunger on a global scale has recently received extra attention because the war between Ukraine and Russia interrupted the export of wheat from

Ukraine. Note that Ukraine used to provide as much as 10 percent of the global share of wheat exports. Although enough food is produced to feed everyone on this planet, international political conflict, climate change, natural disasters, and the recent COVID-19 pandemic have all exacerbated global hunger: approximately 828 million people do not have enough food and 50 million people are facing emergency levels of hunger, especially in Yemen, South Sudan, Ethiopia, and Nigeria.

We can take one further step to discuss the disparity of wealth as the primary source of hunger. The chasm between the poor and the rich, not only within a given country but also internationally, has become bigger every year. For instance, in Mexico, the 15th largest economy in the world, the plight of its lower classes has worsened in recent years. Just yesterday its president, Obrador, who was elected a few years ago with a slogan of "first the poor" declared poverty as the top priority to attack for his administration.

The Gini Index is a measure of income inequality. It summarizes the entire income distribution for a given population. The value ranges from 0, indicating perfect equality to 1, perfect inequality. For reference, in 2018, it was 0.25 for Denmark and 0.63 for Sierra Leon. In 1967, the Index of the United States was 0.38. It increased rather linearly to 0.49 in 2018. There is no indication that the Index may be leveling off in the near future: see Entry # 284. "Whipped together lessens pain," for more.

The trend that the poor become poorer and the hungry become hungrier, together with polarizing societies, is a perfect stage for social unrest and mass migration all over the world. In addition, we witness virtually everyday mass shootings, infernos of wildfire, record-breaking temperatures and floods, wars, and the COVID-19 pandemic. If I sound too alarming, here is my apology in advance, but I cannot stop thinking that the end of this world might be very close. If there is a silver lining in this gloomy picture of the future, it is that my wife and I do not have any children who will have to face such a future.

The world of contemporary literature shows many spooky fictions. *On Such a Full Sea* by Chang-Rae Lee, for instance, depicts the urban lives of the haves and the have-nots. The latter exists mainly for the rich and lives in labor settlements: see Entry #254, "In-laws sing my song." Likewise, *The Testaments* by Margarette Attwood and *Klara and the Sun* by Kazuo Ishiguro also deal with some strange future societies. (07/17/2022)

451. Give a disease and offer its treatment.
병 주고 약 준다.

Purdue Pharma, incorporated in 1991, focused on pain management medication, calling itself a "pioneer in developing medications for reducing pain, a principal cause of human suffering." Their products included hydromorphone, oxycodone (in MS CONTIN and OXYCONTIN), fentanyl, codeine, etc.   The addictive nature of their products, especially those containing oxycodone, creates a significant risk to the abuser; they can result in overdose and death. Although the company was fully aware of such potential harm to society, the company aggressively promoted the products mainly via the medical community. Sales reached an astronomical figure. By 2017, the cumulative revenues had increased to U$35 billion.

OXYCONTIN abuse first emerged in 2000. In 2012, *the New England Journal of Medicine* published a study that found that "76 percent of those seeking help for heroin addiction began by abusing pharmaceutical narcotics, primarily OXYCONTIN" and drew a direct line between Purdue's marketing of the product and the subsequent heroin epidemic in the US.

In 2018, Purdue Pharma patented a new approach for controlling cravings and treating addiction to opioids such as OXYCONTIN. In short, Purdie Pharma gave addiction problems as well as tried to remedy them. This is the crux of the above proverb.

As a footnote, in 2020, the company had reached a settlement with many states, potentially total worth U$8.3 billion, while admitting that it "knowingly and intentionally conspired and agreed with others to aid and abet" doctors dispensing medication "without a legitimate medical purpose." Last year, the US House introduced a bill that would stop the bankruptcy judge involved from granting members of the Sackler family, the collective owner of Purdue, legal immunity during the bankruptcy proceedings.

The main culprit in the gun violence that is currently prevailing in this country is, of course, the gun itself although gun lovers and the NRA (National Rifle Association) maintain that it is humans to commit the violence. Both mantras are semantic at best as no violence will be realized without guns or humans. The Second Amendment to the US Constitution recognizes the individual right to keep and bear arms. So long as the US citizens strictly adhere to the outdated principles underlying the Second Amendment and gun manufacturers sell more sophisticated arms, the violence will continue.

Just last week, on July 17, 2022, a deadly shooting occurred at a mall in a suburb of Indianapolis, killing three innocent shoppers and wounding a few victims. One unique feature of this incident was that a 22-year-old bystander who was carrying a handgun legally shot and killed the gunman. He was immediately hailed by the police as "nothing short of heroic" and became a Good Samaritan. His older brother declared, ".... he's an amazing kid and I've never been more proud of anyone in my entire life. What he did was selfless and amazing."

Gun-right supporters and the NRA have maintained that the best way to stop gun violence, especially at schools, would be to arm ourselves and hire school guards who can shoot. To me, it is twisted logic but many people buy into the suggestion and the above incident will undoubtedly strengthen the argument with a lot of noise. It is nothing but giving disease and trying to solve the trouble with the same cause of the disease.

The pharmaceutical company I used to work for in my "previous life" serendipitously discovered that a drug candidate we were developing for lowering blood pressure showed an interesting side effect: it stimulated hair growth. So, the management decided to go for what seemed to be a more lucrative field of hair growth rather than the blood pressure business: see more in Entry #47, "Have you ever seen hair without skin?"

A frustrating aspect of this new venture was that hair growth was rather minuscule and that one has to continuously use it to maintain whatever appeared on the bold head. A general consensus was that these are not a big issue as bold men are rather desperate and that continued use would mean more profits.

Here, had the company tried sincerely to mitigate the agony of bolded men by studying the fundamental mechanism involved in hair loss, I could have stayed put and worked for them. Their seeming delight to learn that men have to continuously use the treatment did not sit well with the ideal young man I was at that time. As I was leaving the firm, they went to the market with a great deal of fanfare and promotion in the market. I do not know what happened to the product. I no longer see their advertisements nowadays. (07/23/2022)

452. The candlestick in a sanctuary.
전당 잡은 촛대 같다.

Imagine candleholders in a huge auditorium or sanctuary hall, especially when it is empty and prone to echoing. Or you might have noticed their presence just before going through meditation or prayer in a cathedral. They are, for all purposes, just sitting there as quietly as the surrounding. If we personify them, they are like people in a noisy crowd who are sitting in silence with few words, not necessarily out of apathy but in preference for listening rather than talking.

Once we decide on this line of interpretation, we realize that the proverb has many derivatives introduced already, like Entry #10, "An empty wheelbarrow makes more noise." However, I also notice a strange use of the verb, 잡다 (은) in the proverb. The word means to seize, hold, capture, or arrest. Then, a direct translation may read as "like a candlestick that is seizing the sanctuary." Does it imply a burning candle in a dark hall?

The villa drifts in darkness. In the hallway by the English patient's bedroom the last candle burns, still alive in the night. Whenever he opens his eyes out of sleep, he sees the old wavering yellow light.

For him now the world is without sound, and even light seems an unneeded thing. He will tell the girl (Hana) in the morning he wants no candle flame to accompany him while he sleeps.

The above sentences are almost at the end of the 1992 novel, *The English Patient* by Michael Ondaatje. The book won the Booker Prize and has remained one of my favorite novels. It was also adapted into a 1996 film. The story involves four main characters: a badly burned "the English Patient," a Canadian nurse Hana, an Indian Sikh Kip, and a damaged British spy, Caravaggio, who happens to be an old friend of Hana's father. They are brought together toward the end of the Second World War at an abandoned hospital more or less by happenstance in a small Italian village.

The English patient turns out to be a Hungarian Count, whose memories as a mapmaker during his desert explorations in Africa come and go along with sedation by morphine. Nobody, including himself, knows his name until Caravaggio establishes his true identity. Hana's only living family she loves dearly is her stepmother. The lover of her mother dies with severe burns and yet Hana could not help. Now Hana puts all of her energy into caring for the English patient. Kip, trained in England, worked as a sapper, clearing unexploded ordnance around the villa. Kip and the English patient become friends with the shared knowledge of the topography of Tuscany. Kip also develops a relationship with Hana but tries to kill any white man, including the English patient, upon believing that the US could drop atomic bombs only on the Asian race.

Soon after Kip fails to shoot the English patient out of affection and friendship, he leaves the villa for good. The above scene describes the room the patient is in. The candle is the only witness of the dying man. Indeed, the candlelight in a temple, sanctuary hall, or simple church must have witnessed various events like weddings, baptisms of infants, funerals big or small, etc., and yet remains silent.

The word *jeon-dang* (전당) has another meaning, a pawnshop. According to my wife, my interpretation is wrong, saying that the proverb refers to something that is of little use or function, literally like a candlestick on the shelf in a pawnshop. However busy and crowded a pawnshop might be, the candlestick sitting on the shelf is just sitting there. If we follow this line of thinking, the candlestick in the proverb personifies quiet, and perhaps less sought-after, people in a crowd. This was similar to my original thought. The candlestick might have its own intrinsic value but so long as it is in a pawnshop, it is of no use.

According to mass media, for the past 18 months, Vice President Kamala Harris has not shown the leadership expected from her position. Several of her successful travels to foreign nations are often attributed to other delegates such as Secretary of State Antony Blinken and Defense Secretary Lloyd Austin. Many, including myself, begin to wonder if she was just a political partner who helped Biden get elected. To be fair, President Biden should show his full support for her whenever the chances arise. Otherwise one may wonder if she is just a candlestick in a pawnshop. (07/25/2022)

453. Plenty to see, little to eat.
눈은 풍년이나 입은 흉년이다.

What I see in the farm field with my own eyes clearly indicates that we are having a bumper year but what I eat indicates a lean year. How come? This proverb reminds me of what I kept on hearing from the CEO of a Korean pharmaceutical firm for which I used to serve as a consultant: I smell something delicious from our R&D folks, but my dinner table is almost empty. How come? He was a business-minded manager and his words were a subtle way to exert pressure on drug development. He always understood that I would transmit such messages to scientists with whom I would soon sit down for nitty-gritty technical discussions.

When pharmacologists discover an interesting potential use for a new chemical entity from chemists, their employer would apply for and obtain a patent. Currently, the term of a new patent in the United States is 20 years from the date on which the application for the patent was filed. This used to be 17 years when I worked as an industrial researcher. The lengthy development includes not only animal studies for safety and efficacy but also costly human clinical studies.

If a company moves fast and all developmental efforts work out perfectly, they may enjoy about five to 10 years of exclusive market. Even with the additional exclusivity granted by the Food and Drug Administration, the company may not have long dominance in the market for a given indication. Exclusivity is given to promote future innovation in the industry. Once this period is over, generic products emerge from opportunistic manufacturers that invest little R&D efforts. Thus, the cost of a generic product is lower and the patient can enjoy medicine at a lower price.

Due to the time restraints for the exclusive market, the CEO always feels they are sitting on a "cushion of needles" and scientists have to work very hard to expedite development. If one out of 10 drug candidates eventually makes it to market, it would be considered a successful batting average. At a given time, what we casual bystanders and the CEO see or smell is one thing but what they are about to gain in their pocket is a different matter. The final product is so close and yet seems to be far away. Indeed, we live in a highly risky professional world.

There are many instances in our daily lives to find what we see to be quite different from what we have anticipated. Singles meet through various Apps but they may find the date is far from what they had imagined. I find movies to be disappointing compared with the original book. What we eat at a restaurant is usually not as good as what we envision from the pictures on the menu: looks and taste of melons, book cover and its contents, reviews of a product online and what is delivered, and betrayal of the first impression, etc. The list can continue. See more cases in Entry #302, "Nothing to eat at well-publicized feasts."

In some rare instances, we find what is delivered is better than what we were promised, a lucky break. A few years ago, a friend brought a bag of green grapes at a picnic that looked quite sour but it was one of the best grapes I have ever tasted. Since then we have bought green grapes many times but have always been disappointed. I believed that the intermittent but recurring headache I had experienced was from a slowly growing tumor in the brain but it turned out to be from occipital neuralgia.

Earlier this year, my wife and I bought a bag of apples at the Maui airport. They didn't look quite appealing but we were unexpectedly delighted by their taste. We wanted to bring them home but the authorities from the Hawaii agriculture department told us we cannot carry them to the mainland. We thus ate the whole bagful of apples in front of their inspection station. They told us the name of the apple but I forgot what they were. They looked like typical apples but are a bit smaller than usual and had a firmer texture than I had anticipated, with a sweet watery thing with such a nice flavor!

Thanks to the lockdown from the COVID-19 pandemic, we are now accustomed to purchasing nearly everything online. It looks like the only items we buy regularly at a store are those we eat. Even for those groceries, our local store is more than happy to deliver. Not long ago, my wife wanted to order for me a few pairs of pants through Amazon. She showed me several pictures on their website but none of them looked any good. So we ordered just one pair. Later we found it perfect and hence we hurriedly ordered a few more of the same but with different colors. In summary, the above proverb goes in either direction. Sometimes what we see is a lean year but we can receive plenty on the dining table. (07/26/2022)

454. Swallow if sweet, spit if sour.
달면 삼키고 쓰면 뱉는다.

There are many unprincipled people in our world. These people chomp on what is sweet but spit out in a hurry what tastes bad. That is, they take in whatever comes their way if they think it is valuable and useful. They do not think about the long-term effect of their action. Corruption erases principle. Here, I present three cases where people become corrupt: one because of money and the other two because of political power.

LIV Golf is a professional golf tour financed by earmarked $2 billion from its $620 billion Public Investment Fund of Saudi Arabia. LIV stands for the Roman numeral 54, which is the number of holes golfers play, rather than the typical 72 holes. The league was formally launched in October 2021 and played for the first time in June 2022. The former professional golfer Greg Norman is the CEO of LIV Golf.

Because of the large sum of money offered as awards and rewards, many prominent players have left PGA for LIV. For instance, it is said that Dustin Johnson, winner of two major championships, was paid U$150 million for committing to the LIV series. Tiger Woods declined to join LIV Golf and turned down a deal that was "mind-blowingly enormous; we're talking about high nine digits" according to Greg Norman. High nine digits mean a sum close to U$ one billion. Phil Mickelson was rumored to have received U$200 million by committing to the LIV series.

These golfers established their name and fame through PGA and yet they are leaving for LIV for various self-justifications. On the move, Johnson said, "I chose what's best for me and my family." Kevin Na, the only Korean American golfer who joined LIV Golf, offered a very lengthy explanation but it all boils down to money. I wish all of them just to cut to the chase and state it is the money they are going for. Considering the bad track record of human rights in Saudi Arabia, receiving their "blood money" looks awfully bad but the defectors do not seem to care.

Cameron Smith, a 28-year-old Australian golfer, let be known of his participation in LIV just a day after he won the 2022 British Open Championship. They behave like flies gathering around dung. I may sound a bit too harsh but what else could I say about their loyalty or integrity?

The following story deserves a briefing on the early history of the Joseon Dynasty of Korea. Se-jong the Great (1397- 1450) was the fourth king of Joseon. He is considered one of the best kings in our history and is quite famous for his invention of the Korean alphabet. He was succeeded by his oldest son, Moon-jong. This king prematurely died in the second year of the throne at the age of 37, leaving a 13-year-old king, Dan-jong. As Moon-jong foresaw his impending death, he specifically requested all his men to take good care of the young king, Dan-jong.

In 1453, the first year of King Dan-jong, his uncle Sooyang-daegoon (수양대군, 1417 - 1468), or younger brother of Moon-jong, summarily removed the young king and the king's loyal court officials including one of his own younger brothers, and he then became the King Se-jo. This internal rebellion is known as Geyujeongnan, 계유정난. While many loyalists lost their lives, many traitors "sold" their integrity to join the rebel.

One of the turncoats was Sin Sook-ju, 신숙주 (1417 – 1475). Sin was an outstanding scholar as well as a diplomat. He helped Se-jong the Great develop the Korean alphabet, for instance. He was a good friend of Sooyang-daegoon, close enough that he could have stopped the latter from killing King Dan-jo and his followers. Instead, he conspired with Sooyang-daegoon. In short, Sin discarded the principle that he had preached throughout his life and joined the rebels for what could be the only reason, his political power. For many following generations, Korean parents prohibited their sons from consuming a vegetable side dish called *sookju-namool*, 숙주나물, because both names share the same pronunciation.

Another example, this time from the States in the present time, would be a Republican Congresswoman from New York, 38-year-old Elise Stefanik. She is currently the third-ranking Republican in the House. She used to be so disgusted by Donald Trump that she would barely mention his name. But nowadays they seem to be bosom buddies. Apparently, her loyalty to Trump is in such a state that she is often mentioned as a potential Trump running mate in the 2024 election.

Her sudden transformation has become a source of sadness and anger among her former colleagues and also raised much speculation as to the motive. For the conversion, she was rewarded for replacing Liz Cheney as chair of the House Republican Conference, but she was forever branded as an individual whose "ambition unmoored to principle." (07/28/2022)

455. One slack summer day brings ten-day hunger in the winter.
여름에 하루 놀면 겨울에 열흘 굶는다.

This proverb is self-explanatory, reminding us of Aesop's Fable, "The Ants & the Grasshopper." If you goof around when the time is ripe for work, you will pay dearly for your laziness sooner or later. This is a common theme of many old sayings: see, for example, Entry #169, "A tree with deep roots survives drought." Instead of trying to repeat the standard interpretation, we will address a subject that can be tangent to the above in which one can easily overwork "to death." This is particularly true in the education of children in Korea, as pointed out in Entry ##99, "All fields are fertile to diligent farmers."

Lately, there have been so many brazen sex scenes as well as utmost violence in streaming movies that my wife and I seldom watch a movie together. Besides, we have different tastes in films anyway. But, in the past few weeks, we have been able to watch a Korean TV drama series together. Its title is *Extraordinary Attorney Woo*. Last night's episode was about the suffering of children from overburdened schoolwork.

Hack-won (학원) is a small private academy for school children. This type of after-school academy is quite popular in any neighborhood in Korea. Their sole purpose is to provide kids with supplementary lessons so that children can score high on various competitive tests at school and eventually pass the entrance exams for higher educational institutes.

These crammers send out a small van to a school and wait at the gate to pick up students immediately after their final class. They are delivered to *hack-won* where serious remedial and supplemental lessons are crammed into children. Their classroom is often locked from the outside and students may need approval for bathroom breaks. Dinner is invariably something that they can purchase at a corner dime store. Children hate every minute but they usually do not know what they are missing. Besides, they are lambs in front of their tiger moms.

The TV drama introduces a young man, perhaps in his early 20s, whose single mother runs such an academy. He believes in "all work and no play makes Jack a dull boy" and shows deep sympathy for the kids under his mother's constant guidance. One afternoon this young man gives a drink that is peppered with sedatives to the driver of the van that belongs to his mother's academy for the kids. As the driver falls to sleep, the young man steals the van and, instead of heading for his mother's school, "kidnaps" a dozen of kids and goes for fun in the woods. The young man, self-declared the Director of the Children's Liberation Army, becomes a fast friend of the children, and the kids are having the greatest time in ecstasy. His action is very like what Jack Nicholson does for the patients of a mental hospital in *One Flew Over the Cuckoo's Nest*.

The incident infuriates the parents, or mothers to be exact, for the lost lessons and wasted time of their precious children. Mothers sue the academy in no time at all and the case goes to a court of law. However one may look, it is a case of kidnap in court but, for others, it is a case of compassion for a young man who empathizes with the children's lack of free time. In the end, Lawyer Woo and the defendant call the children who have participated in the escapade for the witness. The case was dismissed in the end in favor of the young man and the children.

It is indeed a difficult task for parents to maintain a delicate balance between the study and play of their child. Korean parents will do anything to secure their children's later education at, say, Harvard or MIT. Parents justify their sacrifice for the prospect that their children can now receive the type of education that they never had. They are thrilled with the vision that their sons and daughters would enjoy a successful and happy life, which seems guaranteed by their education. How can anyone blame their desire? See Entry #99, "All fields are fertile to diligent farmers."

If a child grows up without an adequate period of childhood, how could it affect the rest of their life? A teenage sensation at the start of his career, the Swedish tennis player Björn Borg enjoyed unprecedented stardom and consistent success during the 1970s. Borg won four consecutive French Open titles and six consecutive Wimbledon finals. In short, he won everything except the US Open despite four runner-up finishes. He retired at the age of 26. I seem to remember reading about one regret that Borg expressed: he wished he had a "normal" life as a child. As I look back now, I am wondering if his calm demeanor on the court, which earned him the nickname of the "Ice Man" or "Ice-Borg," is something to do with his earlier life. In 1981, when he lost the Wimbledon final, he said, "What shocked me was that I wasn't even upset." (07/29/2022)

456. Gangtaegong, fishing with a straight hook.
강태공의 곧은 낚시질.

This story is from a Chinese legend. Once upon a time, there lived a scholar who read and studied all day no matter what was happening outside. Before going out, for instance, his wife would ask him to keep an eye on their vegetable garden as the weather turned ominously dark and threatened. Sure enough, torrential rain poured down like a wall of water but he was not aware that their vegetable garden was completely washed away.

Other times, he would go out fishing all day but come home emptyhandedly. One day, thinking he might be hungry fishing all day for their sustenance, she brought his lunch to the river but found find him deep in sleep. Not surprisingly, the fish basket was empty but she surprisingly noticed that the hook on the line was straight without any bait. Furious at his absentmindedness, the wife eventually left him for good.

Years later, the man passed an important nationwide test and overcame many challenging tasks to become the King's most trusted confidante. It was during the Chu Dynasty of China which ruled the land around 1000 BC. On his way back to his hometown one day, he came across his wife in tattered clothes carrying a bucketful of water on her head. She begged him for forgiveness and wanted to come back with him again. Upon hearing her plea, he asked her to empty the water to the ground, which she did. Then he asked her to collect the water back, which she couldn't, of course.

The man's name is Gangtaegong, 강태공, in Korean pronouncement. Abiding what appeared to be idling time to other people, *Gangtaegong* had waited for the ultimate recognition by none other than the king himself. It is said that he was almost 70 years old when the king discovered his outstanding qualification.

A lesson one may learn from the above story would be not to give up mental exercise no matter how lazy it may appear to other people. Appearance-wise he was asleep but he must have been in deep thinking. That he was using a straight hook without any lures indicates that he did not want to be interrupted by the excitement of a fish being hooked, or by a thunderstorm. We have to give him some credit for his concentration.

I can speak for myself only, but I cannot carry on serious thoughts while my eyes are closed. I will fall asleep in no time at all. My typical posture during meditation or thinking would be just staring empty space in front, just looking but seeing nothing. A casual walk or strolling alone on a deserted trail offers a good opportunity also. Other people may twiddle their thumb while sitting on a rocking chair and gazing distance without much focus, or shave a wood stick with no obvious purpose. No matter, the story of Gangtaegong emphasizes the importance of thinking.

What I do not like about the story is the way his wife was treated. Obviously, she did not see much of her future with this good-for-nothing man. Leaving him was her prerogative and nobody should treat her later like asking for impossible tasks like collecting spilled water. It looks like misogyny at its best but I suppose we cannot condemn what happened several millennia ago with the 21st-century standard.

A semi-scholarly paper written for laymen that I came across on the topic offers the true meaning of the story by quoting a Chinese sentence written in metaphor, 태공조어 원자상구(太公釣魚 願者上鉤). Now that Taegong is fishing with a straight hook and without any bait, only those fish who wanted to die will be caught. Who would voluntarily wish to be caught?

Taegong was in fact waiting for someone who would recognize his greatness in the military as well as in cultural matters. Belatedly he was discovered by King Moon-Wang or 문왕 and soon appointed as King's advisor. Moon-Wang was succeeded by Moo-Wang, who continuously benefited from Taegong's service. That is how the Chu Dynasty was founded. *Taegong* lived his life as a feudal lord of the Chu nation.

All in all, the above Chinese story amply illustrates the stark difference in mentality between old China and the contemporary Western world. Here, every yo-yo is anxious to promote themselves for the 15-minute fame, screaming many nonsensical speeches. A few days ago this man, Alex Jones, who claimed that the massacre at the Sandy Hook Elementary School had been a hoax, declared bankruptcy in a preventive move against the pending suit from the victim's parents. If you recall, in the massacre killed by a madman were 20 innocent schoolchildren and six adults.

What amazes me most is the finding that such an unimaginable claim receives so much attention from mass media and commands so many believers and followers. As far as I am concerned, they are fish that wants to be snared by a straight hook. (07/30/2020)

457. Complaining of short breath while holding the nose.
코 막고 숨 막힌다고 한다.

If you are holding the nose, of course, you will have a hard time breathing. All you will have to do for recovering normal breathing is just remove your fingers from the nose. The proverb says that oftentimes the simplest solution is just in front of you: there is no need to seek a complicated and convoluted approach. As the next Entry #458 indicates, the darkest spot in a room is just below the candle, meaning that adversity, just like holding your nose, is lurking over much closer to you than you may believe. Two more somewhat related proverbs are Entry # 109, "You cannot see your own eyebrow," and #141, "One feels a splinter under a fingernail, but not a troubled heart."

A person who cannot or refuses to see a simple solution to a given problem is either blind or too sophisticated. The recent shortage of infant formula has become a national crisis, and everyone asking what went wrong with the supply chain involved. President Biden had to assure mothers, saying that more will be forthcoming from European nations. Some commercial airliners volunteered for delivery. A major manufacturer in the nation, which had been shut down because of some hygiene-related issues, was urged to reopen the shop as quickly as possible.

While such a crisis is taking place, I found myself asking what happened to the mother's own milk. Since when have we replaced it with a formula? Infant formula is supposed to mimic the mother's milk at one to three months postpartum. It usually contains cow's milk as a protein source, various vegetable oils for fats, some carbohydrates, and a mixture of vitamins. What is missing in the formula are the immunoglobulins, or antibodies, that offer infants immune protection.

Human milk contains all of the five classes of antibodies, in particular so-called secretory immunoglobulin of type A, sIgA. Collectively they offer a newly born infant with immune protection. Some of these intact antibodies enter the baby's bloodstream from the ingested milk in the gut. This unusual absorption window "closes" when a baby begins weaning. Infants who are bottle-fed have no way of acquiring such "passive immunization."

Pediatricians have long known that infants who are breastfed contract fewer infections than those who are given formula. The popularity of breastfeeding in many countries has in fact made mothers defer the time of beginning infant formula. This seemingly simple and yet more beneficial approach to the formula supply problem would be like removing a hand holding the nose for better breathing in the proverb.

If a solution is too straightforward so that even school children can understand, adults or politicians frown upon the approach simply because it is too simple. These sophisticated people accept only those solutions that can satisfy their immediate interests.

The Youth Climate Movement is an international network of youth organizations, which boasts more than 25,000 volunteers from all over the world. It collectively aims to inspire, empower and mobilize a generational movement of young people to take positive action on climate change. As far as I can tell, what they recommend for the current establishment to do is most relevant and free from any baggage of private interest. Rightly so since the future is theirs, not ours. The guiding principles for their policies must sound too simple for the old powers that be to listen to. What a shame.

If we examine each and every problem we are facing now as a crisis without reviewing the failed attempts in the past, a new fresh approach may turn out to be the simplest solution. For example, a solution to gun violence should start with confiscating firearms from private citizens and establishing a set of new guidelines. In the end, we may realize that the Second Amendment of the US Constitution must go.

As to illegal immigration, the US government should invest in the well-being of the nation from which people are leaving. Why would anyone leave their homeland if their lives are free of hunger and political oppression? Constructing a modern Great Wall is a band-aid approach at best. If there isn't any demand for drugs like fentanyl or heroin in this country, I can guarantee that there won't be any drug smuggling and associated crimes. Sending DEA (Drug Enforcement Administration) officers to the country of drug origin is based on a wrong starting point.

Unfair taxation, skyrocketing health care costs, suppressed labor movement, the cost of higher education, student loans, etc. are all suffering from unfocused temporary remedial, incremental patching jobs. All of us are very good at complaining but do not have the willpower to do what we ought to do. Examine the wisdom of the above proverb. (07/31/2022)

458. Darkest is beneath the candle.
등잔 밑이 어둡다.

If you light a candle right in the middle of an empty room, you will notice what the above proverb is saying is absolutely true. The light intensity is inversely proportional to the square of the distance, which is commonly known as "the inverse square law." Thus, one can say the brightness at two feet away from a candle would be four times less than at one foot away. Regardless of what science says, candlelight brightens every corner of the room, but cannot shed light on its own shadow, leaving a dark spot just at the bottom of the stem. It is like we cannot see our own eyebrows.

While the proverb describes the absolutely correct observation, what it implies could be up to the reader. A standard interpretation would be that we often see things some distance away far better than those quite close to us. In Entry #101, "Even the monkey can fall down from trees," I introduced a renowned astronomer who knows every constellation in the dark sky gets tripped over a small rock protruding from the ground, only six feet away. In a similar vein, many crimes occur by a person close to the victim, as in Entry #174, "My ax injures my foot."

In the case of the murder of a woman, for instance, detectives first suspect her husband or boyfriend as a potential offender. Indeed, as high as 30% of women were slain by the victim's husband or boyfriend. Of these, just over 50% were by their husbands. These are rather old statistics from 1992, but the trend must remain the same nowadays.

The following story was all the rage while we lived in Chapel Hill, North Carolina because the "murder" or "accident" took place in Durham, another college town nearby. In the wee hour of December 9, 2001, Michael Peterson made a 911 call, saying that he discovered the dead body of his wife Kathleen in full blood at the bottom of the staircase. He later claimed that he had been outside by the pool till 2:40 AM and that Kathleen must have fallen down the stairs after consuming alcohol and Valium. He was a writer with a few novels under his name and worked as a columnist for a local newspaper. His column often criticized local police and Durham County District Attorney for their ineptitude. Kathleen was a successful executive at Nortel Networks Corporation.

Michael Peterson was first convicted in 2003 of murdering Kathleen. However, eight years later, he was granted a new trial after the judge ruled a critical prosecution witness gave misleading testimony. In 2017, Peterson submitted an Alford plea to the reduced charge of manslaughter. He was sentenced to time already served and freed. The so-called Alford plea is a guilty plea whereby a defendant in a criminal case does not admit to the criminal act and asserts innocence but admits that the evidence presented by the prosecution would be likely to persuade a judge or jury to find the defendant guilty beyond a reasonable doubt.

Peterson and his first wife had lived in Germany for a while, where they were very friendly to a single mother with two kids, whom they adopted later after the widower died in a nearly identical manner. She fell down to the staircase and Peterson was the last person to see her alive. This together with his somewhat exaggerated military career and his being bisexual cast a dark cloud over his struggle to prove his innocence.

In favor of his stand was the key witness for the prosecutor. He was an analyst working at the North Carolina State Bureau of Investigation whose report for the case was flawed to an unacceptable extent. As both sides were struggling with the lack of water-tight evidence, the Alford plea was a reasonable conclusion.

The betrayal by a spouse or a close friend would be the most common incident of "the dark spot under the candle." More shocking may be the case where parents are slain by their own children for whatever reasons might be involved. The following story may illustrate the case point.

In April this year, an old couple in their 60s and 70s was found dead of gunshot wounds. They were discovered by police who visited for a wellness inspection. This happened in uptown Chicago, on a Sunday morning in an apartment building. Based on the camera footage of the building, the following scenario was established.

Friday night, the father and 33-year-old son arrived to play cards with his mother. Two other guests were already at the apartment. At about 3 AM Saturday, the hosting old lady was seen on camera walking out of her apartment with the two guests, escorting them to the elevator. She then walked back into her apartment. The only people remaining now at the apartment were the three family members. At 6 AM, the son left his mother's apartment, appearing to stop to lock the door. I wonder how his parents reacted when his son confronted them to kill. (08/01/2022)

459. Excessive meddling.
오지랖이 넓다.

Once in a while, we hear a sad story that an old person dies alone, which nobody notices for a few days or even a few weeks until a strange odor sips into the neighborhood. The children of the deceased, who live far away, are hurriedly contacted for funeral arrangements, etc.

My elderly mother-in-law lives alone in an apartment in Tokyo. She and her neighbor, another old lady, have apparently made a pact to see every morning if the other is still alive. If the curtain of a small window of their apartment is raised, it means the occupant is okay. This seemingly standard practice among the elderly hardly constitutes meddling in other's life. One cannot insist "My death is none of your business," and the neighbor's intervention is more than warranted.

Compared with Westerners, Koreans are more prone to poke their nose into other people's business. The tendency was only recently frowned upon, as individualistic ideals arrived in modern Korea. In the old days, our ancestors lived in tightly woven, collective communities, which must have promoted a kinship among not only neighbors but also by extension in the general population. See also Entries #80, "A mother dislikes her daughter-in-law's heel;" #275, "For gossip, even a guy on a double crutch comes forth;" and #355, "Placing persimmons and pears at a *jesa*."

The above idiom expresses excessive meddling once again. Here, an interesting word used is 오지랖 *ojirap* or 앞지락 *apjirak*. This authentic Korean word means the front of an outer garment. The word was somehow transformed to mean interference, meddling, and even gossiping. I spent some time investigating how it might have drifted to "meddling," but I was not able to find any satisfactory explanations. The idiom just says "a wide, or generous, garment front."

One source said that a wide garment front can hide what is underneath and thus offers the liberty to talk about other's business (presumably beginning with other's clothes). My Ever-smart wife suggested that the coat is so wide that it will inevitably touch and often sweep off stuff from the selves or tables. I do not like either of the explanations.

There is a wide range of perceived interference with the business of other people, from bona fide assistance based on good intentions to outright unsolicited meddling. The pact between the two old ladies presented above would belong to the former case. Telling the players of a chess game what moves they have to make would be pure interference. In between these two extremes, where to draw a line between help and meddling depends on a person. Bering Korean DNA, I am quite liberal asking many personal questions to strangers as I believe it to be the best way to get to know people. In May 2016, I met Kirsten and Aya Kotake just after Leon headed Santiago on el Camino.

This Swedish lady Kirsten married a Japanese sailor who deceased some years ago and thus their daughter's name carries a Japanese name. Kirsten had been retired for a while but Aya was working for an advertising firm in New York City. The duo apparently meet regularly for trek together on a section of the Camino. Aya had to leave the trail for her work and I walked with Kirsten for several days before she also took off for Sweden.

Kirsten never showed any sign of discomfort or displeasure with my probing questions about her interesting life with a Japanese "drifter," her own expression. In fact, she seemed to find a sounding board in me. As it turned out, Mr. Kotake had married earlier and left a sizeable inheritance for her and Aya. Then, a legal challenge from the family of Mr. Kotake's first marriage came forward and Christen explained the situation quite in detail. Do remember, time was most abundant on the trial. The floodgate opened for her and I offered my own perspective of life and wisdom.

My friends have now become immune to my tendency of overstepping into their own space. Their basic attitude seems like, "OK, you can ask all you want but I have the right to filter your invading inquiries." That is fine with me also. The point is that they know my shoulders are always available for their cries. If this isn't a sound foundation of friendship, what is?

Apparently, the "interference" from Koreans is the major "complaint" by foreigners. I am wondering if this isn't a simple misunderstanding by Westerners of the eagerness on the part of Koreans to be in a closer friendship, just like my behaviors with Kirsten and Aya. There is no doubt in my mind that poor communication skills in English must play an additional role in the misunderstanding. The only advice I can offer to foreigners is that they be a bit more patient and try a bit harder to gauge the true meaning of our behaviors. (08/02/2022)

460. Slap on the face in return for kindness.
제 것 주고 뺨 맞는다.

One of many instances I feel life is not fair is when my good intention is paid back in malice, not because of misunderstanding but by deliberate betrayal. According to the above proverb, one can even get slapped on the cheek after offering goodwill. In my experience, this type of utterly ridiculous incident happens usually when a monetary or short-term interest overrides one's honesty or vocational integrity.

My wife and I have lived in this town for just over four years. Since we purchased a new house, we needed to hire people who can modify the house to our taste before we move in. As pointed out in Entry #116, "The crayfish sides with crabs" and #125, "Blood is thicker than water (and the arm always bends inwards)," it is quite natural for Koreans including me do business with other Koreans in this town, which boasts as many as 20,000 Korean expatriates. All being equal, why not help other Koreans?

The realtor lady we hired was a Korean and the men who laid hardwood floors and shutters over more than 30 windows were also Koreans. We immensely enjoyed and appreciated their excellent work. On the last day when I wrote the final check, the man who put the floor advised me rather casually not to expect that all Koreans in this town would be as nice as we appeared to assume. He knew we were from a small town with a very limited Korean population. When prompted to elaborate, he mentioned several cases of fraud and cheating by Koreans upon other Koreans, mainly among acquaintances in Korean churches.

But still, I had faith in Koreans and hired a Korean handyman for a variety of small jobs. Mr. Yoon was recommended by the Korean lady who cuts my and my wife's hair. He was somewhat talkative but clever enough to quickly grasp the mechanics involved in each of the following six assignments. First, I had him cut a sheet of plexiglass of 1/8" thickness to a certain dimension. He said no problem as he had a special scissor for the job but missed a straight line quite badly. Later I was able to salvage some parts. The second job was mitigating squeaky noise when the garage door is opened. He had a spray can of a lubricant but he just showed me and asked me to get one when I go to a hardware store next time.

The electric plug for the garbage disposal under the sink gets disconnected quite often due to its vibration. He just placed a short extension cord to dampen the vibration. This clever idea worked and is still working. He also replaced the bathtub faucet, which became loose later causing quite an irritation on my part. See more later.

Earlier we had people lay a hardwood floor even for the small, skewed store space under the staircase, but it does not have a light bulb. Mr. Yoon said that he can tap the outlet on the outside wall and started to drill a hole from inside. It badly missed the spot and had to drill another hole, having to patch the original one.

I just let Yoon do these trivial jobs without my presence, but my wife in an attempt to be a nice host kept on offering drinks like orange juice and ginseng tea from a pouch, *hongsamwon* (홍삼원), along with some cookies. Surely he was treated better than me.

The last job was fixing the icemaker in our Samsung refrigerator. It was only three years old but quit making ice. Indeed, the inside was deposited with a thick layer of ice. Before Yoon showed up, I had purchased a new unit and defrosted the inside, all in advance. I thus naively assumed that he can just replace the malfunctioning old part with the one I had purchased. I was also running a how-to video from YouTube on my cell phone while translating the instruction from English to Korean. He was able to take out the old unit but placing the new one took all afternoon, eventually breaking off the hooking part on the refrigerator. Being clever, he was able to improvise some band-aid jobs and finally made the icemaker work.

A few weeks later, the shower faucet he had installed came off, pouring out water around it. I sent him a text message and waited for three days before I sent him a nasty message: "In my long life of about 80 years, I have yet to come across a repairman as incapable and irresponsible as you are," all in my broken Korean. He later sent me a message saying in a protesting and irritated manner that he did not see my note until then. I later told my hairdresser to be careful from now on when she recommends Yoon.

In the end, both my wife and I felt that Yoon was just good at getting a job and paid but was not responsible for his work. He knew that I know he was lying when he said he did not see my message. He lives and dies with text messages as it is the main way he gets referrals. We had a sour taste in our mouths for a while from the feeling of betrayal but eventually forgot about the whole episode. (08/03/2022)

461. Hiccup during yawning.
하품에 딸꾹질.

How often does a hiccup interrupt and ruin body-stretching and relaxing yawning? I do not know the answer but it could happen albeit rarely. Instead of a hiccup, it could be the displeased stare of your boss at work. Here, not only stopping but also trying to hide yawning is one of the most inconvenient and irritating occasions. It is like when someone touches your abdomen right in the middle of yawning. It almost sounds like coitus interruptus by an intruder into the bedroom.

A standard interpretation of the above epigram is that there are events that would proceed in turns and twists but in the end fail to happen to anyone's satisfaction. It may be equivalent to one of the extended versions of Murphy's Law: "Anything that can go wrong will go wrong and at the worst possible time."

About a year ago, I saw the strange movie *Magnolia* which stars some familiar names such as Tom Cruise. It was strange because I could not form a unified impression from what appeared to be a multitude of seemingly unrelated and unfocused stories presented in parallel. Very confusing, to say the least. Frogs and a gun falling from the sky later in the movie were as improbable as the following scenes at the beginning of the movie. It is about a guy who could not successfully commit suicide by jumping from the building because he was shot by a stray bullet to death while he was still falling down in the air. His yawning was interrupted by a hiccup.

A suicidal teenage son, hoping that one of his parents would be killed during their drunken ritual gun-waving arguments, secretly loads a shotgun. Sure enough, the mother, not knowing the gun was loaded, shoots the gun at her husband in a rage. The bullet misses him and goes outside through the window. It hits and kills her son who has just leaped to his death off the top of their apartment building and is dropping fast passing by the window at that moment. He wouldn't have died, as there is some builder's netting that could stop or at least slow down his free fall. His mother is convicted of the slaying. This was supposed to be a true story of an extreme coincidence but apparently invented by a forensic scientist named Don Mills, for a speaking engagement (from an undated issue of *the Guardian*).

So, what would be the odds that a flying son gets killed by a bullet from her own mother? Such a coincidence seems beyond the realm of statistical probability. What about the odds involved in a car accident in which a pedestrian gets killed by a car that is traveling in the wrong direction on a one-way street? Likewise, have you ever met a guy who got struck by lightning twice let alone once, or who won a big lottery twice? See more in Entry #36, "An unlucky man breaks his nose even when falling backward."

An example of a bad event becoming worse at every turn would be the early phase of the Korean War. On the evening of June 24, 1950, the rain began that continued to the next morning when the North Korean People's Army, or In Min Gun, crossed the 38th parallel that had been dividing the Korean Peninsula. Their multi-prong attacks were so swift that the South Korean army and the US military were forced to retreat to Busan Perimeter within a few weeks of the invasion. It runs roughly 100 miles north and south, 50 miles east to west, bordered by the East Sea on the east, the Korean Strait on the south, and the Naktong River on the west.

The American commander in the Far East, General Douglas MacArthur, had been heavily preoccupied with how best he could serve in establishing a democratic nation out of Japan and was greatly surprised by the invasion. In fact, the US diplomat John Foster Dulles was in Tokyo also to discuss a future peace treaty that would end the American occupation of Japan. He actually visited Korea on June 18, just a week prior to the invasion. MacArthur assured Dulles, who later became the US Secretary of State, that all is under control. This is in spite of some disturbing reports on the North's move along the 38th parallel by the CIA, then the Office of Strategic Services, an agency that MacArthur and his staff didn't care much about.

Per *The Coldest Winter* by David Halberstam, there was a briefing on the eve of June 25, where MacArthur told Dulles, "This is probably only a reconnaissance-in-force. If Washington only will not hobble me, I can handle it with one arm tied behind my back." Then he added that President Syngman Rhee had asked for some fighter planes, and although he thought the Koreans could not use them properly, he intended to send a few along, just for morale purposes. I may sound somewhat ungrateful for what the US military force did for Korea but the War could have run differently had MacArthur been a bit more alert early on. This opening scene was soon followed by a disastrous performance of the Korean army, resulting in a hurried retreat to Pusan Perimeter. (08/05/2022)

462. Raising a tiger cub to fret.
범을 길러 화를 받는다.

The cub of any animal always looks cute. It doesn't matter if the animal is a fearsome lion or a docile rabbit. Think about a bay golden retriever, for instance. How soft their body is and yet they are playful without any bad intention. Look at the long line of ducklings following their mom. Or see how the baby dolphin closely follows her mother.

So, this man purchases a tiger cub and brings it home. Enjoys immensely his new pet all day: feeding, playing, walking the neighborhood on a leash, showing off, and even taking care of the cub's poop. Then a few days later he begins to worry about what to do with the tiger when it grows up. This is a matter of his own safety. Now, the baby tiger becomes the source of constant worries, days in and days out. In effect, this man invites his own worry, maybe not now but worrying about the future in advance.

According to one particular Korean proverb, endless trivial worries are considered one of the three main causes of death: see Entry #248, "Three causes of death: ruthless sun, an endless feast, and trivial worries." They will not let you have a peaceful mind and incessant doubts will give a person an ulcer (not true scientifically) let alone sleepless nights. Self-doubt and lack of self-confidence will lead them to a hesitant and reluctant life.

Now that I've been retired for the past 10 years, there isn't any job-related pressure: the only thing to do nowadays is make a honey-do list, decide what we will have for dinner, when we do the laundry, who is going to do the dish and grocery shopping, etc. In fact, I find myself mellowing down very much in recent years and trying not to allow unnecessary worries to develop. I have been indeed very proud of not letting trivial matters bother me anymore. The following episode may prove the point.

After getting tired of seeing our garage congested with two cars idling most of the time because of the lockdown from COVID-19, in September 2020, we got rid of both a Hyundai Sonata and an old BMW and bought a new Genesis. The salesman sweet-talked us that we would save a few thousand dollars if we apply for a short-term car loan, which we did. five months later, in February 2021, we paid off the balance of the loan. Then, constant headaches began, which could have been ever-lasting worries.

Only yesterday, August 5, 2022, I was able to receive the car title. It has taken 16 months to complete the paperwork, all because incapable people were often lying and passing the buck in routine mannerisms. The worst part is talking to the customer service people at Genesis Finance. After punching in a long number in their automatic answering phone system, I get to talk to a person if I am lucky. Including the 800 number and my birth date, the total number of digits I have to enter into their phone system is 37. Besides, I have to enter the 14-digit loan number and my street address.

Once the verification step is over, I ask them to find my car title with a long explanation of the problem. For some reason, stupid if I may add, the person on the line would submit my request via an email to folks in their Title department and I am forbidden to contact them directly. In the end, they would ask me to contact them again in a week or so to see if they have solved the problem. I tried to call them every week.

Once they realize that my inquiry is beyond their pay scale, they would transfer my call to so-called Special Agents. These people would ask me about the nature of the problem and I had to explain the whole thing again. Eventually, in June this year, one of the Special Agents submitted a formal report to their Care Department requesting an in-depth investigation. In the meantime, I was asking for help from the car dealer here in Las Vegas. They tried but to no avail. I also visited the local DMV a few times to learn that Genesis Finance failed to forward the electronic title to Nevada DMV electronically. I also submitted a formal complaint to Nevada DMV in April 2022. They said they would respond in eight to 10 weeks.

In July, luck was on my side as both Tanisha from Nevada DMV in response to my complaint and Tana from the Care Department at Genesis contacted me nearly at the same time offering help, more out of sympathy. These two "angels" found the source of the problem: it was the corrupt original electronic title. As I said earlier, I received the paper title of our car yesterday in regular mail. Interestingly, no one asked me to pay the fee involved. If I remember it is $20. Did they admit their negligence?

In retrospect, my blood could have been constantly boiling in the past 16 months. I do not know if my mental state has been from resignation and abandonment but I have been calm most of the time. Since my wife has been more upset, at some point and on I did not even bother to tell her anything about the episode. In short, I am very proud of myself for the way I handled the issue. (08/06/2022)

463. Like mixing water with water, alcohol with alcohol.
물에 물 탄 듯 술에 술 탄 듯.

If one mixes water with water or alcohol with alcohol, nothing appears to have changed. As such, this idiom describes a situation where one's act, intention, or statement is not clear to others. It could be intentional or unintentional. Chinese in the old days, often with inscrutable metaphors, are quite famous for being ambiguous on some sticky occasions. This is particularly true if they think that the consequence of their words or acts could come back to haunt them in vengeance.

Such enigmatic behaviors are wish-wash at best but can allow people to avoid an awkward situation. It could be a matter of self-defense and could save one's life. An unintentional vagueness may well be just a reflection of one's insipid personality or simply a poor ability to express oneself clearly. To me, the latter is forgivable as an honest mistake from Inability, while knowingly lying can be quite irritating as in outright cheating. See Entry #82, "Say the words; chew the meat."

Appearance can be deceiving. If we mix cold water with warm water, what we see may remain the same but a new temperature will result. Likewise, if we let South Koreans mingle with folks from the North, all of us would look homogeneous at first glance but the mentality of each group will be completely different. Besides, mixing one liquid with another liquid itself can be tricky. You never, for instance, add water to concentrated sulfuric acid unless you want to see a dangerous reaction from the sudden evolution of heat from the mixing. Since the acid is almost twice heavier than water, added water reacts with sulfuric acid on the surface.

Mixing two liquids inevitably entails dilution unless the two liquids are identical in composition. The dissolved substance in a solution is called solute while the liquid that dissolves the solute is solvent. The behavior or properties of the solute can dramatically vary depending on the extent of dilution, or the solute concentration.

As briefly introduced in Entry #175, "Oil droplets on water," a surface active substance consists of two parts: hydrophilic "head" and hydrophobic "tail." When first introduced into water, these molecules stay on the interface of air and water: its head is comfortably submerged in water while the tail stands up in the adjacent air trying to escape the "hostile" aqueous environment. As more surfactant molecules are introduced, they have to reside in the bulk phase of water as the interface of air and water is completely covered by the surfactant molecules.

Albeit reluctantly because of the hydrophobic tail, individual molecules have to be in the bulk of water. As more molecules come into the system, the bulk phase itself will become more congested. At some critical point in concentration, they spontaneously form molecular aggregates known as micelles. The critical micellar concentration of the solute is defined as the concentration at which micelles are formed, generally sphere in shape, where hydrophobic tails stack together inside while hydrophilic heads are in direct contact with the bulk aqueous phase. The physicochemical properties of the solution, such as viscosity, completely change.

When the number of people in a given cohort reaches a critical mass, their collective behaviors would and could be quite different from those of individuals. Just think about the herd mentality prevailing, say, in an underground resistance movement. The brainwashing of Patty Hearst by the Symbionese Liberation Army (SLA) offers an example.

Around 9 PM on February 4, 1974, there was a knock on the door of apartment #4 at 2603 Benvenue Street in Berkeley, California. A group of men and women busted in with their guns drawn. They grabbed a surprised 19-year-old Patty Hearst, beat up her fiancé, threw her in the trunk of their car, and drove off. Thus began one of the strangest cases in FBI history. The SLA wanted to destroy what they called the "capitalist state."

Patty Hearst was from a wealthy, powerful family; her grandfather was the newspaper magnate William Randolph Hearst. The kidnapping stunned the country and made front-page national news. The kidnappers began brainwashing their captive, hoping to turn this young heiress from the highest reaches of society into a poster child for their coming revolution. Just two months later, the SLA released a tape with Hearst saying that she had joined their fight to free the oppressed and had even taken a new name. A few weeks later, she was spotted on bank surveillance cameras wielding an assault weapon during an SLA bank robbery, barking orders to bystanders and providing cover to her confederates.

Patty Hearst was captured in San Francisco on September 18, 1975, and was charged with bank robbery. One could say that her joining SLA was hardly water mixed in water. (08/11/2022)

464. Bad ending with a bad start.
시작이 나쁘면 끝도 나쁘다.

If a person starts a project in the wrong way, the final outcome would be more likely bad. Even with what appears to be a perfect start, one can end up with a disappointing result. Conversely, if one is lucky, good fortune comes along regardless of the beginning. Thus, the above proverb involves both probability and fate. In terms of odds, this proverb is not as certain as "A bent stick with a bent shadow (Entry #276)."

"Prepare for the worst, hope for the best" is a popular phrase to ease our pain when adversity occurs in spite of our best efforts in preparation. By saying "for the worst," this idiom tries to lower our expectations even with our best efforts. An implication is that there is nothing we will regret when we know for sure that we have honestly invested our best effort in the beginning. The agony of failure happens only when we know we did not put our best efforts into the preparation.

Shortly after midnight on March 13, 2000, Louisville, Kentucky police officers executing a search warrant used a battering ram to enter the apartment of Breonna Taylor, a 26-year-old emergency room technician. She was shot and killed by police officers.

The police had been investigating two men who they believed were selling drugs out of a house that was far from Ms. Taylor's home. But a judge had also signed a warrant allowing the police to search Taylor's residence because the police said they believed that one of the men had used her apartment to receive packages. Taylor had been dating that man on and off for several years but had recently severed ties with him, according to her family's lawyer.

Taylor and her boyfriend had been in bed but got up when they heard a loud banging at the door. He later told the police he feared it was Taylor's ex-boyfriend trying to break in. After the police broke the door off its hinges, he fired his gun once, striking a policeman in the thigh. The police responded by firing several shots, striking Taylor five times. One policeman shot 10 rounds blindly into the apartment. The raid was compromised by poor planning and reckless execution. It was a good illustration of a "bad ending with a bad start."

The other night I watched on Netflix a documentary film, *D.B. Cooper*, a fascinating story of a perfect crime. On Thanksgiving eve, November 24, 1971, Cooper boarded a Boeing 727 aircraft that was to fly from Portland, Oregon, to Seattle, Washington, a mere 30-minute trip. He was carrying a briefcase and a brown paper bag and sat in the last row. Shortly after takeoff, Cooper handed a note to a flight attendant situated directly behind him in a jump seat and whispered, "Miss, you'd better look at that note. I have a bomb," briefly showing her dynamites in the briefcase.

Cooper demanded refueling, $200,000 (equivalent to $1.3 million in 2021), and four parachutes at the Seattle Airport. He also mentioned that the 35 passengers would be released once his demands were met. The president of Northwest Orient authorized payment of the ransom and ordered all employees to cooperate fully with the hijacker's demands, while the plane maintained a holding pattern for approximately two hours. In Seattle, the flight attendant brought him a large bag of money in full view of the passengers. With the money in hand, Cooper finally agreed to release the passengers.

At approximately 7:40 pm, the Boeing 727 took off with only Cooper, one flight attendant, and three crew members. Now they are on their way to the Reno–Tahoe International Airport. Once in the air, the flight attendant told him she cannot lower the aft staircase for fear of being sucked out of the plane. In the end, Cooper told her he would lower the staircase and open the rear door all by himself. Now that he no longer needed her assistance, he allowed her to go to the cockpit but asked her to close the curtain partition behind her. Before she left Cooper, she begged him to "Please, please take the bomb with you."

At approximately 8:13 p.m., the aircraft's tail section experienced a sudden upward movement, indicating the rear exit door was opened. D.B. Cooper simply disappeared into the dark and chilly night from a plane traveling slowest possible speed at approximately 115 mph (185 km/hr) and at about 10,000-foot (3,000 m) altitude. A small portion of the ransom was found along the banks of the Columbia River in 1980, which triggered renewed interest but ultimately only deepened the mystery. The man purchased his airline ticket using the alias Dan Cooper but, because of misreading his signature, he became known as D.B. Cooper.

His thorough preparation for the "harmless" heist would be a case of a "good ending" from a "good start." (08/11/2022)

465. Treasure in livelihood is a quick eye.
살림에는 눈이 보배라.

By "quick eye," the above proverb implies a "quick study" who can observe the good things happening in other households and tries them at home. A young woman may ask her friend where she purchased the one-piece blouse as it looks so good on her friend. She may ask another friend about a particular piece of furniture, say, a coffee table, as she really likes the furniture. A man in the market for a new car may ask about his friend's car as he wants to buy the same model. A guy who is getting a divorce may ask his friend for a referral for a lawyer since his friend has already gone through one divorce.

Such an exchange of information and recommendation is so common nowadays that online e-commerce is invariably accompanied by third-party reviews of a given product or service, either rated by the number of stars or brief descriptions. It has thus become essential for us to have a "quick eye" or become good students with a thorough investigation prior to purchasing a good or receiving a service for a satisfactory result.

Although the original proverb deals with individuals in terms of their domesticity, it can also relate to communities, societies, and even nations. Imports or adoption of trends from foreign countries begins with imitation. If the imitation turns out to be satisfactory, everyone involved would prosper and be happy. Take democracy for example. After the Second World War, Japan quickly adopted the political and economic systems primarily from the US and has prospered nicely for several decades. They even imported baseball, which has become a national pastime.

The old Korea, till the dawn of the 19th century, was most anxious to please China and everything from China was also good for our ancestors. Many nations that adopted the Industrial Revolution quickly extended their imperialism to the Korean peninsula also. Just to name a few, there were Japan, Russia, the US, France, and by then very much weakened China.

Powers that be in modern Korean governments were fractured into many cohorts like pro-Japan, pro-Russia, pro-China, pro-America, etc. Internal fighting and conspiracies of one faction against another with the help of foreign powers continuously weakened the nation. In the end, the

Korean peninsula was under Japanese occupancy till 1945 when the Second World War ended. Everything Korean began to change forcefully to everything Japanese.

At the peak of their hysterical effort to annihilate anything Korean, they prohibited speaking the Korean tongue in public and Koreans had to adopt a Japanese name: mine was Dokudakke. Presented below is how Joseon Dynasty succumbed to Japan, which eventually led to such a dire situation as described above. Essentially, the nation failed to maintain a "quick eye" toward the rapidly changing outside world.

The 25th king of Joseon, Cheoljong, died in 1864 without a male heir. Thus Gojong ascended the throne rather hurriedly at the premature age of 12. His appointment was supported by the powerful Andong Kim Clan. Because of his young age, the nation was effectively run by Gojong's father, Daewongun. This old man was the main proponent of isolationism and was responsible for the persecution of native and foreign Catholics, which brought about expeditions from France and the US, in 1866 and 1871, respectively. This was the beginning of foreign interests in Joseon.

The traditional influence of China effectively ended when they lost the First Sino-Japanese War (1894–1895). The resulting Treaty of Shimonoseki stipulated the abolition of subordinate relationships Korea had with China. In 1897, Joseon became the Korean Empire. The new nation tried to become a strong and independent nation by implementing domestic reforms, strengthening military forces, developing commerce and industry, and surveying land ownership.

Russian influence was also severely curtailed after they lost the Russo-Japanese War (1904–1905). Korean Empire had now effectively become a protectorate of Japan. Since then many intellectuals and scholars set up various organizations and associations, embarking on movements for independence. In spite of these patriotic efforts from the grassroots, in 1907, Gojong was forced to abdicate after Japan learned that he sent secret envoys to the Second Hague Conventions to protest against the protectorate treaty. In 1909, the independence activist An Jung-geun assassinated Ito Hirobumi, former Resident-General of Korea, at the Harbin Railway Station, China. This prompted the Japanese to ban all political organizations and proceed with plans for annexation.

In summary, Joseon did not have a "quick eye" when it was most needed. (08/13/2022)

466. Trying to comb the hair of a turtle.
거북이 등의 털을 긁는다.

The turtle is covered with a hard and shiny shell that provides the animal with protection from predators. There are absolutely no hairs on its back or belly. Then, why is the above proverb mumbling about combing its hair? That it is utter nonsense is the whole point. The old saying thus says, "Don't be a fool trying to find something in the wrong place." No matter how much effort we may invest, people would ridicule us as an idiot as they know for sure we will fail to find whatever we are looking for so long as we are at it in the wrong place.

Kirkus Review is a professional service provider offering an independent review of a book written by indie authors like me. The reviewer wrote the following critique for my most recent book, Volume IV, *The Dragon is easier to Draw Than a Snake.*

> *The author endeavors to make them* (Korean proverbs) *comprehensible to a Western audience. To this end, he often draws on American culture to explain them. The book is brimming with references to the likes of Malcolm X, Anna Nicole Smith, and Al Capone as well as the Super Bowl and Covid-19. But while the accounts provided by Moo-Jung are often remarkably sensitive, many readers will tire of the repeated references to the turpitude of Donald Trump and the corruption of the Republican Party. Rather than achieve a modern contextualization of the proverbs, such political partisanship makes them feel historically bound and sacrifices an element of their timelessness.*

I had known all along that someone would complain about my excessive (ab)use of Trump and related stories. To be honest, I was just lazy and Trump and his Republican followers were low-hanging fruits easy to pick for numerous ridicules. Subsequent to the Kirkus Review, I have been trying hard to stay away from Trump et al. in writing this Volume V. Indeed I have not talked about Trump much well into the two-thirds of this book. It is rather remarkable if I may say so. Then, the following breaking news erased all my determination. My lament.

In May 2021, the National Archives and Records Administration (NARA) contacted Trump's team in the hope to locate important documents that were missing when Trump left the White House in January. Several months later, in January this year, NARA received 15 boxes of Trump White House records from his Mar-a-Lago residence in Palm Beach, FL. In February, NARA asked the Department of Justice (DOJ) to investigate if Trump violated the Presidential Records Act. In May, the DOJ investigators subpoenaed NARA for access to the classified documents retrieved from Mar-a-Lago. It was the first public indication of the DOJ using a grand jury in its investigation.

In June, four investigators, including a top DOJ counterintelligence official, visited Mar-a-Lago and met with Trump's attorneys, requesting for further security of the basement room where documents were being stored. They also demanded surveillance video from Mar-a-Lago. On August 8, Monday, in a major escalation of the investigation, FBI agents removed 11 sets of classified documents including some marked as top secret. The public learned of the "raid" by way of a written statement from Trump.

Immediately, Republicans cried foul about the search warrant. Their protests ranged from "Biden himself must be investigated," "Attorney General Merrick must either resign or be impeached, "Defund the corrupt FBI," "Biden and his appointees targeted their political opponents," "Choke down the FBI," etc. House Republican Leader Kevin McCarthy said that Garland should preserve his documents and clear his calendar, implying that there would be an oversight probe when Republicans take back the chamber in the midterm elections. He maintained that the DOJ has reached an intolerable state of weaponized politicization.

Then, on August 11, Merrick Garland announced that DOJ would ask a judge to unseal the search warrant documents, for the sake of transparency, sending the ball to Trump's court. Upon Trump's agreement, the whole nation became aware that the seized boxes contained top-secret files. With this new turn of the event, hawkish Republicans were notably more restrained and the contrast grew starker between Republicans advancing a knee-jerk defense of the former president and those who are simply calling for additional disclosures from the DOJ.

These still unfolding stories are one of the most absurd stories that I have encountered in my long life. It is as bizarre as the hairs on the shell of the turtle. And the reaction shown by Trump supporters is akin to attempting to comb the turtle's hair. (08/15/2022)

467. No Hercules under lashes.
매 위에 장사 없다.

Torturing for maximal pain always wins anyone perhaps including Hercules, a Roman mythological figure famous for his strength. As such, torture is still considered the best way to extract valuable information from a captured enemy or a spy, especially during a war. This is in spite that it is prohibited under international law for all states under any circumstances. Besides interrogation, torture is also used for punishment, terrorizing for deterrence, and confession from, say, a political prisoner.

The popularity of torture throughout human history clearly establishes its success rate, which in turn implies that most of us would succumb to the pain, eventually confessing what the torturer wants to hear. This is the essence of the above proverb.

We feel physical pain as the sensory nerve is stimulated beyond a certain threshold, which varies from person to person. I know I have a very low pain threshold, say, compared to the old-day Vikings. In turn, my wife still has a lower threshold than me, especially towards a thermal stimulus. In essence, pain motivates an individual to withdraw from damaging situations and avoid similar experiences in the future. For example, my wife gets up to jack up the thermostat to 80° in the middle of sleep from 72° and it stays as such. What a torture!

When we suffer from excruciating pain, we often wish we were with a very high pain threshold like Hercules or no pain at all. As they say, be careful with what you wish. The following story by David Cox is from the April 27, 2017 issue of *BBC Future*.

At the Institute of Human Genetics in Aachen, Germany, Dr. Ingo Kurth is preparing for a rather unusual appointment. She's collecting blood samples from Stefan Betz, a 21-year-old university student who suffers from a genetic disorder so rare that only a few hundred people worldwide are estimated to have it.

Betz has congenital insensitivity to pain (CIP). It means he can place his hand in boiling water or undergo an operation without an anesthetic, and yet feel no discomfort whatsoever. In every other way, his sensory perceptions are normal. He sweats when a room is too hot and shudders at the biting chill of cold wind. But like almost all who suffer from CIP, Betz finds his condition a curse rather than a blessing.

"People assume that feeling no pain is this incredible thing and it almost makes you superhuman," Betz says. "For people with CIP, it's the exact opposite. We would love to know what pain means and what it feels like to be in pain. Without it, your life is full of challenges."

From an evolutionary perspective, one of the reasons scientists believe CIP is so rare is because so few individuals with the disorder reach adulthood. "We fear pain, but in developmental terms from being a child to being a young adult, pain is incredibly important to the process of learning how to modulate your physical activity without doing damage to your body, and in determining how much risk you take," Kurth says.

Physical torture coupled with psychological coercion can often lead crime investigators in the wrong direction. The so-called *Central Park Five* can attest to the point. One spring evening in 1989, a 28-year-old white woman was jogging in Central Park, New York. She was found beaten and raped and was in a coma for 12 days. Five black and Hispanic boys, aged between 14 and 16, were interrogated for at least seven hours without their parents before they made videotaped confessions to detectives.

As the DNA evidence from semen found at the scene didn't match any of the five boys, prosecutors relied solely on the initial interrogations. But the Five took back those statements, saying that they had been coerced by police into giving false confessions. One defendant, in a 2016 interview with *the Guardian*, said: "The fear (from hearing beating next door) made me feel really like I was not going to be able to make it out."

In 2002, another inmate, who had been convicted of a string of rapes and a murder, confessed that he sexually assaulted the victim when he was 17 and that he had acted alone. He was able to tell police details about the attack that wasn't public knowledge and his DNA matched that from the crime scene. Eventually, the five men were cleared of all charges having almost served their full sentences. On their release, the Five filed a civil suit against New York City and received $41 million in the settlement. (08/16/2022)

468. The rolling pearl on the jade tray.
옥반에 진주 구르듯.

Imagine that you have just rolled several pearls on the tray made of jade. What would you expect to hear in this quiet room? Soft but well-defined clean sounds of pearls landing and bouncing on the jade will be followed by an almost imaginary and inaudible sound of actual rolling. In terms of clearness and cleanness, this sound would be the purest. Thus, the above expression is often used for representing a beautiful voice or an articulate speech from a person.

Here, the tray made of jade is referred to as *ock-ban*, in which *ock* (옥) and *ban* (반) means jade and tray, respectively. Because of its high value in the tradition of Korea and China, jade can simply represents precious or ornamental stones in general and symbolize beauty and grace. An *ock-ban* must have been a very expensive item and could well remain as a treasure of a family from one generation to another. Its solid and well-polished surface would be best for bouncing off pearls as depicted above.

A pearl is a hard, glistening, object found once in a while inside of a living shelled mollusk such as an oyster. Chemistry-wise, it is calcium carbonate, $CaCO_3$, which is deposited upon an invading irritant. They come in many shapes, with perfectly round ones being comparatively rare. Throughout human history, natural pearls have been highly valuable objects of beauty and are usually used in expensive pieces of jewelry. These two rare objects, one from the sea and the other from the mountain meet in the proverb and ask us to think about the sound of their encounter.

I used to play golf, in fact, quite a lot, before I realized I had zero talent in the game. One of the facts that prompted me to quit is that I just could not hit the ball cleanly. The sound of it would always leave me with a bad echo in my ears after hitting or trying to hit the ball. It was particularly discouraging when you watch and hear on TV how professional golfers hit the ball at tee-off. The sound from their striking the ball would be equivalent to pearls hitting the *ock-ban*.

Shot Heard 'Round the World was a game-winning home run hit by New York Giants outfielder Bobby Thomson off Brooklyn Dodgers pitcher Ralph

Branca at the Polo Grounds in New York City on October 3, 1951, to win the National League pennant. The sound from the homerun was heard on the radio by millions across America as well as thousands of American servicemen stationed in Korea.

In 1951, I was just a small boy right in the midst of the Korean War, not knowing what I did not know. However, during the 1988 World Series, I was glued to the TV, especially following closely the performance of Kirk Gibson, who had just left my team Detroit Tigers for the Dodgers. In Game 1 against the Oakland Athletics, Gibson hit a home run at the bottom of the ninth inning with the full ball count to win the game. The moment is often described as one of the most exciting moments in World Series history.

Having injured both legs during the National League Champion Series, Gibson was not expected to play at all. However, with the Dodgers trailing by a score of 4–3, a runner on first base, and two out in the ninth inning, manager Tommy Lasorda unexpectedly inserted his hobbled league MVP as a pinch hitter. Gibson, limping back and forth between a pulled left hamstring and a swollen right knee, made his way to the plate to face Oakland's future Hall of Fame closer Dennis Eckersley.

Gibson quickly got behind in the count 0–2, but laid off a pair of outside pitches that were called balls. He then somehow managed to have a ball account at 3-2. With an awkward swing, Gibson used pure upper-body strength to smack the 3–2 backdoor slider over the right-field fence. He hobbled around the bases and pumped his right fist as his jubilant teammates stormed the field. The Dodgers won the game, 5–4. I still remember the sound off the bat followed by a roaring crowd.

In its most common use, the proverb is about a beautiful and clear voice, for example, of a soprano. In my lifetime, we were exposed to such opera sopranos as Renée Fleming, Maria Callas, Joan Sutherland, Jessye Norman, and the like. But I would like to add another name to this list.

Jo Su-mi studied singing and piano at Seoul National University. In 1983, she made her professional recital debut in Korea but left Seoul for further studies in Rome. In 1988, Jo made her La Scala debut. Since then, she has performed at major opera houses all over the world such as Vienna State Opera and Metropolitan Opera. I've just listened on YouTube to her duet with Plácido Domingo, singing the Korean ballad, *Enchanted Mt. Geum-Gang*, or그리운금강산. Her voice here was the very epitome of the proverb. (08/19/2022)

469. Ordering diapers during the first trimester.
아이도 낳기 전에 기저귀 장만한다.

A young couple is expecting their first child. They are being bombarded with advice, suggestions, and recommendations from their acquaintances. All of these are in addition to Instructions from their obstetrician and know-all in-laws. Excited and yet they are approaching the once-in-their-life event with resolute rationale. As soon as they learn of the pregnancy, they start to make a list of baby gear to acquire. It includes not only essential staples such as diapers, bottles, and wipes but also an expensive baby carriage and even a device monitoring the baby's heart rate and oxygen levels.

The anxiety of first-time parents renders them easy prey for various online sales pitches of stuff that they may not need. Assuring words from their physician and their self-confidence erase any unthinkable possibility of miscarriage or stillbirth. The baby's room begins to fill wlth stuff several months before the expected date of birth. They are fully aware that babies were born and survived okay for thousands of years without any of those on their shopping list, but they can't help. It is the subject of the above proverb, as expressed with tongue in cheek.

Nothing wrong, in fact rather commendable, to be prepared for the arrival of the first child. But the proverb says that we should not overdo it in preparing for something that comes far in the future, as far as nine months in advance. The parents could wait till the third trimester before starting the acquisitions. In this context, the above proverb is similar to Entry #182, "Having kimchi juice before the rice cake served," or "김칫국부터 마신다."

All living organisms, ranging from weeds in the wilderness to humans, maintain the instinct of self-preservation. It is indeed the definition of life, and directly related to the reproduction of species. In human terms, every parent wants an uneventful birth and a healthy baby. Following birth, parents do their best to protect them and offer them the best tools such as education for survival in a competitive society. In the end, the parents depart the world knowing they have done their best in raising their children who can prosper perhaps better than themselves. This ceaseless effort is impossible without love. In a nutshell, it is the crux of humanity.

In spite of what the above proverb was telling with tongue in cheek, people believe that developing precautionary measures for an important future event cannot be too early. They are painstakingly careful in acquiring all possible items far in advance, like ordering diapers during the first trimester at the expense of mockeries from others. Without advanced preparedness, they say, we cannot achieve goals without last-minute compromises. Some take great care in preparedness mainly because they want to avoid agonizing regrets later in case of a disastrous outcome. Once they know they have done their best, there is nothing to regret.

Unlike first-time parents who are wholeheartedly agreeing on what to prepare for their future baby, the world seems to have a hard time with what to do with the current and future climate change. Note that this ominous future is as certain as the arrival of a baby. At the time of this writing, we have the biblical scale of rain and flood in the desert town of Las Vegas and unexpectedly in Seoul, drought and heat waves in China and Europe, the wildfire of California, and consequential famine and immigration all over the Southern Hemisphere.

For the past several decades, scientists have known and repeatedly warned the world of what we are facing. The Paris Agreement of 2015, which was adopted by nearly every nation, addresses climate change and its negative impacts. The agreement aims to substantially reduce global greenhouse gas emissions in an effort to limit the global temperature increase in this century to 2 degrees Celsius above pre-industrial levels. Then-president Barack Obama envisioned for today's children "A world that is safer and more secure, more prosperous, and freer."

However, less than two years later, President Donald Trump withdrew the US from the Agreement. It was part of his broader effort to dismantle decades of US environmental policy. Skeptics in the media and governments deride global warming as a monumental hoax, while those who believe in the evidence for human-induced climate change accuse the skeptics of being industry-funded hacks. Meanwhile, efforts to impose cuts on greenhouse gas emissions are failing to get off the ground. Fortunately, following President Biden's day-one executive order, the US re-joined the Agreement. Seven years had elapsed since the Paris Agreement.

The Inflation Reduction Act, which passed the US Congress earlier and was signed off by Biden last week, authorizes as much as $370 billion for improving energy security and climate change. (08/25/2022)

470. Ten big mouths couldn't form a single word.
입이 열이라도 할 말이 없다.

Early in the morning of June 28, 1950, just three days after the North Korean army started to invade the South, all three bridges over the Han River were let exploded intentionally to slow down the advancement of the invaders. The river circles the southern perimeter of Seoul and the move was then considered prudent. This incident was briefly introduced in Entry #348, "The more you bang the drum, the more noise you create."

However, it was later determined that the blasting was almost seven hours premature, resulting in little time for citizens and military personnel to escape Seoul. It resulted in a significant loss to not only six South Korean army divisions and several tens of policemen but also heavy military equipment. A crude estimate was that 44,000 South Korean soldiers were captured or killed by the North Army. More to the point was that as many as 1.5 million citizens, including our family, were not able to flee to the South and had to suffer a great deal of hardship under the North occupation for several months.

A hurriedly assembled investigation later found Colonel Choe Chang-sik ultimately responsible for the fiasco. Choe was arrested on August 28 and executed by a firing squad on September 21. Choe was born while the country was still under Japanese occupation. In 1942 he graduated Japanese Military Academy and was appointed as a second lieutenant in engineering, a position he also held when Korea became independent in 1948. Within a year he was quickly promoted to colonel, reflecting the unsettling time involving Korean independence. He was found guilty as a colonel in the court-martial.

In 1962, 12 years after the explosion of the bridges, his son requested a re-trial and was successful in clearing his father's name posthumously. In 2013, Choe's mortuary tablet was finally restored and placed in the National Memorial Garden. The truth thus prevailed albeit many years later, certainly better than never. In 2020, at the 70th anniversary of the explosion, there was a special monument dedicated to the event and his son was invited. He declined the invite saying that he doesn't want to even look at a newly built bridge anymore.

As expected, the unfortunate event has been a subject of continued debate. On one hand, Choe maintained that he had just followed an order from his superiors, Shin Sung-mo and Chae Byung-deok. These generals later became the Secretary of Defense and Field-Marshal, respectively. On the other hand, someone must be responsible for the loss of lives and military properties incurred from the explosion. Why were none of his bosses ever tried? Where does the inquiry stop in the rank and file? We saw a similar defense from many war criminals at the Nuremberg Trials including those executioners at the Auschwitz concentration camp.

There were many people involved in the explosion of the bridges over the Han River including Choe's superiors and all the way up to then-President Syngman Rhee. As I read about the event unfolding now, what bothers me most is where these people had been during the trial of Colonel Choe. Indeed those "ten big mouths did not say anything," as they were all anxious about keeping their own necks.

The American debacle at the end of and after the Afghanistan War, in terms of both military strategy and foreign policy, was similar to but worse than that of the Vietnam War. In the case of the latter, at least Vietnamese seem to currently enjoy freedom for seeking prosperity. What is happening to the social status of Afghanistan women nowadays, for instance? What about one-time collaborators we abandoned behind as if we have never met before? Where are those planners involved in the development of the country? Indeed, it seems that "ten big mouths could not say anything,"

On August 8, FBI agents retrieved many classified documents from Trump's residence, Mar-a-Lago. Immediately, Republicans and Trump supporters cried foul about the "raid." See more in Entry #466, "Trying to comb the hair of a turtle." Just yesterday, on August 26, the redacted affidavit underlying the search warrant was released to the public, although prosecutors made it clear that they feared the former president and his allies might take any opportunity to intimidate witnesses or illegally obstruct their investigation. Now that the whole episode has become more serious as people begin to speculate a possible indictment of the former president, dead silence has been prevailing among those earlier protesters. Their big mouths fail to form a single word.

The proverb reminds me of the lyrics of *Mrs. Robinson*, sung by Simon and Garfunkel, "Where have you gone, Joe DiMaggio?" (08/27/2022)

471. A vicious dog, ever with a scarred snout.
사나운 개 콧등 아물 날이 없다.

I do not know why it was the case, but we used to see dogfights all the time when we were kids in Korea. If they reflect the mindset of their owner, it makes sense as Korea at that time, after the Independence from Japan and during Korean War, was a difficult place to live in peace. As a child, I perceived that everyone was out there for their own interests and for their own well-being only. Our dogs probably inherited the same trait from us and were often on edge with an empty stomach. To support my speculation, I do not hear much about dogfighting in contemporary Korea.

A dog that is always busy with dogfights or hard playing with other dogs seldom carries an intact nose. The nose of such dogs gets another fresh scar before an old one heals. Thus, at a given time we see a scar on the snout or dried blood in the body. This is the direct translation of the above proverb. Controversies or scandals often follow a provocative and contentious person. Famous figures may be included here for no other reason than just being famous. They can be an entertainer, politician, athlete, lawyer, artists, or even academicians. In this sense, the above proverb would be similar to Entry #81, "Big trees face more wind."

Alan Morton Dershowitz, born in 1938, is a famous lawyer, jurist, and political commentator on the subject of Jews. From 1964 to 2013, he taught at Harvard Law School, where he was appointed, at the age of 28, as the youngest full professor of law in its history. He was involved in several high-profile legal cases. As a criminal appellate lawyer, he has won 13 of the 15 murder or attempted murder cases he has defended.

He has represented a series of celebrity clients, such as the boxer Mike Tyson, Patty Hearst who was kidnapped by but later converted to the Symbionese Liberation Army, and Jim Bakker, a convicted fraudster and the host of the television program *The PTL Club*. His most notable cases include his role in 1984 in overturning the conviction of Claus von Bülow for the attempted murder of his wife, Sunny, and as the appellate adviser for the defense in the O.J. Simpson trial in 1995. His hourly fee for legal services was estimated to be around $10,000 in 2017. That he has been successful and famous is quite an understatement.

More recently, Dershowitz was a member of Harvey Weinstein's defense team in 2018 and of President Donald Trump's defense team in his first impeachment trial in 2020. He was also a member of Jeffrey Epstein's defense team and helped to negotiate the original non-prosecution agreement in 2006. The film producer and convicted sex offender, Harvey Weinstein, was accused by over 80 women in the film industry of rape, sexual assault, and sexual abuse over a period of at least 30 years.

Jeffrey Epstein was a New York-based financier with high-profile ties to the world's ultra-wealthy and powerful. Accused of sexually abusing many underage girls, he was finally arrested and charged for soliciting a minor for prostitution in Florida in 2008 and became a registered sex offender. Of his 18-month prison sentence, he served 13 months. Dershowitz was involved in this case. However, in July 2019, Epstein was arrested again. This time on federal charges of sex-trafficking minors. While awaiting trial, he was found dead in his jail cell on August 10, 2019.

Dershowitz's involvement in such sleazy and notorious cases reminds me of flies being attracted to dung. It has been quite a ride for him considering free publicity and fame. One successful case will lead to another and soon he has become what he is now with high name value and fortune. Along the way, has he been successful in staying away from some shady characters he was defending?

In discussing cancel culture, Dershowitz claimed that after he defended Trump, he has been shunned on Martha's Vineyard, his longtime summer getaway. Apparently, someone was beaten up on the beach just for reading one of his books.

In May 2021, one of Epstein's underage victims, Virginia Giuffre, accused Dershowitz of rape in a sworn affidavit and in the Netflix documentary on Jeffrey Epstein, *Filthy Rich*. According to Giuffre, she had sex with Dershowitz at Jeffrey Epstein and Ghislaine Maxwell's direction when she was just 16. Yes, she is the same girl who posed for a picture with British Prince Andrew. Most recently, just a few weeks ago, Dershowitz snapped during an interview with *The Hill* when confronted about a massage gift he received at Jeffrey Epstein's house. He immediately fired back saying that his wife scheduled the massage.

Why has there been so much noise lately regarding one of the most famous and successful lawyers in this country? I do not understand why he chose to socialize with Epstein, his client. (09/02/2022)

472. A soliloquy learned by ears.
얻어 들은 풍월.

Every Sunday, Fr. Bill, the chief priest in our Catholic church in Las Vegas, would read the gospel purely out of memory prior to delivering his homily. When I saw him doing it for the first time about five years ago, I was duly impressed. This old man, only a few years younger than me, seems to have an excellent ability to memorize those scriptures.

The only part I remember from Lincoln's Gettysburg Address, which we learned by heart during our senior year in high school, is the often-quoted last sentence, "…. and that government of the people, by the people, for the people, shall not perish from the earth." Likewise, I remember only "I have a dream" in the eponymous speech by Martin Luther King, Jr. It was from the context of freedom and equality arising from a land of slavery and hatred, but I cannot quote adjacent sentences.

What a shame. When I think about citing such catchphrases as often as I have been in casual conversations, there is a certain level of superficiality involved in the cliche. It is like pretending that I know the plot of an opera in and out simply I recognize an aria from it. Here is another one: "To be or not to be, that is the question" from *The Tragedy of Hamlet, Prince of Denmark* by none other than William Shakespeare. Do I know when and fully understand why Hamlet uttered these words? No. Out of self-pity, this time I try to better understand the context from which these words came out of Hamlet's mouth.

In Act 3 Scene 1, Prince Hamlet converses with Ophelia, a daughter of Polonius, the chief counselor to King Claudius. If you recall, Claudius is Hamlet's uncle who killed his own brother to become king himself. Besides, he marries Hamlet's mother. Hamlet attempts to kill his uncle, while there seems to be a mutual attraction between Ophelia and Hamlet. To gauge Hamlet's erratic behaviors towards Ophelia as well as the king, Polonius asks his daughter to return Hamlet's love letter. The king and Polonius, in hiding, want to observe how Hamlet behaves when Ophelia tries to return the letter. Thus Hamlet's long soliloquy begins. It is known as the "nunnery scene" and deals with death and suicide, bemoaning the pain and unfairness of life and the equally terrible alternative.

To be, or not to be; that is the question:
Whether 'tis nobler in the mind to suffer
The slings and arrows of outrageous fortunes,
Or to take arms against a sea of troubles,
And, by opposing, end them. To die, to sleep –
No more, and by a sleep to say we end
The heartache and the thousand natural shocks
That flesh is heir to – 'tis a consummation
Devoutly to be wished. To die, to sleep.

...

Thus conscience does make cowards of us all,
And thus the native hue of resolution
Is sickled o'er with the pale cast of thought,
And enterprises of great pith and moment
With this regard their currents turn awry,
And lose the name of action. Soft you, now,
The fair Ophelia! – Nymph, in thy orisons
Be all my sins remembered.

Now, I feel somewhat satisfied as I understand better than ever the context of the soliloquy. And yet, I still feel inadequate to talk about the masterpiece in casual conversations. Then, I also realize that I cannot become a scholar of William Shakespeare during the remaining days of my life. The point is that there are a lot of people, including myself, who learn long poetry, or any subject for that matter, quite superficially by hearing someone reciting them rather than studying in depth.

An interesting word in the above proverb is *poong-wol* 풍월or (風月). The original Chinese characters mean wind and moon for 풍 and월, respectively. Together, the word is translated into delightful poetry or song. I use it to mean a soliloquy. The word *poong-wol* is often used in a derogatory nuance as one may refer to a homily as a lullaby. Another Korean proverb says tongue-in-cheek, "A dog belonging to a *seo-dang* can recite a long soliloquy." See also Entry #87, "Too much scrutiny leads to a blind son-in-law." Here, *seo-dang* is a children's school in old Korea where kids start to learn Chinese characters. An old dog that hangs around the schoolyard hears children's loud reading of a poem so many times that the dog can memorize and recite it. The dog may be able to, but we may ask how much the dog understands the poem. (09/04/2022)

473. A son-in-law is a guest of one hundred years.
사위는 백년 손이라.

As a parent of a married daughter, you ought to treat your son-in-law with utmost care and respect, even feigning affection. Since we do not have any children, I cannot say anything for sure based on experience but I can empathize with the parents since any bad relations with him would directly affect the well-being of your own daughter. The same could be said also with her siblings. A brother's affection for his kid sister, i.e., his nephews and nieces, could be more protective and fearsome than their parents.

The patriarch Vito Corleone (played by Marlon Brando) in the 1972 film, *The Godfather*, has only one daughter Connie (Talia Shire), who marries good-for-nothing Carlo but is abused by him. Vito's oldest son, hot-tempered Sonny (James Caan), physically attacks and publicly humiliates Carlo. When Carlo abuses her again, Sonny speeds to their home but is ambushed and murdered by enemy gangsters at a highway toll booth.

Later, after the last son of Vito, Michael (Al Pacino), takes over the organization, he gets Carlo's confession of playing a part in Sonny's murder. Michael verbally assures Carlo of his safety but has his man garrote Carlo to death. When confronted by Connie as well as his wife Kay (Diane Keaton), Michael flatly denies any involvement in the death of his brother-in-law. It is the beginning of the deteriorating relationship between Kay and Michael, one of the major developments in the story.

When a couple is dating, the father of the girl may not completely approve of the young man his daughter is seeing and expresses opposition to their plan for matrimony. Being more sympathetic, her mother may try to maintain a neutral stand and eventually persuades her husband to agree with their daughter's wedding. After their marriage, the relationship between the father and his son-in-law may stay as it has been, resulting in an awkward and often tense one. This is quite an unfortunate situation for all parties involved but seems quite common. Nonetheless, the father does not have any other choices but has to pretend to be all is well. The subtle but steady pressure from his own wife is not trivial either and the husband has to offer an apparent surrender.

On the other hand, the seemingly cold relationship between the father and the son-in-law could completely turn around in a more amicable and favorable direction. Maybe they finally clear up any misunderstandings they might have had and shake hands man-to-man once and for all. Heck, the father may even ask the son-in-law to join his firm and eventually makes him a partner in the business. This is the scenario with a happy ending.

So, the above proverb is saying that whether you like it or not your son-in-law is and must be treated as a guest of honor and should remain as such for 100 years, *bag-nyun-son* (백년 손). Here, *bag-nyun* means 100 years and *son* means *son-nim* (손님) or a guest. One hundred years mean practically "forever" or "until you die."

If one asks me to name one other matter that we ought to treat as *bag-nyun-son* throughout our lives, I'd say in a heartbeat that it is fact, truth, and honesty. Before retirement, I had been an experimental scientist, spending almost 40 years in a lab. The raw data we obtained never tells a lie. Even with a failed experiment, one has to accept it and keep on moving forward. There is always a certain level of temptation to "cook" the data as the positive results can bring a research grant as well as publicity. This may well mean the expansion of his or her laboratory.

One day in the late 1990s, I was reviewing a grant proposal submitted to the National Institutes of Health (NIH). A set of data that the Principal Investigator (PI) had submitted as the Preliminary Studies section of the application lacked experimental details and was full of dubious claims. I could not prove with absolute certainty that those data were fabricated but, deep in my mind, they were. Reviewers were encouraged to contact the NIH administrator in such a situation, but I did not. I just gave a poor score for the application. The PI's name was, without any doubt, a Korean name. As a footnote, later the NIH no longer accepted unpublished experimental data. The change implied that the NIH would no longer honor the integrity of the applicant, a sad day for the world of science. See more in Entry # 100, "A long tail gets stamped," or "꼬리가 길면 밟힌다."

Cheating has become a mainstay in almost all aspects of modern living. My wife purchased an electronic eye massager via Amazon. She liked it so much that she ordered three more the next day. Then, just yesterday, she ordered one more yet for another friend. The price was changed from $53 to $65 and eventually $75. (09/06/2022)

474. A blind man gets upset when reminded of his handicap.
눈먼 소경더러 눈멀었다 하면 성낸다.

This man has poor eyesight and he is fully aware of his disadvantage. There is no reason to remind him of the fact that everyone knows about. It would be like rubbing salt into the wound, which makes the unpleasant situation even worse as it may appear to highlight one's failure or faults. Some wicked people, most likely a sadist, may do such things just to be cruel to others. The above proverb actually deals with a blind man, making the case even more inhumane to the point that the blind man gets upset and angry at you. Later in his room, he may shed some tears alone.

Similarly, we don't say someone is fat simply because they are a bit obese, neither in front of them nor behind their back. You may suggest they wear roomy clothes in a generous fashion. That would be the extent of diplomatic advice you can offer to your friend. Generally speaking, we should not talk about any deficient physical attributes of a person, like body weight, boldness, height, skin color, or any handicaps. It is just a matter of etiquette from compassion toward other human beings.

On the other hand, one should not take advantage of the goodwill of the general public and assume a certain level of entitlement. Yesterday, I read the following story in a web-based news outlet. This man was flying in from Greece to possibly the East Coast of the States. Since it was a long flight, he purchased a preferred seat. I do not know how much he paid, but Korean Airlines sells such a premium seat from Las Vegas to Incheon Airport in economy class at a price of $70. Sitting beside the man were a gentleman and two kids. Their mother was not able to obtain a seat next to her family for some reason, probably she chose the seat rather late.

She asked the man if they could exchange their seats so that she could travel together with the rest of her family. The man said no and the lady was upset, muttering "asshole" before storming back to her seat at the rear of the plane. Apparently, he also mentioned that her family problem is not his concern. Later this man posted the episode on one of those social media sites and many responded by condemning the lady.

Both my wife and I agreed with the general sentiment that she should not have asked a total stranger for such a favor. Some also pointed out that the whole family would not have had any problem sitting together at the back of the plane where she was sitting, had they looked for people who wanted to come to the front of the plane. Or she could have offered to pay the man for what he had paid for his preferred seat. We both felt that her blatant request was a bit out of the line of civility. If I had been him on the plane, would I have accommodated her wish? Most likely not, although I might have felt some level of guilt for lack of kindness on my part as well as resentment for her aggressiveness. Either way, the occasion must have been inconvenient and irritating.

Affirmative Action in the US is, among many goals, to eliminate discrimination based on racial minorities and women in education and employment. In some instances, it grants special consideration in, for example, admission to college. Although many states such as California and Michigan have made it illegal, most states mandate the policy. It has certainly forced the issue of diversity on the college campus to become the front and center topic in many public debates.

In 1996, California banned Affirmative Action. The following year, the number of Black students enrolling at UC at Berkeley dropped by nearly 50%. Does this sudden drop in enrollment of Black students imply a salient feature of entitlement associated with Affirmative Action? Would such a sentiment be the main reason why in 2020 Californians decisively rejected a ballot initiative to reinstitute race-based affirmative action?

I have always sympathized with minority students who are well-qualified for admission to any college on their own merit, for they may get misunderstood that their admission was solely due to their racial status. If I were one of them, I would resent the situation quite strongly. As for me, this may well be the main reason to stop Affirmative Action. See Entry #91, "Being equal, go for a pink skirt."

Harvard University is being sued by an Asian-American student organization for discriminating in admissions. The plaintiff pointed out, "An Asian American in the fourth-lowest decile has virtually no chance of being admitted to Harvard (0.9%), but an African American in that decile has a higher chance of admission (12.8%) than an Asian American in the top decile (12.7%)." Is this not discrimination? The US Supreme Court will hear the case this October. In a strange and convoluted way, Affirmative Action appears to create its own discrimination, effectively highlighting one's weakness or fault, just as the proverb asks us not to. (09/98/2022)

475. Full and short months follow each other.
한 달이 크면 한 달이 작다.

We are currently using the so-called Gregorian Calendar which is based on the Earth's revolution around the Sun. Each month is either 31 or 30 days while February lasts only 28 days. In a leap year, which comes around every four years, we have 29 days. These are the years that can be divided by four but not all century years are leap years. Here, only those that can be divided by 400 are the leap years. Thus, the year 1900 or 2100 is not a leap year, although it can be divided by four. One year as defined by these seemingly arbitrary rules, is 365.2425 days long, approximating the exact 365.2422 days for one revolution of the Earth around the Sun.

The upshot of the above explanation is that the top of and the valley between the knuckles of a hand mean 31 and 30 days, respectively. This is indeed in accordance with the above proverb while serving as a metaphor for the ebb and flow of a nation or a person. An almighty nation such as the Roman Empire is also subject to a perilous period of downfall. Likewise, the hegemony that the US is enjoying now on the global stage may well be numbered also.

Conversely, a nation that has been struggling for a while with a poor economy, social and political unrest, and uneven wealth distribution must have some upswing period for better prosperity. Take Korea as an example. People have been "whispering" in recent years that Korean GDP (Gross Domestic Product) would soon surpass that of Japan, a historic competitor of Koreans. With all the hardships from the Korean War and political instability, we seem to be posing a leap to prospering years ahead.

As pointed out in Entry #2, "Sunny spots and shadow change places," the above proverb can also symbolize the fluctuation of one's well-being from an egalitarian viewpoint. Presented below is such a case.

Baek Seong-hak (백성학) was born in 1940 to parents who had fled Japanese oppression for Manchukuo, China. After liberation from Japanese occupation, the family moved back to their hometown in the South Province of Hamgyung-do, in what is now North Korea. When the Korean War broke out, he had to flee yet again, this time from communists to South Korea.

During this period of chaos, he somehow lost his parents and became an orphan. In 1952, he was brought to a US military base by an American soldier, David Beatty. While working as an errand boy at the camp, Beatty taught him basic colloquial English. He also managed to get burned all over the body from an oil fire, barely surviving.

After the Korean War Armistice, he worked at a hat factory learning the trade. In 1959, at the age of 19, he founded Yeong-an Hat in a depleted central part of Seoul, Cheong-gye Stream nowadays. His business began with just 70 felt hats at a strip stall. At that time, the Cheong-gye Stream was known as Cheong-gye Cheon, a fowl-smelling, slow-moving, stagnant body of water, serving almost as the sewer system of the populated city of Seoul. Just one year later, the business took a quantum leap and settled into a permanent factory on a more bustling part of Seoul Jong-ro Street. It had now four sewing machines, one molding machine, a clerk, and other basics.

They produced Panama hats for the first time in Korea and exported them to Japan and the US in the 1960s. Soon his factories were established all over the world from Costa Rica to Sri Lanka. In 1990, he also branched out to the US with a sales department. It is said that Michael Jordan wore a Yeong-an hat after one of the NBA championship games. In 2001, the company was elected as the manufacturer of a World-Class Product, a prestigious designation bestowed by the Korean government, and achieved the top share in the global hat market. Currently, Yeong-an is a company with more than 9,000 employees and 2 trillion won (U$ 1.5 Billion) in sales.

Baek expanded his business acumen to other successful ventures such as manufacturing buses and forklifts. His charity in social work includes developing so-called Baek-hak Villages for underprivileged seniors and orphans not only in Korea but also in Kenya, Ghana, Laos, Cambodia, Bangladesh, Nepal, etc. Most recently Baek spearheaded an aid campaign for the Ukrainian War. He said, "The war in Ukraine is our business. This is what we went through 72 years ago."

There are two footnotes to Baek's life story. In 1989, Baek was able to reunite with Beatty in Philadelphia after so many years of disconnect. Their friendship lasted until Beatty passed away in 2011. In 1960, I met Baek when he was struggling to establish his hat business in Cheong-gye Cheon through a mutual friend, Park Jong-hyuk. I am sure he would not remember our encounter but I do. I would not have remembered him either, had he not become so famous with his life of ebb and flow. (12/24/2022)

476. Even a dog doesn't get sick in early summer.
오뉴월 감기는 개도 안 앓는다.

A direct translation of the above proverb would read, "The flu of May and June cannot afflict even a dog." As written, it may sound like a dog is prone to sickness all the time, which is obviously not the case. It just happens that, unlike nowadays, dogs would collectively represent a lowly animal that everyone looks down upon in old Korea: see Essay #279, for instance, "Even a dog recognizes its owner." I do not know why dogs deserve such a low social status in old Korea, but it may well be to do with the lack of room in our ancestors' minds for a "luxurious" hobby like raising a pet dog.

The proverb implies that we are healthiest during the early months of summer. Here, "we" means every living thing on the earth ranging from weeds to humans. We can establish the idiom by default. The winter months affect us with various respiratory diseases such as COVID-19. Living in a confined, often congested, environment due to cold temperatures outside must be the culprit for facilitated infections. The hot summer tends to bring about various intestinal ailments like diarrhea. This is undoubtedly due to the rampant proliferation of pathogens aided by warm temperatures and humid air. Months of spring and fall are okay but can be chilly depending on the physical condition of our bodies at a given time. Also, note that the daily temperature fluctuates wildly during the spring and fall.

May and June are the months when everything comes out in full vigor: tree leaves are shiny green, flowers are at their pinnacle, birds start to have new families with healthy babies, and we seem to enjoy life with renewed purpose. It is thus understandable for the above proverb to declare that everyone should be healthy during the months of May and June. Or is it?

I cannot pinpoint exactly when my allergy began, but I do remember I started immunotherapy, commonly referred to as allergy injection, while I lived in Michigan. That would be early in the 1970s. This experimental approach aims to develop tolerance in my body to the source of an allergy reaction, or allergen(s). This sounds like a fundamental solution compared with taking, for instance, antihistamines just to alleviate terrible symptoms like sneezing and itching eyes. The first and most challenging task would be to identify the allergen. In the standard scratch test, 64 potential allergens are introduced intradermally in an 8-by-8 matrix onto the back. A few days later, the physician determines which of the 64 results in significant swelling in the skin. This is a typical delayed hypersensitivity test. Both in Michigan and later in North Carolina, my allergy was from multiple sources including various weeds, plant flour, and house dust mites.

A cocktail, or so-called serum, is prepared by mixing those allergens that caused swelling. Each week and later intermittently I receive intramuscularly this prep in incremental doses, starting at 0.05 ml to almost 1.0 ml. I cannot tell if this modality works or not as I do not have any baseline data as a negative control. I just wanted unconsciously to believe it has been working, or better than not having the injections.

Then, soon after a winter vacation in Mexico, my skin developed rashes along the beltline of my swimming pants. They were red and itchy. My physician said it is most likely caused by the wet swimming suit I was wearing in the ocean and gave me an ointment containing an anti-inflammatory steroid. They also found me allergic to metal nickel, which was part of the alloy used in my glasses frame. I taped with Scotch tape the metallic part of the temple that is rubbing the side of my face. That solved the problem and later I bought a new pair of glasses that have a plastic temple.

In yet another extension of my allergy problems, my skin has lately become itchy with no obvious reason or cause. The last immunologist I saw before I left the States for Korea diagnosed the problem as hives and suggested taking Allegra and Benadryl every day. I do not take the latter and take 90 mg of Allegra (fexofenadine) twice a day. If I forget the medicine, my whole body becomes itchy, which implies that I have slowly but surely become a slave of modern medicine.

As far as my memory serves, I did not have any allergy problems till I left Korea for North America. That was 1967. Since I gave up the hope of finding the culprit or the allergen, I retort to having some broad hypothesis like the source of the problem is environmental and the problem will thus disappear if I leave the States where I had lived and developed allergies. On December 15, we arrived in this Silvertown in a village far from bustling Seoul, where I grew up till my late 20s. Here, we enjoy high-quality air and water. My hope is high that I may not have any allergy problems any longer. The past two weeks have been disappointing though, still taking Allegra.

This rather lengthy story defies the major thrust of the above proverb. My old body is perhaps beyond its realm. (12/26/2022)

477. Breaking a gourd dipper that is begging for a penny.
동냥도 아니 주고 쪽박만 깬다.

The coins of the Joseon Dynasty (1392 – 1897) used gold, silver, and brass for each of the three different face values. *Nyang* (냥) is of high value but *dong-nyang* (동냥) made of brass is not: See more in Essay #121, "No investment is worthier than children's education." Let's just call *dong-nyang* penny.

A beggar is asking a nobleman for a *dong-nyang*, or a penny. The beggar puts forward a small vessel made of gourd for collecting the expected penny. See, for more on gourd dipper, Essay #74, "Leaky dipper at home leaks also in the field." Traditionally, a gourd dipper was carried by a poor man like this beggar for such a purpose as collecting pennies. It is not unlike a street performer placing a hat in front of an audience of passersby.

Instead of throwing a few coins onto the gourd dipper of the beggar, this rich man steps on the dipper to destroy it! What kind of a man does such a cruel act to a poor man who is begging for pennies for his sustenance? He is as bad as, if not worse than, Scrooge from *A Christmas Carol*. This is as bad as the incident that happened in Toronto on December 18, where a gang of eight teenage girls killed a 59-year-old harmless and defenseless homeless man apparently just for fun. It was the consequence of what police call "swarming," in which total strangers gather via social media at a public place to do some random act like unplanned murder or attack of other strangers.

The other night, Christmas Eve to be exact, over a hundred migrants arrived at Vice President Kamala Harris' residence on three separate buses all the way from Texas after a 36-hour journey. It was one of the coldest Christmas Eves on record in the Washington area and the migrants were clad in a T-shirt or wrapped in a light blanket. They were sent there by the Texas Division of Emergency Management, which follows the directive of Governor Greg Abbott's office.

"They have been doing that for a few months now; it's all for the spectacle," a representative from the Migrant Solidarity Mutual Aid, a volunteer NGO, said of the governor's office. "The cruelty is the point. It's awful to use people in this manner, for political reasons." Somehow, the above proverb reminds me of this recent incident.

Republican governors along the southern border have been doing such deliveries to Democratic-led cities and towns in protest of the open immigration policies of the Biden Administration. Admittedly those southern states have been burdened with record levels of immigration, but it infuriated the White House: "Governor Abbott abandoned children on the side of the road in below-freezing temperatures on Christmas Eve without coordinating with any federal or local authorities. This was a cruel, dangerous, and shameful stunt."

We, law-abiding taxpayers, are helplessly at a loss just watching aghast the "games" these politicians are playing with migrants as a pawn. By taxpayer, I meant we effectively hire them to run the government for the best interest of the nation as well as humanity. What the politicians are doing is as bad as the nobleman crushing the gourd dipper of the beggar. This is like the Jewish moneylender trying to cut out a pound of debtor's flesh in *The Merchant of Venice.*

Not helping the beggar is one thing, but destroying the gourd dipper, which could have been his major possession, is totally unwarranted. The girls of Toronto could have just left the homeless man alone, but why did they have to kill him? There have been some such nasty people in human history as another Korean proverb attests to: "Pouring ash over the steamed rice that you don't want to eat," or "다 된 밥에 재뿌리기." There must have been many hungry people who could have benefited from the cooked rice.

The extent to which such malice is shamelessly displayed is beyond my comprehension, especially among public servants, like Abbott. To them, their own success is not satisfactory enough, but the failure of others must be guaranteed. It's like one political party praying for a bad turn of the economy so that they can win the next election. I wouldn't be surprised if Republicans cannot stop smiling, at least in private, if and when the gas price under Democratic administration begins to skyrocket.

But most of all, I cannot understand the people who keep on electing such mean-spirited politicians who seem to have a heart made of stone. A fortnight ago I left the States where I had lived for the past 55 years for Korea where I was born almost 80 years ago. While I am most grateful for the professionally fulfilling life of the past, I cannot deny the feeling of relief from leaving the country that seems to be moving in the wrong direction. Although I prefer not to see, speak, or hear about the affairs of the US and its people, I just cannot avoid something like the above story. (12/30/2022)

478. Having a hiccup while yawning.
하품에 딸꾹질.

In spite of the fancy words for yawning, oscitation, and studying yawning, chasmology, its physiological origin is not well understood. Maybe that is why scientists need such esoteric terminologies. Yawning is often associated with tiredness, sleepiness, and boredom. But, then, how does one explain paratroopers yawning just before they exit their aircraft and athletes yawning before intense exertions like basketball players right in the heat of a game?

Yawning is usually accompanied by an instinctive act of stretching several parts of the body including the arms, neck, shoulders, and back. Yawning is a relaxing exercise and hence people do not want to get interrupted during yawning. One of my pastimes is pretending to poke the belly of the stretched body of my wife at the onset of her yawning. It would invariably nullify any pleasure associated with yawning and displeasure on her part. The provocation is the very crux of the pleasure on my part.

Likewise, a hiccup, or singultus, is another involuntary act of which physiology is not well elucidated. We don't or can't really control them. When I suffered hiccups, my mother used to ask me to drink water from a bowl on which two chopsticks were placed in a cross and to drink water from each of the four openings exactly the same number as my age. I still do not know if it was the amount of water I drank did the trick or if the psychology involved mitigated the hiccup, but it always worked.

What then happens to the yawning at its climax if a hiccup starts? They are certainly incompatible and do not happen together or in succession in reality but speculation on its consequence would be welcomed. It would be like coitus interruptus without ejaculation. No fun, period. A standard interpretation of the above clause is that difficult times can come in series as a streak of bad luck. This being said, it would be similar to Essay # 17, "When it rains, it pours." Let us examine two cases of simultaneous or serial yawning and hiccup, one almost inevitable and the other easily avoidable.

The decade beginning in 1945 consisted of two major events for young Korea, fresh from the liberation from Japanese occupation: political unrest that eventually divided the Korean Peninsula and the subsequent Korean War that may remain in the foreseeable future. My parents had to, for instance, flee from the communist regime of North Korea with their eight children in tow. That the relocation as a refugee family has affected my life is an understatement. As I see it now, I resent the lack of everything and anything in the lives of my generation. We grew up as the so-called Lost Generation for good reasons. If this isn't simultaneous yawning and hiccup, what is?

A series of disasters that one could have avoided is perhaps best illustrated by the sorry state in which Donald Trump finds himself nowadays. Yesterday, the US House of Representatives finally made public the tax return from Trump, his wife, and his sprawling real-estate business organization. It showed that he paid $750 in federal income tax in 2017, his first year in office. He paid no tax in 2020 as his income dwindled and his business losses mounted. Just for comparison, my wife and I paid federal taxes, $29,184 and $21,474 for the years 2010 and 2021, respectively.

This recent revelation followed two presidential impeachments, the 2020 election loss to Joe Biden, the embarrassing loss of the Republican senatorial and gubernatorial candidates in key states whom he handpicked in the 2022 midterm election, and criminal referral by the House Jan 6th Committee to the Department of Justice for his role in the attack on the US Capitol. The list can continue for a while further with some other personal matters, especially in terms of interaction with women. In summary, many scholars and historians rank him as one of the worst presidents in American history. Had he behaved as most law-abiding citizens do, he could have mitigated all of this silly coincidental hiccup and yawning.

Other examples may be the debacles of the Denver Broncos and the meltdown of Southwest Airlines during this Christmas season. In the former case, after several seasons with dismal records, the Broncos brought in Russel Wilson from Seattle in a five-year deal worth more than $240 million. But their losing streak continues to a record level. Nobody seems to know what to do and pundits suggest that Peyton Manning, the legendary Broncos quarterback, should somehow get involved in the organization.

Southwest Airlines left more than a million passengers stranded at various airports missing family connections or flights home during the holidays, not to mention still missing luggage. Federal regulators believe that the meltdown is not simply due to the bad weather we experienced during the holidays. They are pointing fingers at outdated crew-scheduling technology. Oh, really? (12/31/2022)

479. Asking a cat to look after fish.
고양이에게 생선을 맡기다.

We all know pretty much what would happen to the fish. But those fish in a tank, especially with a lid at the top, would be safe although the cat can scratch the glass in an attempt of pouncing a goldfish inside. Indeed, watching a cat watching fish in a fish tank is a pleasant way of idling time.

In contrast to dogs, cats remain a mysterious pet animal, at least to me. Many years ago, when I was a bachelor, I owned both a cat named Duke and a basset hound named Bilbo Baggins. Duke was always the smarter one and showed very little respect to Bilbo. The dog was a pure breed with a registered pedigree while Duke was a total hybrid of unknown ancestry. One day, Duke was hanging himself upside down with his four paws firmly lodged in the belly of Bilbo during a fight and Bilbo was screaming with his lungs out in pain. After that incident, I noticed Bilbo became afraid of Duke although size-wise the hound dog was several times bigger. I felt sorry for Bilbo but he wasn't the smartest dog in the world. When we walked the neighborhood, Bilbo was on a leash, but Duke followed us of his own will.

Cats love sitting at a high place. This perching may offer them a hiding place for hunting or a better surveying platform. A cat would love to sit on top of a fish tank to watch fish swimming below but the top lid is usually congested with many obstacles like fluorescence light bulbs, an opening for feeding, lines for an aeration pump, etc.

As a predator, the cat displays some strange behaviors. They can see, hear, smell, and feel the surroundings much better than we do. Who knows, they may hear even the noise from swimming fish inside the tank. They seem to play with their prey by momentarily releasing and recapturing it, a mouse, for instance. With fish flickering and jumping on the dry ground, a cat will have great fun playing with them. If the cat is hungry, it will eventually eat the fish leaving well-carved-out bones and a head. That will be the ultimate outcome of the fish, which was entrusted to the care of a cat.

There are many similar sayings, especially those involving a wolf and a sheep: *a wolf in sheep's clothing, a small provocation to make the wolf devour the lamb, the wolf bemoans the sheep and then eats it, the wolf's death is the life of the sheep,* etc.

In *I Care a Lot*, a 2020 American film, the main character, played by British actress Rosamund Pike, is a con artist who makes a living by convincing the legal system that some of her wealthy clients cannot take care of themselves. She places them in an assisted living facility, where they are sedated and lose contact with the outside world. She sells off their homes and assets, pocketing the proceeds. The story may be similar to what Britney Spear could have gone through before the conservatorship by her own father and his management team was terminated in late 2021 by a judge in the Los Angeles County Court.

If a nation is under the control of another powerful nation, its impact on the nation occupied for a long period of time becomes a fond subject of discussion among historians. The facts involved remain the same but depending on who writes the history, the account can be quite different. A glass is half full of water and yet one can argue that it is half empty.

The English East India Company was founded in 1600. Thus began the British rule of the Indian subcontinent till around 1950. There are more than 300 years of constant and contiguous influence. An apologist may argue with the achievements of colonialism by emphasizing what could not have happened had Britain not ruled the continent. They may try to establish how India was lacking in the lives of the native at the time of the British conquest and how those deficiencies were remedied by the new rulers.

Such arguments based on literally double negatives do not merit any further consideration. How can one prove one way or another something that had never taken place? Unless there exists a parallel world that could serve as a reference or control as in scientific research, we will never know the answer to "what if." Instead of asking what British rule did for India, we ought to address what British rule did to them.

I have been occasionally exposed to such an argument as to the Japanese occupation of the Joseon Dynasty of Korea for 37 years. Furthermore, I remember hearing once in a while from my father's generation, "it wasn't all that bad." Although they had experienced the suffering, their detriments might not be perceived as such since they did not know otherwise. How could they know what they do not know? It might not have occurred to them that their lives could have been much better.

The only argument I can offer is based on extrapolation: see how Korea has recently become a nation of prosperity without any undue interference from others. (01/03/2023)

480. A maiden unsuitable for a palankeen ride to her wedding.
가마 타고 시집가기는 틀렸다.

Although Western wedding conventions have prevailed in Korea for decades, usually taking place in a church and officiated by a minister, many young couples nowadays decide to go for a traditional Korean wedding. I understand it is indeed a new trend to revive old traditions that my generation might have discarded simply being old and outdated. It seems to coincide with the arrival of prosperity and the desire to restore national heritage with pride.

A traditional Korean wedding can be quite an elaborate and expensive affair. The venue is usually the courtyard of the bride's family home. The groom would ride a colorfully decorated horse throughout the town. It is a parade announcing the passage of an important time in his life. Needless to say, the richer the groom, the more sophisticated the decoration. Likewlse, the bride usually arrives at the wedding site riding on a fancy palankeen. The bride would be sitting almost motionlessly with a downcast eye, modesty at its best but with excitement and anxiety.

The above proverb describes a maid who does not merit riding a palankeen to her own wedding ceremony for one reason or another. Her family is rich enough to afford a fancy sedan. That is, money is the least of her problem. The notoriety somehow precedes her eligibility for a new bride for a particularly well-spoken groom. It might be the town gossip about her prior promiscuity or a rumor of her being infertile or of bad temper. Here, people may whisper behind her family. As is often the case, the groom would be the last person who learned about the hearsay.

Just like any other judgment calls, whether a bride deserves a fancy ride depends on one's opinion. Here, as an example, presented below is how I perceived the enthusiastic reception that General Douglas MacArthur received in 1951 just after he was fired by President Harry S. Truman for his subordination charge based on his own ego and arrogance.

Douglas MacArthur (1880 – 1964) served as General of the Army for the United States as well as a field marshal to the Philippine Army in the 1940s. He also played a prominent role in the Pacific theater during the Second World War and in Korean War. He received more than 100 military decorations from various nations including the Medal of Honor for his service in the Philippines campaign.

At the peak of the Korean War in 1950, the General enjoyed the highest reputation that a military general can only dream of, especially from the recent successful amphibian landing at Incheon, while President Truman, a son of a dirt-poor Missouri farmer, was struggling with an awful approval rate. In October the modest President Truman and the egotistic General MacArthur met for the first time at Wake Island Conference. On the tarmac where Truman was flying in, MacArthur shook hands with the President rather than a salute and declined an offer to stay for lunch with the President. Other attendees found these behaviors insulting, but not the President. He was just annoyed by MacArthur's "greasy ham and eggs cap that evidently had been in use for twenty years."

In March 1951, clandestine conversations between the General and a few European diplomats stationed in Tokyo came to the attention of President Truman via a secret channel, in which the General boasted that he would succeed in expanding the Korean War into a full-scale conflict with the Chinese Communists, a potential prelude to the Third World War. He also sent a letter in a similar vein to the Republican leader in the House, which the latter promptly read on the floor of the Congress.

President Truman's main concern was saving as many lives as possible through a ceasefire while stopping the spread of communism in South Korea. For MacArthur, the war was an opportunity to liberate the North from communist control through aggressive action. He did not think a ceasefire was an appropriate solution. In effect, MacArthur was not only trying to increase public support for his position on conducting the war but also had privately informed foreign governments that he planned to initiate actions that were counter to United States policy.

The President was unable to act immediately since he could not reveal how he learned about MacArthur's chat with foreign diplomats and because of MacArthur's popularity with the public and in Congress. However, following the release of MacArthur's letter by a congressman, Truman concluded he could fire MacArthur without much political damage. President Truman officially relieved Douglas MacArthur of his command. On April 19, 1951, the General presented his final farewell address in a joint session of the Congress, which was interrupted by 50 standing ovations. Did he deserve such a reception? (01/08/2023)

481. The eagle cannot catch a fly.
독수리는 파리를 못 잡는다.

Two guys can argue all day if an eagle would not or cannot catch a fly, but the crux of the above proverb is that an eagle cannot catch a fly even if the bird tries. Then, the argument becomes a moot point. Why or how can such an awesome bird of prey not capture a mere fly? In this context, the above proverb is similar to Entry #69, "A knife cannot carve its own handle (식칼이 제 자루는 깎지 못한다)" and therein such as "A monk can't shave his own head." See also #109, "You cannot see your own eyebrow (가까운 제 눈썹 못 본다);" #113, "Use a shovel for a job for home (호미로 막을 것을 가래로 막는다);" and #218, "A needle beats an ax (도끼 가진 놈이 바늘 가진 놈을 못 당한다)." An opposite but still relevant to the above proverb can be found in #256, "The small hawk catches pheasants (초고리는 작아도 꿩만 잡는다)."

The proverb implies that everybody is, or can be trained to be, good at something suitable for his or her own ability. The ability to perform a given task exceedingly well appears to come from two sources: one from birth and the other from training. Only when both - one may say, nature and nurture - come to full collaboration, the outcome seems stellar. Ceaseless efforts without the gift born with or outstanding potential without its full exploration could well be "a square peg in a round hole."

In June 2022, Lim Yun-chan (임윤찬) became the youngest to win the Van Cliburn International Piano Competition in Fort Worth, Texas, where he also took two special prizes. Besides, he won U$100,000 and career management for three years. His passion for piano is such that he wishes to play piano throughout his waking hours for the rest of his life in a valley deep in the mountain abandoning everything in the bustling society. Lim Yun-chan began piano lessons at age seven when he was to choose an after-school activity. Fortunately, including himself and every music lover, his talent was promptly discovered at age 13 by his teacher and mentor, Sohn Min-soo at the Korea National Institute for the Gifted in Arts.

Can Lim be good at chopping wood for fire or bearing arms for defending the nation? I am certain that he could do both but is it in the best interest of everybody? Conscription in Korea has existed since 1957 and requires male citizens between the ages of 18 and 35 to perform compulsory military service of generally 18 months. The constitution states, "All citizens shall have the duty of national defense under the conditions as prescribed by (military Service) Act." The only exception will be for those with mental or physical incompetence.

Draft evasion is greatly flown upon by the public, especially for children from wealthy families or politically well-connected families. However, artists and athletes who have won government-accredited competitions can be exempted from military service. Under this rule, Lim will not need to serve the conscription. Since the criteria involved in this rule for the exception are rather murky, controversies often follow the government's decision.

Some dubious exemptions are as follows: the bronze medal-winning football team at the 2012 Summer Olympics, the 2008 Olympic gold medalist badminton player Lee Yong-dae, swimmer Park Tae-hwan, the 2014 Asian Games gold medalist tennis player Chung Hyeon, and the 2018 Asian Games gold medalist baseball player Lee Jung-hoo. Son Heung-min, a forward for Premier League club Tottenham Hotspur and captains the 2022 Korean national team, received the exemption in 2008. Nobody seems to complain about his exemption nowadays.

A two-year extension, from age 28 to 30, for notable K-pop artists could also be given by the government for their career. This amendment is rumored to be primarily for the singer-songwriter Kim Seok-jin of BTS. This exemption seems well justified by the humongous impact of BTS on the global music world and the worldwide dissemination of Korean culture. However, some believe that such an exception can form a precedent example for later days. In October 2022, Kim withdrew his enlistment deferral request and will be the first in the group to enter into mandatory military service, with other members of BTS to be enlisted later.

Kim's decision to fulfill the required duty right now is in sharp contrast to the act of another Korean pop singer, Yoo Seung-jun. In 2002, just prior to being drafted, Yoo became a naturalized U.S. citizen. The South Korean government considered it an act of desertion and deported him, banning him from entering the country permanently. Numerous attempts to appeal the ruling have been futile. In July 2020, his visa request was denied once again. Juxtaposed, Kim of BTS was an eagle who decided not to capture a fly in the above proverb, while Yoo who appeared to have fled this country was an eagle that tries but fails to capture a fly. (01/23/2023)

482. A man gets drunk just passing by a barley field.
보리밭만 지나가도 주정한다.

Some alcoholic beverages such as beer and whisky are prepared mainly from barley. Beer is, for example, produced by fermenting and brewing starches from cereal grains such as malted barley. Likewise, whisky is a distilled beverage made from fermented grain mash, primarily of barley. In short, barley is an important source material for various alcoholic beverages. Now a man, obviously a lightweight in alcohol consumption, is already drunk and acts in a drunken stupor, while he is just passing through the field of barley.

The above expression is quite an exaggeration, but a more relevant point would be that it mercilessly mocks a poor guy who cannot drink at all. Indeed, exaggeration is an essential part of most Korean proverbs. Without them for the emphatic delivery of their true meaning, we may have only a few proverbs that have survived the test of time. See, for example, Entry #388, "A belly button bigger than the belly." There is no way this can be true but in some occasions, it can make perfect sense.

Mockery in exaggeration, on the other hand, is rare but still can be found on some occasions in the daily lives of Koreans. Choong-chung Province of the Korean Peninsula is occupied by laidback folks who do not seem to care much about the fast and furious style of life. They move about slowly but seemingly in a deliberate manner and speak their own dialect biding their sweet time. They speak so slowly that we used to joke that the sun would set in the West by the time a guy completes a sentence, sending a hidden message that they are nitwits.

One of the most popular targets of mockery or scoffing is politicians as their acts often deserve being ridiculed and public taunting. The shameless display of the series of 15 votes in four days for electing the House Republican Speaker Kevin McCarthy will be soon followed by the brinkmanship displayed by the right-wing Republicans during the debate for the national debt ceiling. Their behaviors seem to deserve more than just being ridiculed in a gentle and light-hearted way.

Korean politicians do not fare any better either. At this writing, the ruling party with newly elected President Yoon is trying on the court Lee Jae-myung, who was the presidential candidate from the opposing party, for some nebulous reasons unclear to the public. This divisive move is perceived as another political revenge of a one-time political rival of President Yoon. When the latter retires from the service, he will most likely face a similar condemnation. See, for more instances, Entry # 335, "A man with a sword is felled with a sword."

Going back to the proverb in hand, drinking can often facilitate mutual introductions among strangers, say, a new employee at a firm. Oldtimers try to impress the newcomer with a boastful story while the new member is doing his or her best to accommodate all stories direct to them in the humblest way possible. As alcohol is consumed in liberal amounts and the noise level increases proportionally, the newcomer becomes bolder with the aid of their own drinking and starts to reveal themselves without much reservation. The following morning, they will become a family member with a mutual understanding of the intimate details of their lives.

Truth be told, anyone who does not drink or condones the merit of drinking is an eyesore to the otherwise lively party, true at least to me. They are around with clear eyes and thinking ability, absorbing everything around them including some rowdy behaviors of their drunken colleagues. When I see those folks sitting at a corner seat of the table with my own blurry eyes and questionable judgmental function, I would feel that someone is pouring a basketful of cold water over me and find myself abruptly recovering solemness. Then I may hurriedly leave the party with a sour taste.

As I mentioned in Entry #96, "Drinking can be medicinal with proper consumption, but...," there are people who cannot or should not drink at all because of unique metabolic disposition. And that is usually what we hear from timid and somewhat apologetic non-drinkers. It is not always clear if their excuse is really true or just to avoid the noisy and rowdy evening with us. Gradually they will not mingle with crowds of the after-work drinking nights and there appears an invisible wall between them and us.

Korean TV dramas are full of such scenes. A few days ago, my wife and I completed 16 episodes of *Diary of a Prosecutor*, starring one of my favorite actors, Lee Sun-kyun. It is a story of a group of prosecutors who are constantly under pressure from higher-ups. Their immediate boss is always in trouble because of their inept job performance and nagging from his own chief prosecutor. They all survive okay through the nightly drinking sessions that offer mutual empathy and sympathy. It is fortunate that no one was the type depicted by the above proverb. (01/25/2023)

483. Trying to sweat in a cold room after a cold drink.
찬물 먹고 냉동 방에서 땀 낸다.

For me, one way to cure the silly fever from a common cold is burying myself under a heavy set of blankets after drinking a copious amount of whisky. Since the sweating can be unpleasant afterward, I usually wrap my body with a few pieces of large bath towels first. Since my head is completely covered by the blanket, breathing itself requires some level of patience. I try to stay in such an uncomfortable state of folded sweated body position as long as I can, just like in a hot spring. This approach is certainly not for hot-tempered, short-fused people, including me. That is where whisky comes for help.

When I finally get out of the blanket and towels drenched in my own sweat, the cold and dry air immediately hits me for an abrupt awakening. Since the evaporation of sweat takes away the heat from all over my body, instantly I'd feel freshness with a cool head. In most Instances of a headache from a cold, the above procedure works fine to my satisfaction along with a hot shower and laundry of towels and blankets.

Sweating, or perspiration, is indeed a primary means of regulating body heat. The maximum sweat rate of an adult can be up to 2–4 liters (0.5 to 1.1 Gal) per hour or 10–14 liters (2.6 – 3.7 Gal) per day. Sweat is an aqueous solution that contains trace amounts of dissolved inorganics such as sodium and potassium, lactic acid, and urea. Surprisingly it also "excretes" rare elements considered toxic such as chromium and lead. Along with the urinary system, sweat removes soluble wastes.

Besides my own method presented above, there are several ways to induce perspiration: sauna, for instance. For Koreans and Japanese, hot spring, *oncheon* (온천) is most popular. The silver town we now live in has an excellent *oncheon* in the basement, apparently famous for the high quality of water, *jijang-soo* (지장수). I have never enjoyed oncheon in my life. It was because of the inferiority complex of "small penis syndrome." My bosom buddies used to tell me not to worry because every man has such a complex because the penis always looks smaller when viewed from above. At any rate, lately, I began to visit "our" oncheon in the basement there every day for about half an hour. Drinking cold beer afterward is not bad a life at all.

In the above proverb, someone is trying to perspire for one of the beneficial reasons listed above but he is doing it in a terribly wrong way: in a cold room after drinking cold water!

We would certainly consider the man's action silly and idiotic, but what he is doing is his prerogative and won't harm others. Who am I to laugh at him? Isn't he entitled to do his own business in his own way? Perhaps there are more serious matters with grave consequences for everyone on this planet Earth: the war between nations and between religions, for instance. What about climate change and uneven distribution of wealth and prosperity? We discussed a similar topic before in Entry #141, "One feels a splinter under a fingernail, but not a troubled heart."

The reform of the Roman Catholic church and the birth of Protestantism began with Martin Luther (1483 – 1546), a German priest. The main Christian belief is that "God actively continues His work for the salvation of all mankind and that He works through the Living Christ and the Church." However, its interpretation has varied over centuries. This is particularly true in terms of the relationship between the Church and the democratic process in government and industry, creating what appears an unrepairable chasm between the Catholic church and Protestant churches as well as among hundreds of denominations within Protestantism.

The objective of the Irish Republican Army (IRA), created in 1919, was to use armed force to render British rule in Ireland ineffective and thus to assist in achieving the broader objective of an independent republic. Political upheavals have continued in the pursuing years with numerous violent events. After Ireland withdrew from the British Commonwealth in 1949, the IRA started agitating for the unification of the predominantly Roman Catholic Irish Republic with predominantly Protestant Northern Ireland only to face a lack of support from Catholics in Northern Ireland.

The situation changed dramatically in the late 1960s when Catholics in Northern Ireland began a civil rights campaign against discrimination in voting, housing, and employment by the dominant Protestant government and population. Violence by extremists illicitly aided by the Protestant police force against the demonstrators set in motion a series of escalating attacks by both sides.

The violent clashes from both sides formed vivid memories in me, which have had a fundamental question as to the purpose of religion and profound disappointment and resentment of humanity. (01/31/2023)

484. Following friends to Gangnam.
친구 따라 강남 간다.

The title of the music video that Korean rapper Psy released in 2012 was *Gangnam Style.* See Entry #75, "Assaulted on Jong-ro Street, but let off steam at Han River." Here, Gangnam stands for south of the Han River, a river that skirts the southern part of Seoul. In the old days, the district was just full of plain rice paddies with small ponds here and there where I used to go fishing. The place was not like the place Psy depicted: bustling with crowds and neon signs shining brilliant lights everywhere during the nighttime. It was simply "nowheresville" few would visit willingly. And yet, according to the above proverb, you go there since your friends are going.

We often do things with lukewarm enthusiasm just because our buddies are doing them. The more reluctant you are the more vigorous they become in attempting to change your mind. Once you get to participate in the event, you may find yourself unexpectedly enjoying the occasion or conversely feel later that you have wasted your valuable time. Or, you may be condemned as an accomplice in a police station. Either way, the consequence is not really the topic of the proverb however grave it may be.

Examples may include attending a social function such as fund-raising for a cause that your friend is enthusiastic about, filling a missing fourth slot in the golf outing as the regular player cannot come, going to a party where you have only a few acquaintances, attending funeral or wedding of a person you are expected to although you hardly know the person involved, and being forced to show up at a function of an organization where your spouse is an important member. The common factor in these events seems to be that you are not the organizer or the sponsor of the event.

If someone asks me to characterize contemporary society, it is that nowadays all of us want to be at the center of the stage, a me-first society. Why should I be a substitute when I can be the originator, or why a secretary when I can be the president? I want to be a leader, not a follower, period. Everyone wants to talk rather than listen and write rather than read, constantly seeking fame and public recognition for whatever reasons. In sum, it appears more difficult to find blind groups of followers in modern societies in spite of the above proverb.

On April 15, 2013, Tamerlan Tsarnaev and his seven-year younger brother Dzhokhar Tsarnaev detonated two homemade pressure cooker bombs near the finish line of the Boston Marathon, killing three people and injuring hundreds of others. They were Chechen Kyrgyzstani Americans who had maintained a grave resentment toward the United States for having conducted the Iraq War and the Afghanistan War.

The older brother was killed by the police while Dzhokhar was captured. He was sentenced to death in June, after apologizing to the victims. A law enforcement official said that Dzhokhar "did not seem as bothered about America's role in the Muslim world" as his older brother had been. Dzhokhar said that his brother was the driving force behind the bombing and that his brother had only recently recruited him to help. His defense lawyer also emphasized the influence that his older brother had on him, portraying him as a follower.

A report in today's *The New York Times* reads, "A suicide bomber's blast ended more than 100 lives in the northwestern Pakistani city of Peshawar, devastating a mosque in a supposedly secure sector of the city, and sending smoke plumes into the sky and panic through the streets." It was one of the bloodiest suicide attacks to hit Pakistan in years, killing at least 101 people and wounding 217 others. Many of the casualties were police officers and government employees who had gone to pray at the mosque, in a heavily guarded neighborhood.

For years, Taliban leaders recruited Pakistanis who, like the Afghan Taliban, were ethnically Pashtun, while Pakistani military authorities tried to drive the militants out. We will never know how reluctant or willing the bomber was when he committed to the attack for whatever the cause might have been. This, together with the above Boston Marathon Bombing, represents an example, where persuasion in pleading words, commonly referred to as recruitment, could lead to devastating consequences for not only other innocent bystanders but also the attacker himself.

Many years ago, a young woman agreed to accompany her friend and her family to a Buddhist temple deep in a mountain, although the occasion was little to do with her. After praying and meditation, she came across a gentleman and his family during the lunch hour on the temple premises. Somehow they struck up a conversation and that was how my friend introduced her in Korea to me in the States. The rest was the story of our marriage. (02/01/2023)

485. Noisy Cheon-an interchange.
떠들기는 천안 삼거리.

Let us wind the clock backward about one hundred years and imagine that you are heading south from Hany-ang (current Seoul) in the Korean Peninsula. You would come across an important fork less than a hundred miles later, a *sam-geo-ri* in Cheon-an, a city in the Southern Province of Choong-chung, or 천안 삼거리. The road splits into two different directions. If one bears left, the road eventually leads to the southeast Young-nam territory including Busan. Nowadays, National Freeway No. 1 continues all the way down to Busan via Dae-jeon. The other leads the traveler to Ho-nam territory, which includes the city of Gwang-ju. This road heads more or less straight south, after interchanging with No. 25, to Gwang-ju.

In old Korea, this three-way intersection was apparently where the actions were, with heavy foot traffic as well as various transportation means such as horse buggies. And, of course, there must have been the noise from bustling crowds and busy commerce, not unlike Strip in Las Vegas during the night hours or Broadway in New York City during the theater season.

The place was so lively with people and famous for its heavy traffic that there was a folksong starting with "Cheon-an *sam-geo-ri, heung.*" Elementary school kids still sing the melody. Indeed, the city of Cheon-an owes its name value perhaps more to this simple folk song than anything else. Here, both *heung* and *ye-he-ra* mean little but filler sound just to uplift the mood of singing the song and gesture. See below for more about *Neung-su.*

Cheon-an sam-geo-ri, heung	성화가 났구나, 흥
Neung-su willow tree, heung	천안삼거리, 흥
Charmed in self-fancy, *heung*	능수버들은, 흥
Ye-he-ra Ye-he-ra, heung	제멋에 겨워서, 흥
Now, annoyed, *heung*	에루하 좋다, 흥

There are two completely different legends behind the song. In one, a scholar from a small town Go-bu in Jeolla Province was on his way to Han-yang to take the national exam for a government position. The exam was called Gwa-go. For the latter, see Entry #37, "No need to envy others: you take care of yourself." He stayed the night at an inn in Cheon-an *sam-geo-ri*. In the middle of the night, he heard a melancholy melody floating down to his room in the inn played on *gayageum*, a traditional 12-string Korean harp. He followed where the music came from to find a beautiful *gisang*, or geisha. Her name was Neung-su.

When the scholar came back after having passed Gwa-go, Neung-su sang in happiness the above song accompanied by *gayageum*. The last phrase reads, "성화가 났구나, 흥" which defies any rational translation. It could well be their life afterward was happy and good (좋다) as well as often annoying (성화가 났구나) just like any life.

The second version is more realistic. There lived a widower alone with a daughter named Neung-su. Unfortunately, the father was conscripted for government work far away. Before he left the town, however, he planted a seedling of a willow tree. Some years later when he returned home, Neung-su greeted him standing beside the willow tree. And thus born was the name of the *Neung-su willow tree*.

With time, the *sam-geo-ri* has yielded its function as a traffic center to another spot nearby and has become a playground of an elementary school. The original broad roads were permanently blocked off to have a schoolyard. Time has inevitably brought about such a change under the name of development. Nonetheless, one could imagine a busy and bustling intersection full of crowds a few hundred years ago. One may hear the melody from a *gayageum* in the night through the drooped willow trees.

They say that "A decade can change rivers and mountains" (see Entry #48). More to its implication, people change with time not only physically but also in character. A few years ago, I received a Christmas card from an old colleague of mine who used to work in my lab. She was a beautiful and attractive single and many guys including married ones would come to my lab just to hang around her. My lab was a popular spot in the department until she married and left town.

In the family picture she sent along with the card, I barely recognize her but her writing was still reflecting who she was and is now, assuring me that her character has not changed much. I was rather flattered as she confided in me about her relationships with family members. Although she was passing by where we lived at that time, I did not propose to meet up lest my impression would alter. (02/05/2023)

486. Pseudo-fengshui destroys a house.
반풍수 집안 망친다.

There is an expression, a half-baked potato. It'd be a bit too tough in texture to chew and a bit sour in taste. I guess one can bake further but by the time it is over, we may lose the appetite for the potato and have moved on to something else to eat. Here, we would rather keep potatoes uncooked so that we can cook them later more properly. Then, there is always a project that has started in the wrong direction and now we are all in the middle of it. Continuing the project sure looks like going for a certain failure and possibly a disaster, but scraping off it now makes us think about the cost and effort invested thus far. The only wishful thought would be that we could start all over again from the very beginning.

As pointed out in Entry #229, "A lucky family harvests watermelons from eggplant seeds," feng shui plays a critical role in, say, orienting to the most favorable direction of important structures such as tombs, government buildings, museums, community centers, and even in mapping a new city. The more important a project is, the more thorough knowledge of feng shui appears required. The above proverb says that imperfect knowledge in feng shui can ruin if not outright destroy a house and further a household.

The proverb may find its relevance in the contemporary society that is constantly bombarded by the vast amount of information available online, some of which is obviously misdirected or absolutely wrong. The impact of the latter must be what is referred to above as the destruction of a house.

The dictionary may define misinformation as "false information that is spread, regardless of whether there is intent to mislead," disinformation as "deliberately misleading or biased information; manipulated narrative or facts; propaganda," while fake news as "purposefully crafted, sensational, emotionally charged, misleading or totally fabricated information that mimics the form of mainstream news"

No matter what the intent and original purpose of each of the above may be, I cannot stop wishing that we all go back to the old days without the internet, such that the major way of obtaining was via newspaper printed on paper. By the time one finishes the paper, our fingers are all in black from the print and the "sweet" smell of printing oil. Prior to TV, the radio challenged our imagination as we only hear the news. Most of the time, even nowadays, *The New Yorker* magazine refuses to carry any pictures, which may well be its most attractive feature.

Then there is a relatively new term, deep fake, for "a video that has been edited using an algorithm to replace the person in the original video with someone else in a way that makes the video look authentic." This platform is most troublesome as it appeals to our fundamental desire of believing what we want to believe along with "seeing (and hearing) is believing."

There is very little anyone, particularly lawmakers and enforcement agencies, can do in preventing this highly advanced online technology. Even high-tech industries seem to be having a hard time regulating malicious videos as they have to ultimately rely on human judgment. Once a person is victimized, what can we do about the victim after a fake video has been viewed, say, a million times? In the field, fake sex video is considered one of the best ways to ruin someone's, like a politician's, career.

In the absence of any tangible way to teach the public the technology needed in determining what is a fake video and what is authentic, we feel utmost impotence accompanied by sad resignation. Belatedly we can just blame technology. It would be impossible that we now abandon all technological advances made in recent human history. Even if it is possible, one can argue how far we ought to go back. Shall we keep cars? What about TV, cellphone, airplane, etc.?

This is the dilemma alluded to earlier about a project that has started in the wrong way and the crux of the proverb. Imperfect knowledge of feng shui is less desirable than no knowledge at all.

Human greed along with technological advancement is considered the ultimate reason for climate change, which may end human civilization as we now know it much sooner than one may assume. Before such a calamity occurs, we can ask ourselves if there are other technologies we are currently developing that can be stopped now as a preventive measure. I can think of two areas. One is AI (artificial intelligence) and the other would be genetic manipulation. If and when a nation acquires AI as applied to military purposes, even a few months earlier than nations, that nation can have a dramatic advantage in global politics. Genetic manipulation of humanity such as cloning should be stopped all over the world.

To be fair, we all know what should be done or not done, but what is lacking is the will to do so. (02/06/2023)

487. A dead prime minister is not as worthy as a live dog.
죽은 정승이 산 개만 못하다.

During the old days of the Joseon Dynasty (1392–1897), one must first pass the national exam called *gwa-go* to become a serious government employee. With an appropriate pedigree and outstanding performance at a given position, he can be promoted to a senior minister or even a prime minister, *jung-seung* (정승). See more about *jung-seung* and *gwa-go* in Entry #37, " No need to envy others, you take care of yourself." It suffices to say that a *jung-seung* is a high government official.

And yet, the above proverb says that a dead minister is not as worthy as a live dog, implying that death means an end of all perks and fame one used to enjoy and that life is indeed over in vanity. The dog in the proverb stands for a very lowly creature that is used as a reference. Note that the dog did not receive the social status in the old days that we offer nowadays.

Let us take this opportunity to examine the concept of death from two practical, in contrast to philosophical, perspectives. One is what death means to the dead person's family and descendants. The other is how other people perceive the death of the *jung-seung*. Since we cannot know about the afterlife of the deceased, his own experience is a moot point. However, his family and direct descendants must be still proud of him and would receive due respect from others, but only up to a few future generations.

"That guy over there is the grandson of so-and-so, the first prime minister (of the Republic of Korea)." I remember overhearing such a conversation when I was a high school student, but soon we all forget about the familial tree. As I look back, such stories last less than three generations, although the person's name survives a bit longer. We remember the works of Shakespeare, Mozart, Vermeer, and the like, but who cares about their descendants?

If the relationship a person had maintained with the late *jung-seung* was primarily based on business or professional interests, then it would end abruptly as the person does not find any more "usefulness" of the *jung-seung*. He will for sure attend the funeral and memorial services but soon moves on to his own affairs without any input from the deceased. In my case, only a few of my previous colleagues of mine are in contact with me nowadays.

Thinking behind the proverb must go like this: a live dog is still handy and available for amusement if nothing else, but what good is this dead man for? The interaction between the dog and humans goes way back millennia. According to an entry in Wikipedia, the remain of a domesticated dog was dated back almost 14,000 years ago. We now have as many as 450 different breeds, each offering a unique set of characteristics and personalities. Their median longevity ranges from 10 to 13 years. In general, they are intelligent, loyal, and especially good with children. Unlike many humans, including some of my acquaintances, they do not insist on many unruly demands. Most remarkable is their ability to communicate with humans: with eye gaze, facial expression, vocalization, and posture. We usually communicate with dogs by using vocalization, hand signals, and body language.

It is utterly unfair for the above proverb to use the dog as a reference to a lowly animal. Its nuance is that a live dog is better than the dead *jung-seung* but barely. In fact, I often feel that any dog would be a better and more desirable company than any human being including a live prime minister. This sentiment reflects my fondness for dogs as much as my disappointment with humanity on many occasions.

In my previous life as a professor, I tried to work for long hours every day. That was the only way I know I could survive the highly competitive field of biomedical research. Research grants would come only from outstanding research outcome, which requires diligence as well as creativity. It was thus not surprising that the first person I would see in the morning in my office and the last person I see in the early evening used to be the building custodian. Invariably they are black females. I was always nice to them as they are perhaps more important people than my dean or department chair. They in turn showed a great deal of affection.

We used to talk about their personal life, say, about their pregnant unmarried daughter, aging parents, and sometimes the town in the south they left many years ago. The upshot of these interactions was that the trash from my office and the lab were always promptly taken care of. I found this was far better than complaining to our department chair about tardy janitorial service.

What I am trying to convey here is that I have always been in anti-establishment mode throughout my life. Anything but big brass was a welcome company. At the top of the list would be the dog, certainly not the dead *jung-seung* or alive politicians. (02/07/2023)

488. June is the month for grasshoppers.
메뚜기도 유월이 한철이다.

Because I moved back to Korea only a few months ago during the winter season, I cannot tell how grasshoppers survive in Korea nowadays. When I was growing up as a child, we used to catch them in a wild field not far from the center of Seoul City. Then we would stir-fry for a snack. It tasted very good, similar to the taste and texture of dried *sae-woo* small shrimp or krill. Apparently, the grasshopper is an excellent source of proteins and people still consume them avidly in some corners of the world.

Just like anywhere else, the best season for the grasshopper to prosper is summer, in June according to the above proverb. It simply states the fact, but it appears as a cynical way of describing people who are very good at seizing an opportunity as they come along. We are supposed to take advantage of the occasion but not at the expense of others or our own due diligence.

Opportunity is not, in some miraculous way, delivered to one's doorstep. We will have to go out to find it. The ability to see something of serious potential coming his or her way is the key to success once one properly executes the opportunity. Then we can ask ourselves what constitutes that ability. Many words come to my mind but I dare say that creativity and imagination be at the top of the list, especially if they are fueled with dreams. In carrying out the opportunity, other important traits one must have are hard work and willingness to take risks as well as setbacks.

The opportunity in one field may occur differently from that in another field. The specificity must depend on the discipline. For the research opportunity in pharmaceutical chemistry, the field I should be familiar with, studying the related literature diligently is a "must" so that what others are up to and what progress is being made. I found that such an exercise could bring some wonderful collaboration with scientists whom I had never met before. When someone approaches me with a potential collaborative idea, it is one of the most rewarding compliments.

Some 40 years ago, I took a one-year sabbatical from a pharmaceutical firm in Michigan to the University of Chicago Biochemistry Department. My mentor there told me about an unfortunate experience he had had to endure years earlier. The incident was about a stolen opportunity for him to become a true pioneer in the field of enzyme chemistry. Up until the late 1950s, the presence of enzymes had been firmly established but its mechanism of action remains a great mystery. Elucidating the chemistry involved was a hot topic that many biochemists had been pursuing.

My mentor and his colleagues at the University were able to establish water-tight proof for explaining the chemical steps involved in an enzymatic reaction, the so-called double-replacement mechanism. They hurriedly submitted a short manuscript for publication but the review by peers dragged on. To make the long story short, the editor of the journal had been sitting on the manuscript instead of sending it out for third-party reviews, while his own lab ran a very similar experiment that was introduced in the original manuscript. The upshot was that the editor received all the credit for discovering the reaction mechanism. It was an opportunity for the editor but he stole it from my mentor.

How can we determine if a person is successful? If we define a successful person as the person who has the most influential impact in his or her own field, the following list may suffice. In terms of business innovation, Elon Musk is my top choice. In commerce, perhaps Jeffrey Bozo, in information technology Bill Gates and Steven Jobs, Michael Jordan in the sports world, etc. In the world of science, the recent advance in genetics can introduce many successful biomedical scientists. As modern science is so diversified that permanently gone is the era when one person, like Einstein, can outshine the rest. Selecting the most successful person in art and literature is not as clean-cut as in other fields. It carries the nuance of a popularity contest regardless of concurrent financial compensation. Paul Gauguin and Vincent van Gogh come to my mind.

Professional success often has little to do with personal happiness. Of course, we do not have a way to gauge someone's inner happiness but we can guess from a perception. If we define success as a measure of personal happiness, there must be many unknown successful people on this planet throughout history. In most cases of personal happiness, the consequence of human interaction must play a key role. For instance, meeting and marrying a spouse of life-long love and mutual respect would be of paramount importance. Together, they may have a wonderful set of children with a happy family. I cannot tell how one acquires the ability to have a wonderful set of friends with whom he or she can share the deepest feelings and thoughts throughout life. (02/12/2023)

489. Spoiled beans, still inside a *sot* (솥).
팥이 풀어져도 솥 안에 있다.

Sot (솥) is a classic Korean cookware, cast-iron caldron, that is commonly used in preparing steamed rice. They vary in size but all of them have a rather shallow depth, are invariably black, and come with a heavy lid. See more about *sot* in Entry #138, "Startled by a turtle and now by a caldron lid." Again, they are heavy. Once got inside, there is no way to escape a *sot* with its heavy lid closed. Inadvertently, red beans were overcooked in a *sot* but the above proverb says that there are still inside the *sot*. It implies that not everything was lost although it may look that way at first glance.

A tornado passes through a town and its residents moan that everything was destroyed and lost. In reality, that is not true. Valuable small items such as diamond-imbedded rings or necklaces in a jewelry box must have survived. Or some residents were about to demolish the old house to rebuild a new one. They may be rather thankful. So long as there is no human loss, we can always rebuild the town, perhaps with modernization in every aspect of the municipality. It may take some years but we see them coming back better.

In thermodynamics, we learn that the total energy of a given system remains constant no matter what processes the system is undergoing. See more on energy conservation in Entry #346, "Raising the floor lowers the ceiling." Although the red bean was overcooked to almost a state of disintegration into a mass of paste, it may not be a total loss. Overcooked beans may facilitate digestion when consumed or be much easier to chew. No matter what beneficial gain one may realize, one thing is certain: beans are still inside the *sot*.

Alcatraz is a small island 1.25 miles, or 2 km, offshore of San Francisco. In 1934, the island was converted into a federal prison, Alcatraz Federal Penitentiary. The strong currents around the island and cold water temperatures made escape nearly impossible. Although the prison was closed in 1963 and the island has now become a major tourist attraction, the idea of having a prison inside the island was a good one as there shouldn't be any attempt for prisoners to escape the doubly secured encampment. The prison was primarily for those criminals who continuously caused trouble at other federal prisons, mostly notorious bank robbers and murderers including Al Capone.

Indeed, during its 29 years of operation, the penitentiary claimed that no prisoner successfully escaped. Of the total 36 prisoners who attempted the escape, 23 were caught alive, six were killed during their escape, and the rest are listed as "missing and presumed drowned." One could thus conclude that they were red beans inside a *sot*.

Many detective stories by English writer, Agatha Christie, center around a murder in which detective Hercule Poirot or Miss Marple eventually solve the crime. Typically, the last scene is where all suspects are asked to attend a meeting in a room, where the murderer is identified through developing logical stories. Once confined, Poirot or Miss Marple can take their time in establishing a water-tight case. This is a luxury they could afford compared, with, say, a case where a suspect is roaming in New York City.

Likewise, a person on a ship, airplane, train, or similar confinement can be easily arrested because they are indeed "the red bean inside a *sot*." At the time of this writing, there is an ongoing scandal involving left-wing politicians supported by a chaebol Kim Sung-tae for their attempt to visit North Korea. Kim fled Korea and has been staying abroad in Singapore and Thailand since May last year, but he was apprehended about a month ago upon arriving at the Inchon International Airport.

The pathetic state of world affairs in political conflict or wars between nations or different religions is largely blamed on inept their leaders. Some of these heads of the nation or religious leaders appear to instigate crises as a means of controlling their constituents. That is, the war seems essential for them to maintain their power over their followers. Considering their apparent affinity towards war, it may not be a bad idea for the peace-loving 99.99% of the global citizens to round up all those so-called leaders and put them on a remote island all by themselves so that they can fight one another till the end. That would be my day.

Since these leaders are not familiar with fistfights or any other types of physical fights, we can introduce a few tough thugs with nasty demeanors into the group so that they can teach those politicians how to fight. Ideally, we should install a video camera so that we can watch their quarrel in real time if we wish. It would be quite entertaining and we may well deserve that much from their ceaseless fights inside a *sot*. (02/15/2023)

490. A rookie thief forgets when the sun rises.
늦게 배운 도둑이 날 새는 줄 모른다.

Traditionally, in Korea, a small burglary occurs during the night till the wee hours, but it certainly ends before the sun rises. Thieves are smart enough to flee before day breaks. This man has just learned the trade at an old age but loves stealing so much that he forgets when the sun rises. We do not know what happened to this "new kid in the block," but it is likely that he was caught by the homeowner and handed over to a policeman.

Enthusiasm is one thing, overdoing is another. Anyone can be carried away if they over-indulge in something that they immensely enjoy. It can be an affinity to drugs, alcohol, sex, gambling, porn, social network service, work, smoking, food, video game, etc. A workaholic can lead to so-called *karoshi*, as introduced in Entry #96, "Drinking can be medicinal with proper consumption, but…" In 2013, a 31 year-old Japanese female journalist died of *karoshi* working at a frantic pace for covering two elections in Tokyo. Subsequent to her death, *karoshi* became a social issue in Japan.

Indulging in sex and love late in a man's life has frequently manifested itself throughout generations in human history. In modern times, a married couple whose children have all grown up and left home for college often ends up in a divorce as one spouse, usually, the man, finds renewed vigor in the young lover. In the old days in Korea, it was a well-accepted practice that a wealthy *yangban* would adopt a second wife or keep even multiple wives.

"That was fun. Say hi to Snow White." This sentence was found among many emails that Jes Staley sent to the disgraced financier Jeffrey Epstein just after he visited Epstein on Little St. James Island in 2009. Staley is the former JP Morgan Chase executive who had maintained Epstein's account at the bank. He later became the chief executive of the British bank Barclays. But in 2021, the bank pushed him out in the middle of a regulatory inquiry into his years-earlier relationship with Epstein.

The reference of Snow White and other similar nicknames such as Disney Princess were code words for young women or girls: (from an article in the 02/17/23 issue of *The New York Times*). As far as the above proverb is concerned, Staley was the newly minted "thief who forgot when the sun rises," and was eventually subject to various investigations.

198

It is interesting to note that the above proverb refers to an aged man learning a new trick, implying that a young man tends to jump into a pilfering business without any perspectives based on experience. He may hardly know any other occupation as an alternative means of living. Now burglary has become the only job he has ever had and mastered all ins and outs of the trade. He would surely know when to stop the burglary.

An old man, on the other hand, belatedly discovers an exciting new venture and finds it much easier to make a living compared with what he has gone through in the past. He might have gone through numerous sad experiences, perhaps including the departure of his own wife and children one morning. Now that they have gone, he must be glad that he does not have to face and confess what his real nightly job is. Most of all he seems to find a new purpose for living.

Imperialism is the state policy, practice, or advocacy of extending power and dominion, especially by direct territorial acquisition or by gaining political and economic control of other areas, often through employing hard power (economic and military power), but also soft power (cultural and diplomatic power). While related to the concepts of colonialism and empire, imperialism is a distinct concept that can apply to other forms of expansion and many forms of government. (from Wikipedia)

The term, imperialism, was mainly applied to Western and Japanese political and economic dominance, especially in Asia and Africa, in the 19th and 20th centuries. American imperialism or colonization in Far East Asia including Korea arrived late compared with European nations, Japan, and Russia. This may reflect the long-lasting influence of the Monroe Doctrine and the foreign policies practiced by many presidents who believed in the principle of national sovereignty such as Ulysses S. Grant, Theodore Roosevelt, John F. Kennedy, and Ronald Reagan.

This is not, however, to mean that Americans did not have such an appetite. The Philippines would be an example. The recent history involving Iran, Vietnam, Afghanistan, and other Middle East nations gives off a nuance of modern imperialism under a disguise of economic interests. It may well be the old man who belatedly discovered the burglary. (02/18/2023)

491. Acupuncture onto the nostril of a sleeping tiger.
자는 범 코침 주기.

It would be a rude awakening for the tiger if you insert an acupuncture needle into the epithelium of the nostril. You would be extremely lucky if you escape the tiger's assault and survive to tell your friends about the experience. Invariably, they would say how stupid you were and that we usually leave even a dog alone when it is sleeping. Now, you hurt a sleeping tiger with a sharp needle at the most pain-sensitive part of the body.

Had you just walked away, very cautiously I might add, from the sleeping tiger, everything would have been okay. On certain occasions, it would be best if you leave things as they are rather than mess around trying to fix them. See Entry #234, "A hole gets bigger whenever you work on it."

"Let China Sleep, for when she wakes, she will shake the world." Although nobody can prove it, presumably Napoleon Bonaparte made this statement. Between 1959 and 1976 when Mao died, China suffered nationwide famine from the failure of the so-called "Great Leap Forward" and social unrest involving the Cultural Revolution. The post-Mao era, led by Deng Xiaoping, began to enjoy economic liberalization but also a policy of government-controlled capitalism.

China's economy has changed rapidly in recent decades. In 2008, China became the world's second-largest economy, second only to the US. Since assuming power in 2016, Xi Jinping has successfully maintained tight control over the Chinese Communist Party with reinforced discipline but more importantly demonstrated more aggressive moves in relation with the US, the South China Sea, border disputes with India, and the political status of Taiwan. Xi has also expanded China's influence on African and Eurasian nations via various infrastructure developments.

These eye-popping moves certainly attracted much attention from the US, with whom China has enjoyed the largest trade. The tension that has been simmering between the two countries over the military and global trade domination has shown a full display over the spy balloon incidents in recent weeks. A couple of weeks ago, a large Chinese air balloon was spotted drifting over Montana that was later shot down by the US off South Carolina. A few similar but smaller air balloons were shot down again since then.

On the 18th of this month, the US Secretary of State Blinken met with his Chinese counterpart, Wang, in Munich, warning him that the flight of a Chinese surveillance balloon across the United States "must never happen again." Blinken also cautioned Beijing against providing "material support" to Russia's war in Ukraine. In response, Wang said it was up to the US to "solve the damage caused by the indiscriminate use of force" when it shot down the balloon off South Carolina. All in all, both Washington and Beijing were digging in, two weeks after the episode.

It was another reminder that Chinese-US relations have fallen to their lowest point since Richard Nixon opened a channel of communication to China's leadership a half-century ago. I do not know if anyone including the US has ever poked a needle into China's nostril but China seems to be waking up with determination to win the competition in every front one think of with the US for world hegemony.

Asia faces the problem of a declining population. The death rate is higher than that of the new birth in both Korea and Japan. In Japan, almost a third of the population is over 65, compared with 17% in the US. The economies of Korea and Japan are suffering from a lack of available younger workers. One reason for the low birth rates in these countries is the high cost of raising children. In addition, young couples nowadays seem to believe that raising a child is more difficult than ever. This perception may originate from what appears to them a more hostile environment to rear a kid in. This includes both in and outside school. It is thus getting more difficult for women to do both parenting and fulfilling career.

In China, there is another reason: they instituted a One-Child Policy in 1979 to control its growing population. It was only in 2014 that the policy was replaced with a Two-Child policy. Now its consequence is in full display in many aspects of Chinese society. The UN has just released its 2022 World Population Prospect, which concludes that China's population began to decline this year. It may be just my perception but its negative impacts on the future of China appeared thoroughly discussed in recent mass media with celebratory glee in the US.

China now appears to be awakening from the slumber of the economic prosperity of recent years not so much because someone inserted an acupuncture needle into their nostril but because they had developed inadequate policies based on wrongful assumptions. It was almost a self-inflicted wound. (02/20/2023)

492. Cleansing nasal drippings while pulling an arrow.
활을 당기어 콧물을 씻는다.

As an archer pulls the bowstring just prior to aiming, his hand holding the nock at the rear of the arrow invariably passes through beneath the nose. If he happens to drip from the nose at that particular moment, the hand can clean the drippings while pulling the arrow. This is the scene that the above proverb describes, implying that one can achieve two things in one move or one thing with an excuse for running another business. Call it an old Korean version of multitasking.

As pointed out in Entry #370, "Meet the lover, pick the mulberry as well," I have never liked multitasking. To me, its merit has been greatly exaggerated while our lives have become more hectic at a fast-and-furious speed. It appears to promote a large number of shady jobs at the expense of the high quality of a few jobs. You may not catch any rabbits if you chase two rabbits concurrently out of greed. See also Entry #31, "Dig one well at a time." I have been advising young people to take "one firm step at a time," avoiding the fad of multitasking. This is not because I cannot multitask myself but because I simply do not see any point in doing it.

In the 1981 film, *On Golden Pond*, an aging couple, played by Katharine Hepburn and Henry Fonda, was spending the summer in their cottage on Golden Pond. They were visited by their daughter Chelsea (Jane Fonda) and her finance Bill (Dabney Coleman) with his 13-year-old son from his previous marriage. In one scene, which the above proverb reminds me of, Bill is standing with one foot on the boat and the other on the dock. As the boat drifts away from the dock, Bill falls into the water. He was too late to grab onto the boat and too far away to jump back to the dock.

If one tries to appease both opposing parties, such a nonsensical episode can happen. It has never been and will never be a smart move. Even if you were able to clean the nasal drippings, not only the top of your hand pulling the bowstring would become messy but also the upper lip can be smeared with the dripping. You may as well stop the archery completely for a minute to wash off your whole face as thoroughly as you can. Then you can hit the mark with an arrow with a refreshed mind and clean face. What could be wrong with this approach to one's life?

There are things that you absolutely cannot run simultaneously. Saturday morning domestic errands used to include the post office, pharmacy, dry cleaner, gas station, and grocery. I would map out the route before I leave home, usually the grocery shopping at the end. If I can complete all chores before noon, I congratulate myself. If not I tried a better approach next time. The bottom line is that I cannot be in all these places at one time but I can plan in advance with the highest efficiency I could muster.

It is not different from planning a long cross-country road trip. If you try to do many things or visit many places in a strange town you are visiting during the trip, an accident is bound to happen. Why not stay another night? You may say that you cannot afford it because you have only so many or few days of vacation. This mentality spills over to the days in retirement also. I have found it to be the case even though I retired about 10 years ago. I still find Friday afternoon more agreeable and relaxing than Monday morning. Let's call it the remnant of habit.

Often we find ourselves in the middle of complicated relations such that we don't have any other choice but have to do multiple tasks simultaneously. Take current Korea's foreign policy as an example. The multidimensional aspect of international relations comes from the fact that we cannot consider one parameter at a time and try to somehow string them together at the end. Just to name a few, we will have to consider the other country's political system, religion, history, military strength, economy including trading partnership, cultural influence, etc.

Immediately relevant to current Korea's foreign relations would be the above aspects of North Korea, the US, China, and Japan. How we deal with North Korea in terms of military strength would be far from how to take care of cultural and technological influence from the US. It would be impossible to face one issue at a time as a crisis occurs as a band-aid solution. At least that is how I have perceived Korea's foreign policies in my lifetime: juggling many balls in a helter-skelter fashion purely as-needed fashion.

What is lacking appears to be a guiding principle or long-lasting national doctrine that is applied to developing foreign policy. Let's say, we Koreans proclaim that individual freedom and the individual's right to pursue prosperity are of utmost importance in developing a relationship with all other nations and that other nations respect our priority. If we consistently reflect such a philosophy for many generations, there won't be any misunderstanding and need for ad hoc multitasking. (02/21/2023)

493. Blocking eyes with a leaf.
가랑잎으로 눈 가리기.

"Seeing is believing" does not necessarily mean that not seeing solves any troubles. This is in spite of the fact that we close our eyes when we do not wish to witness a certain scene. A basketball game is on the line in the final second when my team player goes for a three-pointer. I cannot stand the outcome one way or another and thus either close my eyes completely or peep through closed fingers. The above proverb says someone refuses to see by blocking their eyes merely with a leaf. Why leaf? I imagine it is because the leaf is as clumsy and fleeting as anything else for the purpose.

There is practically no way to close off all views with a small leaf. It is a silly attempt but the psychology behind it is the subject that the proverb is exploring. A man in front of a firing squad is mercifully offered a black sack or hood so that he cannot see what is happening in the last minutes of his life. Given a choice, would you prefer observing every detail of execution that will soon end your life? Most people would not. Under the hood in the darkness, your hearing may perk up to detect and imagine the preparation.

Seeing or not seeing is an all-or-none event, while hearing depends on a person's hearing ability. In contrast, speaking is actually one's option. The option includes if one wishes to speak at all, what to say, and when to speak. Sometimes, what is not spoken has more meaningful consequences. Any individual has the right to silence when asked to answer questions from law enforcement officers or court officials. Although silence is often considered affirmative, it cannot establish any criminal case without evidence.

Legality put aside, silence is far from establishing innocence. A man, for instance, on his way back to his home after work, kills a total stranger without any motive. At home, an unsuspecting wife does not specifically asks him if he killed someone on the way home. Later he cannot say that he did not confess to the killing, not to mention admitting it, simply because nobody raised such a pointed question. Without any witness or evidence of the crime, he may walk free. The only punishment we can expect or hope for is self-inflicted agony or mental torture from within himself. If the killer is immoral, it would become a moot point. The last resort we have for justice will be the hope that the killer will spend his afterlife in an inferno forever.

Several years ago, my wife and I had some unfortunate experiences with her then-employer, Duke University. She brought the University to the court of the law for what appeared to be an unfair administration of my wife's research grant and concocted evidence presented in defending their position. The episode was introduced in detail in Essay #317, "Beating the boulder with an egg." In brief, it turned out to be an eye-opening occasion of realizing the delicate relationship between justice and the law as they are practiced in the States. Subsequently, I began to realize that most scholars in the law either conclude that justice is only a judgment about the law or do not support that justice is somewhat part of the law.

It was thus a pleasant surprise to find a few days ago an essay, "On the Connection Between Law and Justice," written in 2011 by Anthony D'Amato at the Northwestern University School of Law. It was written in plain English without any convoluted logic so that any layman like me could follow with ease. He developed an argument using a hypothetical case to conclude that "judges should decide cases according to justice." Apparently, he had been promoting the idea that justice is what lawyers should do; justice is what judges should render. "Law" is nothing but a set of tools for exercising justice. He maintained that we should not get so caught up in the intellectual interest of law that we forget that law in itself cannot solve human problems. Like any other tool, the law may facilitate the solution to a given problem.

The hypothetical case he presented consists of an "innocent" girl darting out of nowhere on an oncoming car, with two possible outcomes. In the first case, the driver was able to save the girl by bearing off to the left crossing white double lines. She violates traffic law and was accordingly cited. In the second case, the driver sees the child at the last minute, refrains from crossing the parallel lines, and runs over and kills the child. The case moves all the way to the US Supreme Court along with analyses of existing law, much publicity in the media, and legislation issues. It reads like a plot of a film.

Toward the end of the essay, we find the following: *the real meaning (of written law) is contained in the way the legal system as a whole impacts the social system, namely, to help deliver justice to that social system. To omit considerations of fairness and justice in interpreting statutes is to fail to do justice to the reason for the existence of statutes.* We cannot and should not try to hide justice with a leaf from the common practice of law. (02/24/2023)

494. Having lunch after letting visitors leave.
나그네 보내고 점심 한다.

During the good old days of the Joseon Dynasty (1392–1897), it was a kind of custom that a passing traveler is welcomed and often fed by a villager. You may call them Korean Samaritans as they extend warm hands to a total stranger. However, one finds exceptions to this traditional kindness. Call them Korean Scrooges. Here is a family of misers who wait till their visitors leave for their lunch instead of having lunch together. They might have been anxiously waiting for their guest's departure. They may complain under their breath about the prolonged stay of their house guests, although they may say a few pleasantries of welcome.

If it were an elaborate dinner that the family had planned earlier for their intimate family alone, it would be understandable to put off the fest till the visitors leave. This would be particularly inconvenient if the visitors show up unannounced. But the proverb is referring to a simple lunch that any family should be able to afford without much planning or preparation. Whichever you may see, they are misers, full stop.

Usually, these are the same type of people who visit acquaintances just before mealtime. They are the type who disappears to answer their phone or to visit the restroom when the bill for a meal at a restaurant is about to arrive. Yes, they had devoured wholeheartedly the most expensive item on the menu. Yes, I have come across such people in my long life, including some friends. In many instances, I have also noticed that people with wealth tend to be tight with their money like a penny-pincher. See also Entry #62, "A pear drops to the ground as a crow takes off."

I used to wonder what makes a man a miser. Poverty or lack of financial means does not seem to be the cause as I see many poor people who are quite generous with their compassion from the bottom of their hearts. Is greed then the cause? Not necessarily as we see many successful business financiers are philanthropists. Besides many wealthy and famous people turned out to have lived a frugal life to the point they were often considered misers. Examples may include the billionaire investor Warren Buffett, the co-founder of Wal-Mart Sam Walton, President John F. Kennedy, comedian actor of last century Charlie Chaplin, et al.

In *The Merchant of Venice* by William Shakespeare, the merchant defaults on a large loan provided by a Jewish moneylender, Shylock. This man demands a "pound of flesh" for retribution. The moneylender is particularly determined to revenge the Christian merchant because his own daughter has eloped with the Christian lover and converted to Christianity from Judaism. Is Shylock a miser or simply a man with cold blood? Are they necessarily the same?

In a Korean fable, *Hung-bu and Nol-bu*, we find the older brother *Nol-bu* a terrible miser full of avarice. See Entry #17, "When it rains, it pours." If these brothers share some level of identity in DNA, can we conclude that becoming a miser is a phenomenon of nurture rather than nature? I have a good Korean friend who inherited his business from his rather frugal father. Their business was doing very well and both maintained a well-off life but with austerity. I believe that my friend became tight with money through his upbringing in business. In short, I am still at a loss for what sense I can make as to how one develops the trait of a miser as he or she grows up.

In contrast to the word miser, which always carries a negative connotation, there is more literature as to frugality. Right off the bat, my Korean generation who had gone through the hardship of the Korean War, tend to be frugal but we are not misers and seldom tempted by wasteful consumption. Speaking for myself, I hate waste, have always tried to avoid expensive habits most likely due to circumstantial necessity, aimed for self-restraint in domestic finance, resisted any silly social fashions and trends, questioned dubious advertisements, and sought efficiency in all daily activities. I would recommend these habits proudly to anyone in any generation. But, most of all, I have never considered myself a miser.

Frugal living is practiced to cut expenses, have more money, and get the most they possibly can from their money. According to the Guinness record book, Pavle Kostevski with Aegean and Greek ancestry is the most frugal person recorded. This person entered the hall of fame in the 19th century when he spent only 365 pennies for the whole year. He allegedly was buying only one small piece of bread every day and was living exclusively on bread and salt. He was asking for free salt from the local shops. He also claimed he never drank tea because the tea had fat! He was not poor, owned a big house, a big farm, and a few horses. He inherited this trait from his father. The horses were fed by donations from the locals. He might not have anything to share with anyone. (02/27/2023)

495. One stick for ten blind men.
열 소경에 한 막대.

Here we have 10 blind men but with only one walking stick. One can easily see how valuable and popular the stick would be among them. It would be like the last roll of toilet paper or the last drop of water in the middle of the desert. Just as these are not usually considered valuable items but only under certain circumstances, anything or everything on this planet Earth can be so crucial that they can dictate one's life or death. How would a mere wooden stick be so valuable for those 10 blind men? This is to say, all things can be absolutely needed as they have been.

The circumstance referred to above includes the time component besides place, as in "an extraordinary time of crisis brings about extraordinary heroes." Like Winston Churchill, for instance. My wife and I have been watching on Netflix belatedly the *History of Three Kingdoms* (삼국지) in ancient China from the year about 220 to 300. It is a very long Chinese TV drama, consisting of more than 90 episodes, that tries to convey the waning era of the Han Dynasty (201 BC – 220 AD). The divided country by belligerent warlords was eventually, albeit temporarily, united by Jo-Jo (in Korean pronunciation for 曹操) or Cao Cao (in pinyin).

When Jo-Jo asked a physiognomist to predict his own potential as the future king, the face reader said, "You would be a capable minister in peaceful times and an unscrupulous hero in chaotic times." Jo-Jo was said to have laughed and left. Indeed Jo-Jo has been often described as a cruel and merciless tyrant in literature, but he has also been praised as a brilliant ruler, military genius, and great poet possessing unrivaled charisma. In other words, in any peaceful time, we do not have a great leader.

One of his main rivals was Liu Bei (유비). He was in many ways opposite to Jo-Jo. Liu Bei believed in people and considered their well-being before anything else. In the historic novel, *Romance of the Three Kingdoms* by Luo Guanzhong, Liu Bei is the most admired and loved character. His success was largely from his brilliant military strategist, Zhuge Liang (제갈공명). The latter had been quite reluctant initially in joining Liu Bei's camp because none of the warlords seemed capable of reviving the wavering Han Dynasty.

In the end, however, he decided to help Liu Bei by convincing himself that he could find and make an ideal hero. Both Jo-Jo and Liu Bei became historic figures not so much because they were born heroes but because their lifetimes coincided with a chaotic time in Chinese history.

Liu Bei to his constituents must have been the walking stick to the blind men in the proverb and a shepherd to sheep. I wish I could say the same for Jo-Jo, but for him, political ambition seemed to have taken over his soul. What he needed most was the skill to disintegrate his enemies at all costs. For a while, he was very successful in unifying the nation in his own wicked, and often very crafty, ways.

If a chaotic time or crisis produces an extraordinary leader or hero, can't we have them in a peaceful time? It seems rare indeed but I can find such a leader in King Sejong the Great (세종대왕, 1397 – 1450) of the Joseon Dynasty. In a peaceful time without any real external pressure, he not only established national policies based on our own version of Confucian which had lasted for centuries in the Korean Peninsula but also enacted major legal amendments for the first time in Korean history. But, most of all, he singlehandedly created the Korean alphabet currently known as *hangul*. Its impact on Korean culture has been immeasurable.

I cannot stop wondering what might have prompted King Sejong to proactively develop and establish so many things in such a short life of 53 years. This can be a generic inquiry for all outstanding leaders in a peaceful time. It is patently not like preparing for an imminent invasion of a foreign force or an expected natural disaster where what to do is given by the event. Instead, Sejong must have what is needed in the nation first. For instance, he must felt sorry for the people who cannot read Chinese characters, which must have been the majority of the population. Identifying such needs for a new language mandates empathy as well as sympathy.

Any ordinary person can identify what is needed or to be changed during their lifetime. Even I can voice certain complaints in many daily activities., especially in politics and social justice. Having an opinion is one thing but what to do with it is another matter altogether. That is where Sejong is different from me. He had the willpower to do something for his people but more importantly, he was capable of fulfilling the desire.

In sum, how many people do I know who are bold, courageous, creative, and intelligent, in addition to compassionate towards their contemporaries? He or she is the essence of the stick for blind men. (03/01/2023)

496. A pearl on a pigtail ribbon.
댕기 끝에 진주.

Asian girls, usually till they get married, often fashion their hair in pigtails, either one or two braids, and their end is tied with a fabric ribbon. The ribbon, its shape and color, reflects one's personal taste in beauty. It goes without saying that girls would do their best in decorating the ribbon. In the above proverb, someone placed a pearl on each end of the ribbons. They would be the priceless, emphatic point of the pigtails. An interesting Korean noun for pigtail ribbon is *daeng-gi* (댕기). It is not a common word but is always associated with a girl. As pigtails were most popular in the old days, girls appear in Korean historic epic dramas or films in them with *daeng-gi*.

The centerpiece jewel of a royal crown, the gem on the forehead of a Buddha statue, and Pelé of the Brazil national soccer team are all good examples of the pearl at the end of a pigtail ribbon. For that matter, any of the Korean National Treasures will be just that, a pearl on *daeng-gi*. The Korean government defines National Treasure as any tangible treasure, artifact, site, or building that have exceptional artistic, cultural, and historical value to the country. In this essay, would like to introduce a few.

Nam-dae-mun (남대문, or 南大門), which literally stands for South Great Gate, is designated as the Number One Treasure. It is also officially known as the Sung-nye-mun (숭례문; or: 崇禮門) and is one of the four gates in the Fortress Wall of Seoul during the Joseon Dynasty. It is located between Seoul Station and Seoul Plaza, right at the center of the city. The gate was built in a classic pagoda style by the founding king Taejo of the Joseon Dynasty in 1398. The gate was extensively damaged during the Korean War. In 2006, a 182-page-long blueprint was made for a contingency against any emergencies. See more on this below.

If a tourist, be it a Korean from the rural district or a bona fide foreigner, has not visited this historic site, they cannot claim that they have been to Korea or Seoul. See more in Entry #199, "Speak louder, win the argument." Unless you are a serious scholar in an old structure or something similar, spending 10 minutes would be sufficient. Just take a picture for the evidence of your visit and leave this crowded and noisy area quickly.

In February 2008, a fire broke out at 9 PM, destroying the wooden structure of the gate. It took more than three hours for 360 firefighters to control the fire. A 69-year-old man was arrested on suspicion of arson. He later confessed to the crime. Apparently, this insane man had sprayed paint thinner on the floor of the structure and then set fire to it. Police say that the man had been upset about not being paid in full for the land he had sold to developers. Restoration work started in February 2010 and was completed in April 2013. The gate was finally reopened in May 2013.

Following the South Gate on the list of National Treasures are mainly pagodas, steles, and Buddha statues. An interesting structure, placed on the 31st, is called Cheom-seong-dae (첨성대, or 瞻星臺) in Gyeong--ju. It is an astronomical observatory, a "star-gazing tower," built in the 7th century. It is said that the structure is the oldest surviving astronomical observatory in the world. The tower with a cylindrical body tapered off at the top, is only 9.2 meters (90 ft) tall and less than 6 meters (20 ft) wide at the bottom. There is a square window or entrance to the inside at the midway of the tower. Its original appearance and shape have remained essentially the same for over 1300 years.

My favorite is the Buddha statue at Seokguram (석굴암) Grotto, the 24th South Korean National Treasure. The Grotto is part of the Bulguksa temple complex located in Gyeongju, which is also on the UNESCO World Heritage List. It overlooks the East Sea and rests 750 meters (approximately 2,500 ft) above sea level. Construction began in 742 and was completed in 774. I remember trying to view, during a field trip for our elementary school, the sunrise over the sea. It is visible from near the seated Buddha's perch. It was a cloudy morning and the same thing happened again in 2013 when I visited the place again with my wife. Nowadays, cars are allowed to climb all the way up to the Grotto, but at that time we had to walk up early in the morning just before sunrise, which wasn't an easy task.

The Buddha, 3.5 meters (11.5 ft) in height, is seated on a lotus throne right at the center of the Grotto with legs crossed. The gently placed hands are to symbolize enlightenment. The tranquil facial expression instantly calms the onlookers in the cool air of the cavern. I do not know when or if I could visit the place again but a nagging thought is what's the point. There are too many things to see in such a short life remaining. It would suffice to feel good that such a treasure will survive for additional thousands of years. If they are not the pearl on *daeng-gi*, what is? (03/03/2023)

497. A dog barking at the moon.
달 보고 짖는 개.

Similar to Entry #433, here is a dog barking up at the moon all night for no obvious reason one can fathom. This isn't just a one-night nuisance. It happens every night. During a sleepless night, you may wonder what this dog is up to and come up with a tentative conclusion that the dog is of little use, has no brain to speak of, fails to show any respect to other dogs and human beings, and can go to hell as far as you are concerned. Then you would also realize that this world is full of such people. By the time you get to sleep, you find wisdom that the dog world could be as bad as the world we live in.

Indeed, in Entry #199, "Speak louder, win the argument," I made the following statement to lament the state of the world we have nowadays. "We are in a troubled society if the wrong people win over the right, the fake prevails over the truth, vanity overrides reality, appearance matters more than content, the ugly outshines the beauty, apathy runs over compassion, science is pushed away by fantasy, politics matters more than the national interest, fraud appears as legitimate, and so on and so forth."

One of my fundamental complaints is that there are way too many people who keep yakking away all the time on a matter they are not well versed in. It is tiring and rather exhausting for listeners, especially for someone who knows the topic far better than the talker. Equally worrisome is the trend that an expert, and thus an authoritative figure in a given narrowly defined field unconsciously assume that he or she is equally knowledgeable in other fields. Thus, we have the phrase, "an ugly PhD." Admittedly I also often find myself restraining the desire to speak as if I were an expert, say, in the economy, simply because I had some knowledge in pharmaceutical chemistry.

The American Kennel Club (AKC) has the following statement as to barking. "Some barking is normal, but when barking becomes excessive not only is it frustrating for owners, but it's also a sign your dog may be stressed, or their needs aren't being met. Dogs use their barking as a means of communicating with us when they need things: to go outside, to play, because they are hungry, or because they are concerned about things.

There is always a reason for the barking, and it's our job to figure out what our dogs need." I can figure out that much myself.

Let us superimpose the AKC statement onto our talkative friends. Yes, we all agree that talking is normal and that excessive talking is not. Interesting words I find are "stressed," "unmet need," "communicating," etc. Then it concludes that "it's our job to figure out what our dogs need." In summary, we are to accommodate talkative people with understanding and compassion. The AKC website continues with potential remedies for barking dogs. As one may expect, all is based on compassion.

Of various suggestions, I find the following somewhat interesting: remove distractions, develop alternative behaviors, increase enrichment, and most importantly do not punish. Under enrichment, it says, "Excessive barking can be a sign that your dog is bored. When dogs don't have enough enrichment in their day, they may develop destructive habits including too much barking." What are they suggesting? Do talkative people need some "stimulating activities" like the playing opportunity with a stuffed King Kong?

Having a dog barking too much can be stressful like we get tired of people talking too much. It would be tempting to yell at and punish a barking dog but AKC says never to do so as it becomes a yelling match. In the end, nothing will be improved. Do I have such a temperament of patience?

We seem to have completely lost the art of listening. In my case, it is irritating to find myself focusing on what to say in response to what is being said by another person instead of opening my mind widely so that I can absorb wholeheartedly without much interruption of my own making. This tendency is of course that I am also very anxious to speak. I can proudly say that the situation is getting much better nowadays: I just close up my mouth shut and watch and listen to what others have to say. My poor Korean also helps. The upshot is that they listen when I say something. Ha!

Likewise, we write (like I do now) rather than read, look instead of see, complain rather than praise (as I often do), and get rather than give. This is to say that we are all self-centered, which should be clearly distinguished from being selfish. It is said that even one of the greatest humanitarians we have ever had, Albert Schweitzer, did all those charity works in medicine at a remote place in Africa for his own satisfaction. There is nothing wrong with being self-centered but being too much so is frowned upon.

Nobody, including those pundits at the AKC, would ever know for sure why the dog keeps barking all night at the moon, but obviously, the dog does not mind doing so or even enjoys the company of the moon. We ought to give that much credit to a talkative person. (03/04/2023)

498. Sorry to see a heater gone in the summer.
여름 불도 쬐다 나면 섭섭하다.

I left Korea for the States in 1967 and we just came back only last December "to bury my bone at home." Fifty-five years is a long time to be away from "home." I had lived in six different locations in North America and had owned at least five homes. I also got married. As one can imagine, I had accumulated a lot of stuff during that period, most of which I had to abandon as we moved into a small two-room suite in so-called Silvertown.

Based on the advice from other returning immigrants, we brought back many pieces of furniture, artifacts, clothes, dining sets, our car, and other junk. The idea was that we can always throw away what we do not need in Korea as purchasing new items in Korea can be costly. More than half of my clothes, especially those I used to wear almost every day for work, and much electric equipment (due to the change in voltage from 110 to 220 V) were discarded soon after we unpacked. The key issue was the lack of closet space, which my wife assumed most of.

What I really miss most nowadays are small items. They are inexpensive items so we figured we could easily buy them here in Korea. The problem is that we keep forgetting to purchase those items like a shoe horn, a back scratcher (made of bamboo), a can/bottle opener, even a spoon and fork, simple tools like a screwdriver, and a step stool. Those items that we immediately put in a trash bin after we unpacked our stuff were a checkbook from Bank of America and the US postage stamp.

According to the above proverb, one would miss the heater that they removed at the beginning of summer, the very heater that would dispel the chill from the spring nights. Soon after it was gone, they miss it, not so much because the night was cool but because the space the heater used to occupy looked strangely empty. They have not yet accustomed to it.

Because we lived in Las Vegas, a town built on a desert, for the past five years, we did not need any umbrellas and we left all of them behind. The day we arrived in this village, we had rain, a pretty cold one. A month later when our car arrived, we found one in the trunk. In one corner of a grocery store we used to go to, Vons Grocery, there was a rack for umbrellas, collecting dust. It was a weird scene that I still remember.

Material things aside, what a person misses most would be the deceased, especially loved ones, be it one's spouse, parents, friends, siblings, or even colleagues at work. We can no longer spend time together with them nor can we reminisce about time together in the past. Most of all, we no longer have those people whom we can ask about a particular set of memory. Their departure automatically erases the source of recollecting an event. This is troublesome as I begin to doubt if my own memory is reliable.

Come to think of it, we also miss something associated with smells, songs, and a particular sound of nature. The song, *Night Mist*, or 밤안개 always reminds me of my student days in Vancouver. In 1968, the Korean National Basketball team visited Canada for a series of exhibition games. At the post-reception, the players taught me the song. The song, *Oh, my friend*, or 친구여 is associated with a trip to Beijing. A young lady played the melody on the piano in the lobby for welcoming Korean tourists. See more in Entry #18, "Habits from the cradle to the tomb."

I don't think I have any so-called suppressed memories but sometimes I have a glimpse of a scene flashing by. Was it really what happened many years ago in my life or a blurry scene from a bad movie? Does it matter? But one thing is very clear: whatever I wanted to forget never disappears from the memory bank, like such an experience of visiting a lady's room at a bar after I was totally drunk, or of failing the college admission test. Who could forget where we were when the 9·11 attack took place in 2001? (I was in the lab running an experiment.) See more in Entry #138, "Startled by a turtle and now by a caldron lid."

In closing, the above proverb is saying that we feel sorry and miss even seemingly useless stuff to disappear. It may include a heater during the summertime. In the same token, we may miss a fan in the fall, ice block in the wintertime, seasonal dresses and sandals, hairspray on the shaved head, an abandoned bicycle with flattened tires, stocks of a bankrupted corporate, dull knife, etc. See more in Entry #313, "A fan in the fall."

Then a few years back, I heard the host of a music program on the radio mumbling about the color association. Color association? They must have been talking about a universal symbolism of colors, like red representing passion, blue sadness and depression, yellow sunshine, green nature, etc. What color am I missing nowadays, grey? (03/06/2023)

499. A mother porcupine insists her baby has soft skin.
고슴도치도 제 새끼는 함함하다고 한다.

Porcupines are covered by sharp spines, or quills, that protect them against predation. Quills are considered as hairs that are coated with layers of keratin, a class of structural proteins offering the rigidity of biomaterials such as nails. On contact with its predator, quills are released and inserted into the attacker causing pain. When born, quills are soft but harden within a few days. They are hardly soft but to their mother, they are.

Mothers have tons of right to boast about their babies. After all, they carried them in their wombs for nine months and raise the babies day-in-day-out 24-7, for 365 days. Any seemingly trivial development is a godsend and kept in the mother's memory bank for the rest of their lives. Around the sandbox in the neighborhood is the place young mothers compare notes and emphasize any progress their babies are striding for. The PTA is the place where kids' mothers begin gossiping about bullying, etc.

Mothers begin to lose their grip on children when they are about to leave home for college. Still, anything they hear from kids at college can be a subject of bragging. Maybe their son made a varsity debate team, won a scholarship, or met a wonderful girlfriend. Likewise, their daughter was on a summer trip to Europe, met an interesting Brit, or ran out of money. They would invariably show the pictures that children sent home and make comments about how happy they looked.

All along, the topic of mothers' conversation begins to drift to that of a typical wife. Ceaselessly they go through the life of "their kid's dad" in a fine comb, ranging from what they wore this morning to general habits. If they are close enough they may exchange even some idiosyncratic ritual in the bed, bursting into unstoppable laughter. In all this, hidden is the boasting of their spouse. He might have gotten a big promotion to become a bona fide partner at his law firm or received a huge research grant.

It is also interesting to observe how the conversation takes shape, say, when a group of couples go out for a fancy dinner or some such event. It begins with noble enough a subject like a recent art exhibit or musical event. By the time a few rounds of wine loosen their formality, they would start to talk about their "children's dad," right in front of their husbands. Most of the husbands involved just let the chat proceed without much concern. Once in a while, they may make some sounds like heh, heh, heh, or uh, uh, um.

The situation has been so bad in our case, I have begged my wife never to utter a word about me at a dinner gathering. It is hopeless. My wife goes back to what odd thing I did that morning, etc. Often, I had to kick her under the table to rein her in. Sad.

Most of my contemporaries are now beginning their first octogenarian year and are thus beyond bragging about our sons and daughter. For Pete's sake, they are in their 50s. Instead, their focus is on their grandchildren in high school or even college. Some of them have great-grandchildren. In our informal group chat, we have established an unwritten rule, which stipulates that any bragging grandfathers must donate a large sum of money to our alumni association. The custom seems to be doing just fine for everyone.

Like a mother porcupine claims that their newly born babies have soft skin, we all wish that what we have is the best in the world, or at least we wish it to be the case. Unconsciously we compare our children with those of other parents. This, of course, goes beyond children: money, home, car, and much more. The uneasy and inconvenient truth that we are inferior to others in possession begets envy and even jealousy. And unhappiness, perhaps.

I'm wondering loudly if such a concept as jealousy exists among animals. For instance, would a lioness discriminate pubs from her sister? I think not. If this is one of those things that differentiate humans from animals, I'd say the animal kingdom might be a better place to live. To be fair, in all six kingdoms including bacteria, there must be more fundamental concepts must be in play. They may include competitiveness for survival, hegemony, reproduction, and ownership. Analysis of the relationships among these topics is certainly beyond the scope of this writing.

One's patriotism may be another subject worthy of discussion here under the above proverb. As I remember, for the first several years after I settled in the State, we, Korean students, used to discuss or criticize the current political and foreign policies all night. But, in front of other foreigners or Americans, we were quite defensive of what was happening in Korea. It was like we all of a sudden become a good son or daughter once we leave home: so they say: foreign traveling brings a patriot out of you.

Now that I just came back to Korea after such a long stay in the States, I had anticipated a similar patriotic sentiment towards my previous "home away from home," but it has not happened yet. (03/08.2023)

500. The Great Wall built during an overnight stay.
하룻밤을 자도 만리성을 쌓는다.

One day at the peak of the Korean War, the whole family, except the mother, from one of our neighbors was killed during an air raid. Apparently, they were walking around the Seoul Station (서울역) when the US airplanes came by attacking the train that carried supplies for the North Korean army. If I recall, killed were the father and two children, both a few years older than me. Such a tragedy was not that uncommon during the War but it happened very close to our home. That was the frightening part. The neighbors did what they could to comfort the widow as best as they could.

Sometime later, perhaps less than a month later, the widow came across a man who fled to the South after he had lost all his family also. He was aimlessly wandering on the street of Seoul when she noticed he wasn't just a drifter or a beggar. Out of pity or sympathy, she initiated a conversation – or might have been the other way around, him begging her for something to eat. The outcome was that she had him stay at her place.

A few days later all the neighbors including my parents were informed that they were getting married, making their cohabitation more or less legitimate and proper. If I recall, my parents were saying that it was one of the few pieces of good news in the neighborhood that has been suffering, just like everybody else, from the War.

These two total strangers with a very similar recent familial tragedy must have understood quite well. Comparing stories of deceased families, not only dead spouses but also their respective children with sad but sweet memories with occasional smiles or teardrops on their faces. What was their lovemaking like? It must have been tender but compassionate, sad but with renewed hope and joy. They must have talked and talked all night. Call it a pillow talk that dealt with death as well as new lives together.

The Great Wall of China is now recognized as one of the most impressive architectural achievements in human history. It spans approximately 21,000 km or 13,000 miles, which can be seen by the naked eyes of astronauts in the spaceship. Although it was built primarily for national defense from various nomadic groups, they called barbarians, the Wall also offered convenient border control Including global transportation.

The major portion of the Wall was built over a few hundred years during Ming Dynasty (1368-1644). Now, the above prover is saying that one overnight sleepover can build the Great Wall. This is different from a modern-day one-night hookup following a casual encounter at a bar. The emphasis is that, if they are serious, the couple involved could build a long-lasting relationship during a short encounter. The story introduced earlier involving two war victims may illustrate the crux of the proverb.

Although not clearly stated, the proverb seems to emphasize the importance of sexual encounters in old-day Korea. For a typical male-dominant society, a sexual act would be typically described as a woman "offering" or "dedicating" her body to her new husband, "몸을 바친다." Once done, the woman lost her virginity as if a man "deflowered" her. For most men, intercourse used to mean a long-term commitment, never any other alternative outcome like divorce. Nowadays, young people appear to have casual sex with a stranger as if they change their underwear. The trend inevitably renders the sexual act to become a mechanical activity.

If we accept an analogy between marriage and building the Great Wall, it goes without saying that the first and most important requirement for a successful marriage would be effort. Putting in an effort is of course a conscious act., which can be challenged time after time. For instance, after the exhausting and elaborate wedding, the parties involved may exhale a sigh of relief, especially after coming back from a honeymoon trip. But most of all, the most challenging period may well be everything in a family has become rather routine. After the kids have gone to school and the husband has gone to work, what would the mother do with her long morning hours?

Part of the effort would be being honest with oneself as well as with one's spouse. However painful it may be, confessing lost interest in someone, especially in terms of love or respect, would require as much, if not more, effort than confessing affection at the beginning of the relationship. This is a generalization, which I usually abhor, but amicable split and divorce seem to be the norm in the States but seldom the case in Korea. One can conveniently attribute the difference to social backdrop but exactly what it means may require another chapter to discuss. But we could again generalize that Koreans are more emotional than logical while Americans are more logical than emotional. (03/10/2023)

INDEX (in essay number)